What people are saying about
Developing Knowledge-Based Client Relationships

"Ross Dawson's book offers a meticulous analysis of all key drivers which define successful business relationships. Highly topical, *Developing Knowledge-Based Client Relationships* is a must read for all whose survival hinges on their ability to successfully convert transaction-based interactions into comprehensive long-term partnerships with their clients." —**Marcel Kreis**, Managing Director, UBS Singapore

"Ross Dawson has delivered a powerful and comprehensive view of the future of professional services—and the role that knowledge will play in that future. He recognizes that the introspective days of corporate strategists are over. Success starts with one's external relationships—with customers, partners, and suppliers. The ability to capitalize on knowledge to build effective enterprise relationships has become critical. This book captures that reality and thus serves as a valuable field guide to success in the unfolding knowledge economy."
—**Britton Manasco**, Editor and Publisher, *Knowledge Inc.*

"'Guns don't kill,' the saying has it, 'People do.' Likewise, information doesn't confer competitive advantage. Knowledge does. And knowledge is always someone's knowledge. This book cuts through the cant about the value of data and information and shows that relationships with living, breathing people are crucial to putting knowledge profitably to work."
—**Jay Ogilvy**, Managing Director, Global Business Network,
and co-author of *China's Futures*

"Nowadays almost every consultancy company will claim to be in the business of knowledge management. Yet how many really deliver value through managing relationships with their clients that enhance their clients' knowledge? For those managers and organizations who seek to achieve this elusive goal there is no better guide than *Developing Knowledge-Based Client Relationships* by Ross Dawson. No professional in the business of delivering services to client organizations can afford to ignore this book."
—**Stewart Clegg**, Professor, School of Management,
University of Technology Sydney, and co-author of *Changing Paradigms*

"Dawson's book should be required reading for anyone in a professional services firm. Developing value-added relationships requires that we not only solve our client's business problem, but also make them more knowledgeable. His book will help professional services organizations to rethink how knowledge can most effectively flow within and outside the firm."
—**Peggy Parskey**, Functional Manager, HP Consulting
Global Knowledge Management Initiative

"The mediation of knowledge across cultural boundaries (national, industrial, professional, organizational) is not well understood, let alone practiced by many

professional groups. This is why Ross Dawson's lucid book is such essential reading for professionals operating in the emerging e-service economy."
—**Bill Ford**, Adjunct Professor, Southern Cross University, and OECD/CERI Consultant

"Ross Dawson has identified precisely the area which offers the most promise for future success in organizations—the intersection of knowledge and relationships. Addressing these two key aspects of value-creation in the 21st century, Ross Dawson's intelligent new book offers a practical guide to those who must lead their organizations through turbulent times to an unknowable future."
—**Jan Lee Martin**, Director, The Futures Foundation

"Ross Dawson breaks new ground by providing a methodology enabling professional service firms to translate abstract theory about knowledge management into strategies to improve the depth and quality of their interactions with clients. This book brings fresh insights into management of professional service firms, with best practice examples from sectors as diverse as law and advertising."
—**Peter Leonard**, Technology Partner, Gilbert & Tobin Lawyers, Sydney, Australia

"Ross Dawson's book integrates the two central concerns of every business enterprise today: managing its knowledge and managing its relationships in order to create a sustainable competitive advantage. By showing how the sharing of knowledge is deeply interwoven with the development of relationships, Dawson calls for nothing less than a reinvention of the way organizations think about client or customer relationships, and how these relationships may be redesigned as knowledge-enabled and knowledge-enabling partnerships. Dawson presents a set of sound principles and helpful practical advice that can guide professional service providers and their clients to jointly amplify value creation through mutually beneficial knowledge-based relationships."
—**Dr. Chun Wei Choo**, Associate Professor, University of Toronto, and author of *The Knowing Organization*

"In this insightful and comprehensive exploration, Ross Dawson has skillfully woven together both classic and new thinking about organizations, learning, and knowledge. This book sharpens the focus on the role of knowledge in building customer relationships through numerous examples and comprehensive listings of possibilities. The result is a useful and provocative handbook that can help guide consultancies and professional service firms in developing business offerings, deepening strategic relationships, and identifying innovation and service opportunities. A foundational book for anyone offering knowledge-based services."
—**Verna Allee**, author of *The Knowledge Evolution: Expanding Organizational Intelligence*

"*Developing Knowledge-Based Client Relationships* is a book that provides a clear understanding of a complex but important area."
—**Göran Roos**, Chairman, Intellectual Capital Services

"Dawson is to be congratulated on opening up this new subject area in knowledge management. The examination of the different types of professional services and their characteristics is very useful both to buyers and to sellers of these services. I will certainly use this as a reference book when planning client interaction or collaborating with another provider."
—**Victoria Ward**, former Chief Knowledge Officer, NatWest Markets, and founder of Spark Knowledge

"Ross Dawson has written an important book. Its all too easy to view service industries as compliant advisors. Now there is a need to see the value in cooperative knowledge generation and a requirement to learn how to give freely and learn fast. Truly thought-provoking."
—**Andy Law**, Chairman, St. Lukes, and author of *Creative Company*

"Dawson's book delivers an excellent perspective on the knowledge transfer process and its impact on business decisions and results. It's a must-read for any professional services executive who is serious about winning and keeping customers."
—**Cameron A. Lochhead**, Managing Director, Links Securities LLC

"After all, our customers are our real employers, and the currency of knowledge enlivens the relationships and makes it possible to co-create wonderful new opportunities for all involved. Ross Dawson has put his pen on a key pressure point of tomorrow's economy, and we are all so much better for his knowledge, because now our professional knowledge takes on new meaning and value."
—**Dr. Charles Savage**, author of *Fifth Generation Management*

"At last! A book that talks about the practical challenges and difficulties we all face in applying knowledge management principles in a professional services environment. Ross does an excellent job of describing how knowledge is applied and used in context. He outlines how business knowledge has value in a business relationship, and how that value can be unlocked. This book should be required reading, not only for professional services knowledge workers, but also for aspiring content dot-com entrepreneurs."
—**John G. Peetz**, Chief Knowledge Officer, Ernst & Young LLP

"If the Knowledge Economy means anything, it means that knowledge has become, more and more, what sellers sell and what buyers buy. Few companies have even begun to think through how this fundamental fact changes the nature of customer relationships. Fortunately for them—and for all of us—Ross Dawson has done a brilliant job of examining how all businesses (not just professional services, though that is where he focuses) can build knowledge-based relationships to create new, immensely lucrative ways of doing business."
—**Thomas A. Stewart**, author of *Intellectual Capital*

"If you wish to see the future of business, learn from the professional services firms! Professional services firms have more experience in how to leverage knowledge and in how to create value from 'invisible assets' than any other industry. By focussing

Developing Knowledge-Based
Client Relationships

Developing Knowledge-Based Client Relationships

The Future of Professional Services

Ross Dawson

Boston   Oxford   Auckland   Johannesburg   Melbourne   New Delhi

GLOBAL RELEAF 2000 Butterworth–Heinemann supports the efforts of American Forests and the Global ReLeaf program in its campaign for the betterment of trees, forests, and our environment.

Library of Congress Cataloging-in-Publication Data
Dawson, Ross, 1962–
    Developing knowledge-based client relationships : the future of professional services / Ross Andrew Dawson.
      p. cm.
    ISBN 0-7506-7185-8 (alk. paper)
    1. Business consultants.   I. Title.

    HD69.C6 D39   1999
    001'.068'8 21—dc21   99-045024

British Library Cataloguing-in-Publication Data
A catalogue record for this book is available from the British Library.

The publisher offers special discounts on bulk orders of this book.
For information, please contact:

Manager of Special Sales
Butterworth–Heinemann
225 Wildwood Avenue
Woburn, MA 01801–2041
Tel: 781-904-2500
Fax: 781-904-2620

For information on all Butterworth–Heinemann publications available, contact our World Wide Web home page at: http://www.bh.com

10 9 8 7 6 5 4 3 2

Printed in the United States of America

Part or all of the images used in Figures 3–1, 10–1, 10–2, and A–1, and the illustrations on pages 61, 129, 148, 179, 190, and 208 were obtained from IMSI's Master Clip® Premium Image Collection, 1895 Francisco Blvd. East, San Rafael, CA 94901-5506, USA.

Contents

Preface

I believe that the future of professional services—which is itself much of the future of differentiated business—is all about people, knowledge, and relationships. In my various careers in systems sales and product management, international stockbroking, financial market analysis and reporting, and management consulting, it has always seemed obvious to me that the greatest value provided to clients has been in making them more knowledgeable. The task for my team and me has always been to help clients to know more, to make better decisions, to have greater capabilities. I have experienced developing relationships and the fruits of building mutual trust while working in a number of different countries and cultures. I observed in practice that adding value to corporate and institutional clients is deeply tied to knowledge, relationships, and developing ongoing rich interaction. At the heart of each of the industries in which I have worked the same basic issues existed, and each one was ultimately centered on interactions among people.

Since my youth I have been profoundly interested in the nature of knowledge, including how the mind works, and how it can function more effectively. Fairly early on I came across the field of neurolinguistic programming (NLP), which draws on the principles of cognitive and behavioral psychology, however, it is eminently practical in that it is framed to answer the question, "Is this useful?" For more than a dozen years I have engaged in extensive study and training in the field, and have had the good fortune to study with some of the founders and leading thinkers in the field. From there I extended my study to the more academically accepted field of cognitive psychology, and also found that extremely practical in its business applications.

When I started to develop my ideas on knowledge and relationships, I came across the nascent field of knowledge management. Here were people who recognized that valuable knowledge is about people and interactions among people, and that technology is an enabler for that process rather than an end in itself. But somehow everyone always seemed to be talking about knowledge inside organizations. Knowledge is the primary asset of the organization, so if it is made more productive, it will provide better products and services to clients. This way of thinking appears to me to be substantially missing the point, as it seems to be implicitly based on holding clients in low esteem, and thinking of them as consumers. I have sought those who had thought or written about enhanced knowledge as the source of value to clients, and found just a few scattered allusions to the idea as something important, but with no further development of the theme. It strikes me that this represents an enormous gap in current thinking about knowledge in business, and about the whole nature and future of professional services, so with this book I am hoping to begin to remedy this oversight. Perhaps others will build further on what I have begun.

The book is intended primarily for practitioners—professionals in all industries who are in the frontline of adding value to clients. Professional services are more a way of doing business than a group of industries. Therefore, while I expect consultants, investment bankers, accountants, lawyers, and the like to see immediately the relevance and value of these ideas, I hope professionals—that is, all knowledge specialists—in every sphere of business recognize that these issues are also directly applicable to their industries.

The book is designed around the theme of client relationships, however, knowledge sharing and transfer is equally important inside and outside organizations, and this book is intended for everyone interested in the issues of dealing effectively with knowledge in business. I also anticipate that graduate students of business and related disciplines, especially those who intend to work in the field of professional services, will find this book extremely useful in understanding the underlying nature of these businesses.

Acknowledgments

Many thanks to all those who provided valuable input in conversations and feedback on draft chapters. There are too many to mention, but in particular I would like to thank Sally Andrews, Lesley Brydon, Stewart Clegg, Martin Crabb, Bill Ford, John Grinder, Alan Hocking, Greg Joffe, Sally Jones, Michael Katz, Julia Kirby, Peter Leonard, Cameron Lochhead, Iain McGregor, Tony Morriss, Greg Rippon, Michael Ross, Rudy Ruggles, David Shannon, Tom Stewart, Kees van der Heijden, Stuart Westgarth, and Steve Weber. Forgive me to those I have overlooked!

I would like to thank all the people who kindly gave me their time to discuss their organizations' approaches and initiatives in developing knowledge-based client relationships. These include Christine Burns of Blake Dawson Waldron; Martin North of Booz•Allen Hamilton; Margareta Barchan of Celemi; Keith Reinhard of DDB Worldwide Communications Group; Rick Collins of EDS Australia; Greg Reid and John Peetz, Jr. of Ernst & Young; Valarie Eiland of Fannie Mae; Renee Johnson and Matt Nolker of Giant Step; Nancy Murphy and Sean Baenen of Global Business Network; Peggy Parskey of HP Consulting; Göran Roos of Intellectual Capital Services; John Scott of ksbr Brand Management; Mark Bunke of Manpower; Stuart Roden of Mercury Asset Management; M. T. Rainey of Rainey Kelly Campbell Roalfe; Victor Grijalva and Reid Smith of Schlumberger; Andy Law of St. Lukes; Ian Battye of State Street Bank; Don Creswell of Strategic Decisions Group; Tony Cole of William M. Mercer; and many others.

It has been a delight working with Karen Speerstra, Rita Lombard, Jodie Allen, Michael Abenante, and Scott Rousseau of Butterworth–Heinemann—special thanks in helping make it a reality. Thanks to Angela Fehringer and Andreea Impeciati for the photograph and laughs. And special thanks to Oliver Freeman, Sally Jones, Tony Morriss, and Verna Allee for their support and faith during the early stages of building my business.

Introduction

Normann and Ramírez were right on target when they stated that the essence of strategy is the way companies "link together the only resources that really matter in today's economy: knowledge and relationships,"[1] in their classic *Harvard Business Review* article, "From Value Chain to Value Constellation." Together, knowledge and relationships are the only true sources of sustainable competitive advantage. Moreover, knowledge itself is all about relationships—between people and organizations.

The twin themes of knowledge sharing and relationships are deeply entwined, and ultimately inseparable. Becoming more effective at both sharing knowledge with clients and developing enduring and profitable client relationships establishes a bedrock foundation for achieving sustainable competitive advantage in times of dramatic, ongoing change.

It is now widely acknowledged in the business community that knowledge is the most valuable resource of organizations. The evangelizing work of business people and writers such as Tom Peters[2] and Tom Stewart[3] has helped companies to understand the fundamental importance of knowledge to their sustained profitability in a rapidly changing business environment and the foundations of how to leverage their knowledge to achieve better business results.

Until recently, however, the emergent field of knowledge management has focused almost exclusively on how firms can make their knowledge more productive in their internal processes. This strong internal focus reflects more generally how clients often seem to be regarded as something separate and distant to which services are provided, and from which revenue and perhaps feedback ultimately return. There has been much talk of the "extended enterprise," which includes not only clients, but suppliers, partners, and alliance members. Yet organizations still often do not act in ways that reflect a belief that the flow of knowledge and interaction should freely include their clients and other stakeholders. Knowledge is not just an internal issue; every facet of it is deeply tied to external relationships. And professional service firms are increasingly realizing that sharing knowledge with clients is at the very heart of their business.

Professional service firms can either try to hold onto their knowledge, and perform "black-box" services for their clients, or they can proactively share their knowledge, working with their clients to create value. Both of these models have a future; however, the powerful and accelerating forces of commoditization mean that those who are not prepared to work with rather than for their clients will find that the fees and margins they are able to command will gradually wither away. In today's economy the distinction between commoditized offerings, which are driven by price and cost, and differentiated offerings, which are driven by greater value to the client, is becoming ever clearer, and differentiation is ever more fleeting and tenuous as the undertow of commoditization pulls down.

This book is about professional services in business-to-business relationships because it represents a model for the future of differentiated business. An enormous proportion of business in the future will be commoditized, with many players fighting for advantage, which proves very ephemeral. Here our theme is specifically how to achieve lasting differentiation and premium pricing. Any business that achieves sustainable differentiation will be based on knowledge and relationships; as these are at the very core of professional services it represents a model for almost all differentiated business. The same principles can apply in any industry, but I argue that any business based on knowledge and relationships, that makes its clients more knowledgeable, is in effect a professional service firm. And the common foundation of knowledge specialization in professional services means that every professional service firm has much to learn from others, even those in apparently quite different industries.

What is most valuable to clients is making them more knowledgeable, helping them to make better decisions, and enhancing their capabilities. If a company chooses to outsource a given function by getting an external service provider to do it better or more cheaply than it can, it has implicitly decided that this function is not part of its core and differentiating competencies. This strategy can never add as much value as having a service firm assist the company in enhancing its core competencies, and improving the functions that are its primary source of differentiation and value creation. Adding value to clients at this level can only be done with a highly interactive approach that draws on and develops relationships. Linking and building knowledge and relationships in this way puts professional service firms in a situation that creates superior value on a sustainable basis, and is highly differentiated.

These management trends are being accentuated by the increasing sophistication of clients. The clients of professional service providers are demanding not only real added value, but also respect. They already have ready access to a wealth of information, and they are increasingly telling their service providers that they want not only knowledge transfer, but also self-sufficiency. While this may alarm some professionals, it in fact represents an enormous opportunity to move to a higher level of value creation and partnership with their clients.

Knowledge and relationships are about people. Only people hold knowledge, and all relationships are ultimately about individuals interacting. As such, greater effectiveness in developing knowledge-based client relationships must be based on understanding the nature of knowledge, how people acquire and develop their understanding of the world, and how people can learn to interact more effectively. Rich interaction among people is at the heart of knowledge sharing.

This is certainly not to imply that technology is not a critical factor in the effective delivery of professional services. Technology issues will be fundamental to the future of professional services in three ways: in helping to bring people together in more effective ways, in developing ways of interactively developing people's knowledge rather than simply dumping information, and in contributing to the commoditization of many offerings.

While our focus is firmly on client relationships and knowledge sharing across company boundaries, many of the principles are equally applicable within organizations. Effective knowledge transfer inside organizations, in situations ranging from within small teams to between different operating divisions across continents, is the pivot for leveraging the knowledge assets of an organization. Studying how to transfer knowledge to clients can also provide very valuable lessons for those who focus on developing the internal knowledge capabilities of their organizations. Clearly the issues that confront professional service firms are equally relevant in internal consulting; the boundaries within organizations can be almost as rigid as those between organizations. All issues covered in this book can be applied within companies.

In *Developing Knowledge-Based Client Relationships*, we begin by establishing the foundations on which we will build throughout the course of the book. The first two chapters are perhaps a little drier than what follows, but they provide the crucial building blocks and definitions that will enable us to develop a practical understanding of the changing nature of business. This book is intended to be eminently useful—a practitioner's manual—and one of the primary tools to achieve this usefulness is a wealth of case studies, as well as examples of excellent, innovative practice in a wide variety of industries. There is nothing more practical than seeing how other organizations have successfully addressed the same issues.

In Part I we examine the foundations of developing knowledge-based client relationships. Chapter 1 looks at how knowledge sharing is becoming an increasingly important part of the value added to clients, and introduces the basic terms and definitions we will use throughout the book. Chapter 2 examines the nature of professional services, along with the forces driving change in these industries.

Part II addresses adding value to clients with knowledge. Chapter 3 examines the processes of adding value to information that will be used by clients, and how to develop organizational information and knowledge capabilities. Chapter 4 covers adding value to client decision making, while Chapter 5 discusses adding value to client capabilities. This section provides a number of cases and examples of organizations taking innovative approaches in these areas.

Part III is about implementation—making it happen—and draws more extensively on examples of leading practice in the field. Chapter 6 describes how to manage the portfolio of communication channels with clients. Chapter 7 builds on this strategy to look at effective approaches to structuring client contact in firm-wide relationship management. Taking relationships a step further, Chapter 8 deals with issues involved in co-creating knowledge with clients, while Chapter 9 examines new pricing models that can be used for knowledge-based services. Chapter 10 draws together the various strands developed throughout the book to look at the practice of implementing these approaches, and how to enhance knowledge and communication skills.

The Appendix draws on the field of cognitive psychology and related disciplines to examine the nature of mental models, and how people acquire knowledge. An understanding of these issues is becoming central to the ability to add greater value to clients with knowledge. Here we provide a practical framework for understanding the nature of knowledge, based on contemporary research and understanding, for those interested in an introduction to the field.

The book covers a broad spectrum of industries and perspectives on business, so I must rely on you to relate the ideas and examples presented here to instances directly relevant to your industry and situation. I hope that rather than simply taking the ideas at face value, you will integrate them into your own circumstances and ways of thinking to develop innovative, useful approaches that go well beyond the scope of ideas covered in this book.

NOTES

1. Richard Normann and Rafael Ramírez, "From Value Chain to Value Constellation: Designing Interactive Strategy," *Harvard Business Review* (July-August 1993): 65–77.

2. See for example Tom Peters, *Liberation Management: Necessary Disorganization for the Nanosecond Nineties* (New York: Fawcett Columbine, 1992).

3. See for example Thomas A. Stewart, "Your Company's Most Valuable Asset: Intellectual Capital," *Fortune* 130, no. 7 (October 3, 1994); and *Intellectual Capital: The New Wealth of Organizations* (New York: Doubleday, 1997).

Part I

Knowledge-Based Client Relationships

Chapter 1

Adding Value to Clients
The Increasing Knowledge Component

"The basic economic resource . . . *is and will be knowledge*," affirms the grand old master of management, Peter Drucker.[1] Certainly the business world has been effusive in taking to the ideas or at least the language of knowledge—it seems hard to find an organization that isn't implementing knowledge initiatives, or a software vendor that doesn't sell knowledge management solutions.

If you read through the reams of business literature being produced about knowledge, it is almost invariably couched in terms of organizations having to develop, capture, and apply their "hidden reserves" of knowledge. And if you look harder, you might find something about this approach to knowledge being intended to result in better services and products for the clients out there. In this old and essentially outmoded way of thinking about business, the client is indeed "out there," as some kind of box you furnish with wonderful products and services, and receive in return revenue, and possibly feedback on how you can improve your offerings. Throughout this book we will develop the case that the value added to clients will increasingly be in sharing knowledge with them—making them more knowledgeable—and that this approach is also central to developing the closer and richer relationships on which sustainable competitive advantage is based. In this chapter we will present the foundations and definitions on which we will build throughout the rest of the book.

EXTENDING KNOWLEDGE MANAGEMENT

For our purposes I define knowledge as "the capacity to act effectively." If so, what is knowledge management? Many people say it's an oxymoron: knowledge cannot be managed. However, knowledge management is generally used to refer to any initiatives that focus on knowledge as a primary resource of the organization, and attempt to make it more productive by increasing access to it, developing it, capturing it in databases, or applying it to enhance processes, products, and services. I prefer the term *developing information and knowledge capabilities* as more accurately expressing knowledge capabilities as something dynamic, rather than knowledge as a static asset (compare the term *property management*), and already suggesting the sorts of approaches that need to be taken. This concept is explained in more detail in Chapter 3.

Professional service firms have been among the earliest and most enthusiastic in implementing the principles and practice of knowledge management, as they have long recognized that their key resource is the knowledge held in their staff and structure. Indeed, the leading professional service firms have been leveraging their knowledge effectively for decades. They are now simply formalizing their existing practices, drawing on the increasing wealth of ideas and experience in managing knowledge across all industries, and tapping the potential that new technology offers in facilitating knowledge leverage and transfer. The Big Five accounting firms and the top management consulting firms have all made major commitments to developing their internal knowledge bases, and most have appointed chief knowledge officers (CKOs), who hold responsibility for effectively leveraging the knowledge of their firms. All major law firms are at very least computerizing their precedents databases to give easy access to relevant information across the organizations.

The core of these knowledge management initiatives is in building and developing relationships between people, both by putting people together to share their useful knowledge, and providing electronic media to capture, store, and communicate information which represents the knowledge of people. The relationships on which the creation and application of knowledge are based, however, are by no means just within organizations. Many of these relationships are with clients, suppliers, alliance members, and even competitors.

The key challenges facing organizations today are first, increasing their knowledge capabilities on all fronts—to "manage knowledge" better—and second, extending the field of knowledge management beyond their organizations to encompass all members of the extended enterprise, especially their clients of all descriptions. As we will see, knowledge is increasingly central to the value added to clients.

KNOWLEDGE TRANSFER TO CLIENTS

Knowledge transfer to clients quite simply means making them more knowledgeable. In an economy in which knowledge is the most valuable resource, this avenue clearly has the potential to add the greatest value, and attract the highest rewards. This principle is being acknowledged in the business world, with a flurry of consultants and other professional service firms now proclaiming that they focus on knowledge transfer to their clients, and clients for these services increasingly demanding that real knowledge transfer is built into engagements.[2]

Here I use the phrase *knowledge transfer* as the most commonly used and convenient phrase to express the concept of making clients more knowledgeable. The term can be misleading, however, because the implicit metaphor of the word "transfer" is that of a commodity that can be moved from one place to another. As we will see, knowledge is intrinsic to people, and one person's knowledge will always be different from another person's knowledge. In other words, when knowledge is transferred it changes; this way of creating new knowledge is often highly valuable in itself. The two-way interaction required for effective knowledge transfer means that both parties will always see their knowledge increase, simply through the active process of communication. Throughout the book I will often use the term *knowledge sharing* when it is more appropriate, and this is indeed the direction in which professional services are moving, as we will see in Chapter 8. I will still usually refer to knowledge transfer, as this is the most useful phrase to encompass the key concepts of this book across the broadest range of situations. We will look at the nature of knowledge transfer in more depth later in this chapter; here we will examine its role in professional services, and how it adds value to clients.

Black-Box Services and Knowledge Transfer

The traditional approach to providing services is what I call *black-box* services. These are services in which the outcome or result is of value to the client, but the process is opaque, and the client is left none the wiser for the experience.

In many cases the client will only want the outcome of the service. A simple example is a haircut, in which you want a service performed, and you want the hairdresser to use his or her knowledge and experience to produce what you consider to be a good result. However, you haven't the slightest interest in that knowledge or how specifically that result is produced. Within business services, an example is contract office cleaning, in which you want a clean office with a minimum of fuss, but are unlikely to want to know what goes into achieving that outcome. These are black-box services, and that's probably how you want them.

Knowledge transfer is also a type of service, but in contrast to black-box services one that *does* leave the client wiser or more knowledgeable as a result of the interaction. We cannot easily categorize services as either black-box or knowledge transfer; the difference between them lies rather in the way the services are performed. Many professional services that could be performed to result in valuable knowledge transfer are still often performed in a black-box style; conversely, many services that have traditionally been executed as black-box are now being transformed to result in the client's acquisition of useful knowledge. This trend has become apparent over the last years, and is now gathering strong momentum.

An example is auditing, which in principle provides the client with a simple check mark result that all is in order for regulatory purposes. This black-box approach prevailed historically, but increasingly the major auditors—the Big Five professional services firms—are actively transferring the knowledge they have gained during the auditing process to add value to their clients. Auditing has become a highly interactive process that involves regular debriefings to the client, and incorporates additional services such as comparisons of processes with global peer organizations. As we will see in Chapter 2, this shift of professional services from a black-box style to knowledge transfer has been forced to a large degree by competitive pressures, and the necessity of finding ways to differentiate offerings from others.

On a more personal level, people tend to prefer physicians who tell them what is wrong with them, why their medical problem happened, what their treatment options are, and how they can stay well once they are better. The black-box approach to medicine is for doctors to study their patients, and then advise them to take some unidentified pills. One of the reasons this traditional medical practice style is becoming less common is that people are becoming far better informed and knowledgeable about their illnesses, and are demanding to be treated with respect and to derive real value from their physicians.

The same trends are in place in business-to-business services, where clients have ready access to information, and are getting smarter and more demanding with their professional service providers. Clients are no longer prepared to defer to the superiority of the professional, and seek real value to be added.[3]

The outcome of knowledge transfer is that the client is more knowledgeable. Of course, the critical issue is not whether the client has more knowledge, but how valuable that new knowledge is to the client. Knowledge can be valuable to a client in either or both of two ways:

- Enabling the client to make better business decisions
- Enhancing the client's business capabilities

Chapters 4 and 5 respectively will cover these themes in depth, however, we will introduce them here.

Better Decision-Making

Making decisions and implementing them is where the greatest value is created in an organization. Information and knowledge have value only insofar as they result in better business decisions, in terms of increased shareholder or stakeholder value, or alternatively increased profitability with lower risk. Decisions are the final and critical step in the chain of adding value to information and knowledge. For the purposes of a service provider adding value from outside, decisions in an organization can most usefully be classified into strategic, line, and portfolio decisions.

Strategic Decisions

Strategic decisions are those that determine the direction and positioning of the organization. Unless prescribed by the organization's charter, there are no boundaries on strategic decision making. While there is often input from many levels of the organization, these decisions are usually made by the board of directors or most senior managers, and are based on the broadest scope of information and knowledge about the organization, its business environment, and the relationship between them.

Line Decisions

Line decisions can be made at any level of the organization, from top executives to production workers. They are distinguished from strategic decisions in that they are made within a bounded scope, determined at the strategic level by the allocation of responsibility within the organizational structure. All knowledge workers make line decisions in performing their functions.

Portfolio Decisions

Portfolio decisions are those made in the ongoing management of a portfolio of assets, liabilities, or risks. This set of decisions most obviously applies to financial markets, though it is also relevant to a host of corporate-level functions.

Enhanced Capabilities

An organization's competitiveness is based on its business capabilities—how well it performs the activities that impact its performance. Those capabilities are based on a fusion of effective business processes and skills, both of which are forms of knowledge. An organization's processes are an institutionalized form of knowledge; they are often partially documented, but usually far more simply reflect "the way things are done." Individual skills are also critical in effectively implementing processes, and developing specific skills within the context of an organization's capabilities can add substantial value. Firms that can effectively contribute to enhanced capabilities in their clients are in a prime competitive position.

Prescriptive and Facilitative Consulting

The concept of knowledge transfer to clients can be expressed in many ways, and is by no means a new idea. In 1982, Arthur Turner of Harvard Business School identified eight levels of value in consulting engagements; the top two levels were permanently improving organizational effectiveness, and facilitating client learning.[4] Another formulation is found in the differentiating between prescriptive and facilitative consulting. Prescriptive consulting is telling clients what to do, while facilitative consulting is helping them to do it for themselves. Clearly demand for the latter is increasing.

CLIENT OFFERINGS

The distinction between products and services is rapidly blurring.[5] This trend was made clear in 1993, when *Fortune* merged its traditionally separate Top 500 rankings of industrial and service companies into a single list, implicitly admitting it could not distinguish between the two groups. Not only are product companies increasingly selling services, and service companies selling products, but it is ever more difficult to determine what is a service and what is a product, as more and more offerings demonstrate the characteristics of both.

One suggestion for how to distinguish between the two is that a product is something you can drop on your foot. Perhaps a more useful definition is that a product is something you *receive*, and a service is something that is *done* for you. Digitization doesn't change the dynamics of these working definitions—a physical CD and a music file downloaded onto your hard disk from the Internet are both products. With this distinction machinery, software, manuals, and digitized photos are all products; and a haircut, legal advice, search engines, and after-sales support are all services.

This definition by no means clears up the confusion—in the end most transactions have both product and service components, in that clients usually receive something, as well as having something done for them as part of the overall offering from the supplier. As such it becomes more useful to think simply in terms of *client offerings*,[6] that is, what a company offers its clients in return for payment, in money or other forms of value.

The Components of Client Offerings

Client offerings usually consist of some mixture or hybrid of products and services. We can now take that a step further to suggest that offerings in fact consist of a combination of products, black-box services, and knowledge transfer. Some transactions fall almost entirely within the one category, such as a pencil, office cleaning, and a training course. More commonly (and arguably even in these instances) the offering to the client encompasses all three categories.

While we have distinguished between black-box services and knowledge transfer, services are always some combination of these, usually together with a product component. Even when a service is mainly black-box, it will often have some knowledge transfer component, and vice versa—nothing belongs purely in one category. While black-box services will always play a significant role, a gradual shift will continue to occur in the value of offerings toward the knowledge transfer component.

Characteristics of Products, Black-Box Services, and Knowledge Transfer

Each component of the client offering has substantially different characteristics in terms of the value added to clients. The major aspects of value added to clients by each type of offering is summarized in Table 1–1.

Products can add value in a wide variety of ways. In a business-to-business context, products are often used either in the production of products or services, or to increase efficiency.

The essential role of black-box services is to perform functions that the client does not consider central to its business. Prahalad and Hamel's seminal work on core competencies helped frame a mindset in which businesses limit their activities to what they do best.[7] This is, of course, nothing new—the foundation of economics is that each producer focuses on its comparative advantage to mutual benefit.

The strong shift in the 1990s to outsourcing and business networks has increased the pressure on companies to be very clear in distinguishing between functions in which they hold a competitive advantage and thus perform in-house, and functions others can do better or more cheaply. Choosing to outsource a function essentially means that only its outcome matters, and the knowledge behind it is nonessential. For this type of function, the client usually specifically wants a black-box service, and is not interested in how the function is performed. So in the case of black-box services, the value added is essentially in performing those functions or services better, more effectively, or more cheaply than the client could do in-house. Of course, there are many cases in which companies have made decisions to outsource functions, only to discover later that the knowledge necessary for those functions was in fact also critical to their core competencies.

Knowledge transfer specifically relates to the core functions of the client, in which knowledge *is* important in achieving a competitive edge

TABLE 1–1   Value Added to Clients By Different Types of Client Offerings

Type of Offering	*Value Added*
Knowledge transfer	Better decision making
	Enhanced competencies and capabilities
Black-box services	Noncore functions performed more efficiently and cheaply
Products	Enhanced production
	Increased efficiency

and better business results. Since this process intrinsically relates to the core competences and distinguishing features of the client, it necessarily has the potential to add greater value than in performing functions that the client has decided are generic and wishes to outsource. While the generally accepted notion of outsourcing sometimes includes knowledge transfer as well as black-box components, in its truest sense outsourcing a function means that management has decided it is not central and distinctive to the organization.

One of the critical differences between black-box services and knowledge transfer is that by the very nature of black-box services, the client sees only the outcome. As such, it is relatively easy for competitors to replicate that result, meaning that the services can easily become commoditized. In contrast, knowledge transfer is inherently differentiated, in that the process is often as important as the outcome. We will examine this issue in more detail in Chapter 2.

INFORMATION AND KNOWLEDGE

Information and knowledge are words being bandied about very freely these days, and yet it seems few people can clearly distinguish between the two, preferring to use them almost interchangeably. Many writers have offered definitions that distinguish between information and knowledge, and often draw in the concept of data, as something less complex than information, and wisdom, as something more complex than knowledge. The academic and business practitioners of knowledge management continue to discuss these distinctions and definitions; we will briefly review the debate in order to come up with a clear distinction that is helpful in addressing the issues of knowledge transfer between organizations.

The Capacity to Act Effectively

We do not wish to duplicate here some of the insightful and useful examinations of the concept of knowledge given by management practitioners.[8] What we do want is some sense of what knowledge *means* in a business context. Ultimately, knowledge within the world of business only has any value or meaning if it results in action. One of the most useful insights into knowledge is that of Karl-Erik Sveiby, who gives us a working definition of knowledge as "a capacity to act."[9]

Perhaps more accurately, it is the capacity to act effectively in order to produce desired outcomes in a complex and uncertain environment, or "the capacity to act effectively." Similarly, Tom Davenport and Larry Prusak contend that "knowledge can and should be evaluated by the decisions or actions to which it leads,"[10] while Donald Schön notes of professionals that "our knowledge is *in* our action."[11]

This capacity to act effectively, which requires considering and understanding the broad array of factors in a situation, making effective decisions, and enacting them, is exclusive to human beings. Computers, databases, and documents do not have a capacity to act having considered a diverse range of issues, and will not have this capacity for the foreseeable future. Knowledge is only an attribute of people.

Tacit Knowledge and Explicit Knowledge

Michael Polanyi was a relatively obscure philosopher of science, however, he is now often quoted in the business literature since his work has been rediscovered by practitioners of knowledge management. What has brought about his revival is his exposition of the distinction between tacit and explicit knowledge. Polanyi pointed out that we can know more than we can tell or explain to others.[12] Explicit knowledge is what we can express to others, while tacit knowledge comprises the rest of our knowledge—that which we cannot communicate in words or symbols.

Much of our knowledge is tacit—we don't even necessarily know what we know, and what we do know can be very difficult to explain or communicate to others. One instance of tacit knowledge is a surfer's knowledge of the patterns of swells in the ocean, where and how the waves are likely to break, and how best to catch and ride them. That knowledge is based on long experience, and very little of that knowledge can be readily captured or communicated to others.

Another simple example of tacit knowledge is being able to write a clear and concise business letter. This kind of skill is learned over time, often largely by trial and error. Most people who are good at writing business letters would probably be unable to give others precise instructions on how to do so. It is part of their knowledge, but not something they can easily or effectively explain to others.

Explicit knowledge, conversely, can be put in a form that *can* be communicated to others through language, visuals, models, or other representations. Whatever the surfer could say, write, or draw about his knowledge of the wave patterns, or the business person could communicate about her ability to write letters, would be explicit knowledge. In most business situations, especially in the professions, the bulk of an individual's valuable and useful knowledge is tacit rather than explicit.

Knowledge Is Personal

Since tacit knowledge—the essential component of knowledge—cannot be communicated to others, it is inherently personal and individual. The way in which a person comes to act effectively in any given circumstances is unique, because ultimately it is a product of all his or her experience and responses to that experience. As we will see, knowledge is acquired by integrating it with and relating it to existing experience and ways of thinking. No two people will understand an idea in exactly the same way, because they interpret it in relation to different sets of experience. Understanding that knowledge is personal is critical in framing how we share knowledge with others.

Knowledge Conversion

Nonaka and Takeuchi proposed that the creation and expansion of knowledge takes place through social interaction between tacit and explicit knowledge, and applied this distinction in the context of the "knowledge-creating company."[13] The interaction between these two forms of knowledge results in four modes of knowledge conversion, as illustrated in Table 1–2.

TABLE 1–2   Modes of Knowledge Conversion

| | | *To* | |
		Tacit Knowledge	*Explicit Knowledge*
	Tacit Knowledge	Socialization	Externalization
From			
	Explicit Knowledge	Internalization	Combination

From *The Knowledge-Creating Company: How Japanese Companies Create the Dynamics of Innovation*, by Ikujiro Nonaka and Hirotaka Takeuchi © 1995, Oxford University Press, Inc. Used by permission of Oxford University Press, Inc.

Tacit knowledge is converted to tacit knowledge in other individuals through the process of *socialization*, or sharing experiences. *Externalization* is the conversion of tacit knowledge to explicit knowledge by making it readily communicable. Explicit knowledge is converted to tacit knowledge through *internalization*, which is the process of translating it into personal knowledge; while *combination* is the conversion of explicit knowledge to other explicit knowledge, by creating frameworks for knowledge. We will return to this framework in a moment to explore it from a slightly different perspective.

Explicit Knowledge as Information

Polanyi's critical distinction was to frame explicit knowledge as the portion of a person's knowledge which *can* be communicated by being made explicit, and tacit knowledge as that which *cannot* be communicated directly. However, when knowledge is made explicit by putting it into words, diagrams, or other representations, it can then be digitized, copied, stored, and communicated electronically—in other words, it has become information. Indeed, as we will see in Chapter 3 the most useful definition for information is something that is or can be digitized—in other words made explicit. Information, which represents captured knowledge, has limited intrinsic value, except as an input to human decision making and capabilities. Tacit knowledge remains intrinsic to people, and only people have the capacity to act effectively.

These new insights into information and knowledge enable us to slightly reconceive Nonaka and Takeuchi's framework, by substituting information for explicit knowledge, and simply knowledge—in the business sense of a capacity to act effectively—as tacit knowledge. This clarification of the distinction between information and knowledge makes the knowledge conversion framework more directly applicable to interorganizational interaction.

From this perspective, externalization is capturing people's knowledge—that is their capacity to act in their business roles—by making it explicit and rendering it as information, as in the form of written documents or structured business processes. This remains information until other people internalize it to become part of their own knowledge, or "capacity to act effectively." Having a document on your server or bookshelf does not make you knowledgeable, nor even does reading it. Rather, knowledge comes from understanding the document by integrating the ideas into existing experience and knowledge, and thus providing the capacity to act usefully in new ways. In the case of written documents, language and diagrams are the media by which the knowledge is transferred. The information presented must be actively interpreted and internalized, however, before it becomes new knowledge to the reader.

This process of internalization is essentially that of knowledge acquisition, which is central to the whole field of knowledge management and knowledge transfer. Understanding the nature of this process is extremely valuable in implementing effective business initiatives and in adding greater value to clients. These issues are examined in detail in the Appendix.

Socialization refers to the transfer of one person's knowledge to another person, without being intermediated by captured information such as documents. It is the most powerful form of knowledge transfer. People learn from other people far more profoundly than they learn from books and documents, in both obvious and subtle ways. Despite technological advances that allow people to telecommute and work in different locations, organizations function effectively chiefly because people who work closely together have the opportunity for rich interaction and learning on an ongoing and often informal basis.

The Knowledge Management Cycle

One of the classic ways of thinking about knowledge management is found in the dynamic cycle from tacit knowledge to explicit knowledge and back to tacit knowledge. In other words, people's knowledge is externalized into information, which to be useful must then be internalized by others to become part of their knowledge, as illustrated in Figure 1–1. This flow from knowledge to information and back to knowledge constitutes the heart of organizational knowledge management. Direct sharing of knowledge through socialization is also vital. However, in large organizations capturing whatever is possible in the form of documents and other digitized representations means that information can be stored, duplicated, shared, and made available to workers on whatever scale desired.

The field of knowledge management encompasses all of the human issues of effective externalization, internalization, and socialization of knowledge. As subsets of that field, information management and document management address the middle part of the cycle, in which information is stored, disseminated, and made easily available

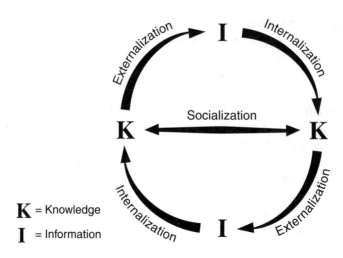

FIGURE 1–1   The knowledge management cycle.

on demand. It is a misnomer to refer to information sharing technology, however advanced, as knowledge management. Effective implementation of those systems must address how people interact with technology in an organizational context, which only then is beginning to address the real issues of knowledge.

UNDERSTANDING KNOWLEDGE TRANSFER

Knowledge transfer is the process by which the useful knowledge held by a person or group is enhanced. This broad definition encompasses any process or direct or indirect interaction that adds value by developing others' knowledge.

I distinguish between two types of knowledge transfer:

- Knowledge communication
- Knowledge elicitation

Knowledge Communication

Knowledge communication refers to what most people think of as knowledge transfer—it suggests that a person or group has knowledge, and communicates that knowledge so that another person or group has the same or similar knowledge. We have already seen that because personal knowledge is necessarily intermediated by our communication and interaction, that the knowledge received will never be the same as the knowledge transmitted.

Knowledge communication can take place in two forms:

- *Socialized transfer*. This is knowledge transfer through socialization, which is direct personal contact and interaction.
- *Intermediated transfer*. Here, a person or firm's knowledge is externalized into information, which is then made available to clients who internalize this into knowledge; the knowledge transfer is intermediated by its capture as information.

Both methods of knowledge communication have advantages and disadvantages, which we will examine further in Chapters 3 and 6. Knowledge communication is necessarily mediated either by information or personal interaction, and any comprehensive strategy for knowledge communication will include both approaches. Effective communication must be based on a solid understanding of the dynamics of externalization, internalization, and socialization.

Knowledge Elicitation

We acquire knowledge throughout our lives, both on the basis of reflecting on direct personal experience, and by learning from others. Isaac Newton didn't acquire knowledge about gravity from outside when the proverbial apple fell on his head—he generated it by combining a new perspective with his existing understanding. It is not just through the communication of existing knowledge that we can add value.

Knowledge elicitation describes the process of assisting others to generate their own knowledge. It suggests that the potential for knowledge is inherent in clients, and that specific kinds of interaction can result in their creating their own knowledge and understanding its value. This happens more often than many people realize—attempts to communicate knowledge often result in insights and learning, just not those that were intended! Increasingly, clients value suppliers that can help them to generate their own knowledge and learning.

One illustration of this principle is found in management games, which are intended far more to get participants to gain insights and think in new ways about their particular situation than to impart specific knowledge or information. Another example is the tendency of fund managers to deliberately seek out research and opinions on financial markets that challenges their thinking. Even if they disagree with the conclusions of the research, they can find the logic or analysis behind it valuable in developing their own thinking, and they are usually more than willing to pay for stimulating ideas.

Socialization, Interactivity, and Bandwidth

Effective knowledge communication and knowledge elicitation are based on rich two-way interaction and dialogue. Engaging in discussion—essentially a process of socialization—is central to the process of knowledge communication, which can rarely be accomplished effectively through the mere exchange of files or documents.[14] Knowledge elicitation is even more dependent on interaction—people generate their own knowledge most effectively in a stimulating environment involving discussion of ideas and perspectives. To a great extent the value and quality of knowledge transfer is a function of the richness of interactions with clients. Alan Webber, founding editor of *Fast Company* magazine, writes in *Harvard Business Review* that knowledge workers create relationships with customers through conversations; in other words, "the most important work in the new economy is creating conversations."[15]

In communications technology, bandwidth refers to the amount of information that can be communicated in a given period of time. The growth of the Internet, for example, is predicated on steadily increasing bandwidth, allowing the flow of richer forms of information such as sound and video rather than just text and pictures.

The concept of bandwidth is also applicable in interaction between people. Telephone conversations allow for the expression of subtleties of emphasis and emotion far exceeding that of the content and meaning of the words themselves, though this can be limited by the relatively low audio quality of the connection. Videoconferencing, in turn, gives far greater bandwidth in interaction between people, by allowing visual as well as auditory information to be conveyed. Even so, the bandwidth achievable by any current technology—in terms of information flow between participants—is many orders of magnitude less than that of face-to-face meetings, which is why video link-ups are still not usually considered to be an effective approach to important meetings. Over time videoconferencing is likely to become more effective and used more frequently, but many of the subtleties of human interaction will still not be contained even within a significantly amplified bandwidth. The requirement for the richest possible knowledge transfer will also increase rapidly, so the airline industry need not overly fear the advance of communications technology.

In practical terms, maximizing bandwidth means developing the greatest degree of interactivity with clients, by engaging in dialogue through all available means of communication. This principle is vital, not just in individual interactions with clients, but in designing the overall structure of client relationships, as we will see in Chapters 6 and 7.

KNOWLEDGE TRANSFER AND DEVELOPING CLIENT RELATIONSHIPS

One of the central themes of this book is that developing client relationships and adding value to clients through knowledge transfer are inextricably entwined. Adding value to clients with knowledge by itself results in deeper client relationships, and to a large degree developing better client relationships yields enhanced two-way knowledge transfer. Both sets of dynamics are central to the ability of professional service firms to differentiate themselves from their competitors.

The Virtuous Circle of Knowledge Transfer and Intimate Relationships

The key link between knowledge transfer and client relationships is intimacy. Client intimacy denotes the existence of rich ongoing two-way interaction and a deep level of mutual trust. High-value knowledge transfer is predicated on patterns of rich socialization and interaction, which in turn find their foundation in trust. Intimate client relationships are based on the ability to add substantial value, which is achieved by effective knowledge transfer, and leads to the openness that allows access to key client executives and the scope for rich interaction.

In this way, knowledge transfer and closer client relationships form a virtuous circle, with each benefiting from the outcomes of the other, and enabling both to develop in tandem within a positive feedback loop, as shown in Figure 1–2.[16] Once this dynamic develops it provides the source of ever-closer relationships with the client, and the potential for ongoing highly profitable business. As seen in this simplified diagram, there are a number of positive feedback loops, all of which compound to support the strength of this approach to business. Not only does the client gain the benefit of the rich knowledge transfer enabled by the intimacy of the relationship, but the service provider has

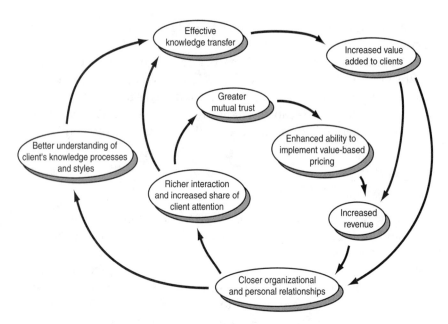

FIGURE 1–2   The virtuous circle of knowledge transfer and developing client relationships.

an excellent opportunity to learn and develop its own knowledge, as well as to identify further business opportunities. If the relationship is strong enough, the service provider and client may choose to engage explicitly in the co-creation of knowledge; this concept is covered in Chapter 8.

Trust and Intimacy

Worthwhile relationships are based on trust. Without trust, neither party is given the opportunity to add significant value to the other, or even to demonstrate its trustworthiness, so there is no scope for a mutually beneficial relationship to develop.

Your clients' trust in you is based on their belief that your actions will reflect a high level of consideration for their interests. They must believe that you will act with their best interests at heart. In everyday situations, this trust is reflected in the degree to which they feel they can rely on you to fulfill their expectations of your behavior. Most importantly, a deep level of trust really reflects faith that in unpredictable situations you will be able to work out arrangements that are mutually beneficial.[17]

In the end, trust is about personal relationships rather than organizational relationships; indeed all relationships are ultimately between people, not organizations. Individuals in client organizations trust individuals who work for their service providers, rather than the firm itself. This is one of the key reasons that professionals regularly take their clients with them when they move to other organizations—the clients remain loyal to the individual professionals, not the firm.

The development of trust is to a great extent a matter of interaction over time. While relationships may begin with a high degree of trust based on the reputation of the individual or organization, it is through consistently meeting expectations that deep trust is developed. This fulfilment of expectations requires interaction—the richer the interaction, the greater the opportunity for experiences that will build trust.[18]

On a more personal level, friendships—in which trust is implicit—form through repeated interaction. The socialization necessary for effective knowledge transfer provides a basis for the development of personal relationships, which in turn results in greater interaction and a richer flow of information and opportunities. The rich interaction necessitated by knowledge transfer naturally facilitates deep levels of client intimacy, again reinforcing the virtuous circle.

A vital outcome of intimate relationships is that new business opportunities are naturally uncovered in the course of interaction. The closer you are to your client, the more likely you are to identify or hear of openings for your services, with far better chances of winning that business without formal competition.

In addition, this level of intimacy results in a deeper mutual knowledge of business objectives and styles. Ultimately, developing client relationships is about matching business objectives in a way that the relationship and associated transactions bring maximum value to both parties. This process of mutual disclosure and alignment of objectives is greatly facilitated by the intimacy necessary for and based on effective knowledge transfer.

Customizing Communication

An important theme throughout this book is that of customizing the communication of knowledge to suit your client. Adapting the way you communicate with your clients to match how they most effectively assimilate knowledge has a major impact on the effectiveness of knowledge transfer. Doing this requires understanding your clients in great depth, including their styles and approaches to taking in information, thinking, and making decisions. The Appendix draws on findings from the field of cognitive psychology to analyze these issues in some detail.

This customization process involves a significant investment of effort, first in coming to understand your clients, and then in applying that understanding to adapting how you communicate with them. The effort is amply rewarded, however, as it results in an increasing ability to add value to the client, and particularly perceived value, since the client can understand and use the knowledge you deliver more easily than that of your competitors, thus deepening the relationship.

Professional Knowledge Cultures

Professionals naturally see their knowledge as their source of wealth—they are very reluctant to part with it, and eager to promote themselves as experts for hire.[19] Knowledge management is largely about getting people to *want* to share knowledge—it is useless putting in elaborate intranets and other sharing technology and systems unless users are motivated to share their knowledge. Considering the difficulty in getting people to share their knowledge inside their organizations, it is not surprising that many professionals are reluctant to share knowledge with their clients.

This culture is rooted in the traditions and education of many of the professions. Some observers define a profession in terms of having strict standards and entrance procedures. These criteria are useful in establishing consistent quality; however, they also induce a mindset of having put in the time and effort required to achieve this differentiating expertise, and a desire to retain that difference. "I'm an expert and you're not, so leave it to me—I know best," accurately expresses the attitude of many professionals.

Why Should I Teach My Clients to Do What I Do?

The great fear of professionals is that if they make their clients more knowledgeable, they are giving away their key productive asset from which they make money. In many instances this is a misunderstanding of the nature of knowledge transfer. Knowledge transfer is often not about teaching your clients to do what you do, but making them better at what they do, which by no means results in doing yourself out of a job.[20]

In other cases, it is true that knowledge transfer is about making clients more self-sufficient, which means that they may rely less on you in the future. The temptation is to avoid this situation, and in some cases the most effective business model may be to protect the knowledge behind the services offered.

Ultimately, however, refusing to transfer knowledge to clients is an unsustainable position. In professional services, the far greater risk is that competitors will offer more value to your clients than you do, so that you will lose all their business. In the past, most professions have effectively closed ranks to ensure none of their members revealed professional secrets, and they maintained their hermetic and privileged knowledge. Today's competitive pressures mean that there will always be participants who break ranks to transfer valuable knowledge to clients, and win business away from others.

In a few cases the client will no longer require further services, as it is now able to perform them without the professional's assistance. However, in most cases the client will continue to seek external assistance on similar or different functions and issues. At that point, the client will return to the providers that focused on knowledge transfer as a key element of their services, and pass over those that have only offered black-box services.

Clients are finding increasingly that knowledge transfer from their professional suppliers is the primary differentiating factor in the value they receive, and they are switching from suppliers that insist on the black-box model of services to those that add greater value by increasing transparency or focusing specifically on knowledge transfer. Client mobility between suppliers is rapidly increasing, so that it will become more and more difficult to maintain relationships with clients to which you decline to transfer knowledge.

Continuously Creating Knowledge (and Value!)

A business climate in which professional service firms routinely transfer knowledge to clients, combined with the rapid global diffusion of information through electronic channels, means that professionals will never again be able to rest on their laurels. Those that attempt to hang onto their hard-accumulated knowledge will see it rapidly slip away, leaving them with just a few dated ideas to peddle in the marketplace.

The only way that professionals can survive in this keenly competitive world is to create knowledge continuously. Freely transferring knowledge to clients means that it is necessary to generate new knowledge and insights on an ongoing basis. Any professional who has not yet understood this will be forced to do so very soon now.

Schlumberger ClientLink[21]

Technical services giant Schlumberger employs 64,000 people worldwide across a range of service divisions, though its history and major area of operations is in oil services. Recognizing the changing nature of the way its clients—the major oil companies—wanted to do business, Schlumberger in 1992 set up the ClientLink initiative, which established a framework for client contact and collaboration. Specific programs that fall within the ClientLink initiative include joint research and development programs with clients, client training, implementation of extranets, client advisory boards, and regular technical conferences. All of these are intended to result in enhanced client knowledge and capabilities.

As an example of how these principles have been implemented, BP-Amoco (then British Petroleum) was experiencing production problems in very long horizontal oil wells.[22] BP and Schlumberger established a joint initiative to develop new techniques for addressing these problems. Both sides allocated significant resources to the project. While the technology that was developed remained the property of Schlumberger, and served as the foundation for a new line of business, BP's reward was the quick acquisition of the knowledge and experience required to develop horizontal oil wells using the new technology. BP CEO John Browne then wanted to disseminate the knowledge more broadly within his company, so Schlumberger established an extranet website for the project that people in both companies could access.

Part of ClientLink is an intranet called ClientLink Solutions Program, which allows field engineers to access solutions developed throughout the organization. Client issues are routed through specific expert reviewers by e-mail, and a very active bulletin board system enables ongoing dialogue with engineers and peers around the world. Much of the knowledge behind this effort is delivered to clients in their direct interaction with field engineers, although Schlumberger has also established the "Connect Schlumberger" client extranet, which provides personalized access to technical information. Schlumberger now frequently provides extranet hubs to meet specific client requirements.

Schlumberger is finding that its clients are increasingly interested in developing knowledge through collaboration, and sharing the resulting benefits. In developing new Venezuelan oil fields in joint teams with its client, Schlumberger has established a base fee for its services based on target production levels, with an incentive fee which can be either positive or negative depending on the actual production achieved and agreed quality criteria.

Fortunately, professionals who transfer knowledge to clients will find not only that knowledge always flows in both directions, so they continuously learn from their clients; but also that the interaction required for knowledge transfer actually generates new knowledge in itself. The most effective way to generate new knowledge is actually in its implementation and transfer to clients. Client work is the key source of knowledge.[23] And as Peter Drucker points out, knowledge workers learn the most when they teach.[24]

In addition, the new dynamics of knowledge creation and transfer mean that effective facilitation, process management, and other primary skills required for knowledge elicitation are becoming increasingly valuable and in demand. Professionals who can help others to create their own knowledge will never find themselves out of a job.

THE SCOPE OF KNOWLEDGE TRANSFER

Knowledge transfer to clients is a vital aspect of the developing knowledge economy. However, it is important to acknowledge that there are many industries and instances in which knowledge transfer plays a minimal role for a number of reasons. Primarily, since knowledge transfer is a key source of differentiation, as we will see in Chapter 2, it is rarely applicable in commoditized businesses. This book focuses on differentiated business—especially professional services—in which knowledge transfer plays a central role. Here we look briefly at some of the parameters regarding the application of knowledge transfer.

Client Desires

The most obvious instance in which sharing knowledge, as opposed to performing black-box services, is not appropriate is simply that the client doesn't want it. Many situations exist in which organizations have specifically decided that they wish to outsource a function, and they want results without being bothered by the details as to how the function is performed. Examples of services where this is common include litigation, property maintenance, graphic design, and similar services.

Professional service firms should be alert to situations in which the client is not seeking knowledge transfer, but would benefit substantially from a service such as input into its strategic decision making. This kind of situation could happen in any of the above instances. To explicitly propose enhancing client decision making and business capabilities can help to develop a far closer and more profitable relationship.

Linking Knowledge Transfer to Perceived Value and Revenue

Creating substantial value for clients is of little use if they receive all of that value without acknowledgment. Service providers must appropriate part of the value they create by linking it directly to generating greater revenue and ongoing superior profits for themselves as well as their clients. One of the key links is that of client-perceived value. Professionals must ensure that their clients perceive the value they receive, and convert that perception to higher fees and increased profitable business from existing and new clients. Awareness of these issues should be built into all aspects of client relationships; these issues will be examined in more detail in Chapters 7 and 9.

Clearly, there are situations that must be managed carefully in order to ensure that the revenue generated is in line with the value of the knowledge transfer to the client. For instance, in a competitive situation, if the applied value of your knowledge can be readily encapsulated and communicated, it is important not to give that to the client for free at the proposal stage. Professionals have always been extremely careful about giving away their advice and knowledge for free, and probably need no reminder to continue to do so.

Degree of Client Sophistication

The degree of sophistication of your clients has a major impact on the way in which knowledge transfer can be used to add perceived value. In general, the more sophisticated the client, the harder it is to add value, and the greater the importance of knowledge transfer in adding value. Usually the most sophisticated clients are those that are most desirable in terms of potential revenue, learning, and prestige. Knowledge transfer is also valuable with less sophisticated clients, although the most effective approaches to achieve this result may be different. Our primary focus here is in working with the more sophisticated corporate, institutional, and individual clients.

Return on Effort

A final critical limitation to knowledge sharing with clients is simply whether it is worth the effort. The time-intensive use of high-value professionals is not merited by the potential revenue from many clients. Certainly knowledge transfer is intrinsic to increasing client intimacy, however, this begs the question of whether it is a client with which you wish to become intimate.

Throughout this book we will be dealing with those situations in which the potential value of clients is indeed worth the personalized effort of increasing intimacy, adding greater value, and building deepening relationships. When this isn't the case, you have by default chosen to be a supplier of commoditized services. Technology now allows the ability to "mass-customize" service to clients; this is an increasingly important concept in knowledge transfer, though it will never be a substitute for personalized attention.

SUMMARY: KNOWLEDGE AND CLIENT RELATIONSHIPS

Knowledge has become the primary economic resource, and business is now shifting its approaches and initiatives to treat it as such. However, the burgeoning field of knowledge management thus far has focused almost exclusively on how organizations can make knowledge more productive in their internal processes. It is essential to understand that knowledge has little value in isolation—it is created from and applied in the context of relationships. Knowledge and relationships are deeply intertwined, and companies' external relationships are intrinsic to their ability to generate knowledge and use it in creating value for their clients and themselves.

Black-box services give a result to the client, but leave them none the wiser. Knowledge transfer, by contrast, *does* make the client more knowledgeable, able to make better decisions, and equipped with enhanced business capabilities. Since black-box services focus on areas that the client considers not essential to its core competencies, and knowledge transfer is intended to enhance the features that distinguish the client from its competitors, knowledge transfer necessarily has the power to add far greater value.

Indeed, in a business context knowledge is the "capacity to act effectively"; this means it is a property of people, not documents or databases. While information systems are valuable enablers to capturing information and making it available, knowledge is created and made valuable by establishing richer direct and indirect contacts and relationships between people.

Developing client relationships is ultimately inseparable from knowledge sharing; adding value to clients with knowledge both necessitates and builds the intimacy out of which enduring and profitable relationships flourish. Those who attempt to hang on to their expertise will soon find themselves supplanted by competitors who are willing and able to make their clients more knowledgeable.

In this chapter we have established the main definitions and foundations of the nature of knowledge and knowledge transfer, on which we will build throughout the remainder of the book. After having examined the relatively theoretical field of knowledge, however, we must understand the business arena in which knowledge is created, used, and transferred. What is the nature of organizations that add value to knowledge and add value to their clients with knowledge? In Chapter 2 we will develop an understanding of the quintessential knowledge organizations—professional service firms—and the challenges they are currently facing.

NOTES

1. Peter Drucker, *Post-Capitalist Society* (Oxford, UK: Butterworth–Heinemann, 1993): 7. Italics in original.
2. In a survey by *Information Week*, clients of IT service firms rated knowledge transfer as the area in which service providers needed to improve the most. Bob Violino and Bruce Caldwell, "Analyzing the Integrators," *Information Week* (November 16, 1998).
3. See G. C. Shelley, "Dealing with Smart Clients," *Ivey Business Quarterly* (Autumn 1997), 50–55.
4. Arthur N. Turner, "Consulting Is More Than Giving Advice," *Harvard Business Review* (September-October 1982).
5. This point has been made by a multitude of writers, including Steven L. Goldman, Roger N. Nagel, and Kenneth Preiss, *Agile Competitors and Virtual Organizations: Strategies for Enriching the Customer* (New York: Van Nostrand Reinhold, 1995); and Michael Schrage, "Provices and Serducts," *Fast Company*, no. 4 (August/September 1996).
6. The term "offerings" has been suggested by Normann and Ramírez, while Davis and Meyer use "offers" to refer to product-service hybrids: Stan Davis and Christopher Meyer, *Blur: The Speed of Change in the Connected Economy* (Reading, MA: Perseus, 1998): 22.
7. C. K. Prahalad and Gary Hamel, "The Core Competence of the Corporation," *Harvard Business Review* (May-June 1990): 79–91.

8. Excellent reviews and practical definitions of knowledge have been given, for example, by Verna Allee, *The Knowledge Evolution: Expanding Organizational Intelligence* (Boston: Butterworth–Heinemann, 1997): 40–55; Karl Erik Sveiby, *The New Organizational Wealth: Managing and Measuring Knowledge-Based Assets* (San Francisco: Berrett-Koehler, 1997): 29–38; and Thomas H. Davenport and Laurence Prusak, *Working Knowledge* (Boston: Harvard Business School Press, 1998): 1–12.

9. Sveiby, op. cit., 37.

10. Davenport and Prusak, op. cit., 6.

11. Donald A. Schön, *The Reflective Practitioner: How Professionals Think in Action* (New York: Basic Books, 1983): 49. Italics in original.

12. Michael Polanyi, *The Tacit Dimension* (London: Routledge & Kegan Paul, 1967): 4.

13. Ikujiro Nonaka and Hirotaka Takeuchi, *The Knowledge-Creating Company* (New York: Oxford University Press, 1995).

14. Bartlett and Ghoshal note that Philips and Unilever have both recognized that the most effective way to manage knowledge flow within large multinational corporations was through socialization processes such as conferences, forums, and training. See Christopher A. Bartlett and Sumantra Ghoshal, "Managing Across Borders: New Organizational Responses," *Sloan Management Review* (Fall 1987): 43–53.

15. Alan M. Webber, "What's So New About the New Economy?" *Harvard Business Review* (January-February 1993).

16. Liedtka et al. make a similar point that in professional service firms there is a "generative cycle" of employee and client development, i.e., knowledge and relationships, but they implicitly treat client relationships as black-box. See Jeanne M. Liedtka, Mark E. Haskins, John W. Rosenblum, and Jack Weber, "The Generative Cycle: Linking Knowledge and Relationships," *Sloan Management Review* (Fall 1997): 47–58.

17. Some researchers use as a base people's understanding of others' motivations to identify three stages of trust: predictability, dependability, and faith. See John K. Rempel, John G. Holmes, and Mark P. Zanna, "Trust in Close Relationships," *Journal of Personality and Social Psychology* 49, no. 1 (1985): 95–112.

18. Ring and Van de Ven have proposed that trust emerges from repeated transactions, and also point out that in close relationships the high risk necessitates high levels of trust. See Peter S. Ring and Andrew H. Van de Ven, "Structuring Cooperative Relationships between Organizations," *Strategic Management Journal* 13 (1992): 482–498.

19. Quinn et al. comment on the challenges of getting professionals to share knowledge, as well as the exponential benefits of companies learning from

outsiders. See James Brian Quinn, Philip Anderson, and Sydney Finkelstein, "Managing Professional Intellect: Making the Most of the Best," *Harvard Business Review* (March-April 1996): 71–80.

20. As Arthur Turner points out, consultants who facilitate client learning will have satisfied clients who will recommend them to others and invite them back the next time there is a need.

21. ClientLink is a trademark of Schlumberger.

22. BP's perspective on this is given in Steven E. Prokesh, "Unleashing the Power of Learning: An Interview with British Petroleum's John Browne," *Harvard Business Review* (September/October 1997): 147–167.

23. See for example Monica Nicou, Christine Ribbing, and Eva Åding, *Sell Your Knowledge: The Professional's Guide to Winning More Business* (London: Kogan Page, 1994): 43.

24. Peter Drucker, *Managing for the Future* (Oxford, UK: Butterworth–Heinemann, 1992).

Chapter 2

Professional Services

Achieving Differentiation in Rapidly Changing Industries

Professional services, for the purposes of this book, are defined as business services based on the application of highly specialized knowledge and expertise. This specialized knowledge is generally, but not always, certified by credentials from academic institutions or professional organizations. This definition enables us to understand the breadth of the field of professional services. It certainly includes the traditional professional service industries such as law, consulting, investment banking, and accounting. But it goes far beyond the traditional parameters to include firms in fields such as advertising, architecture, market research, engineering, public relations, software implementation, independent research and development, and many more; all these clearly provide services based on specialized knowledge.

While the unifying theme behind this diverse range of industries is very simple, it underscores that the fundamental nature of these businesses is the same. Certainly much of the specialist knowledge content is different across industries, but the fact that they are performing services based on distinctive knowledge and expertise results in very similar dynamics operating across all businesses. Professional services maven David Maister affirms that "in spite of many differences, businesses within the professional service sector face very similar issues, regardless of the specific professions they are in."[1]

This book focuses on professional service firms that work with business clients, especially large corporations and institutions. These are the organizations that express most completely the principles of knowledge-based relationships. Professional service firms have been keenly aware for decades that they are in the knowledge business and have long focused on developing their abilities in leveraging knowledge; they also fully understand that their relationships with clients are the foundation of their current and future success. The themes and examples that we develop in this chapter and throughout the book relate primarily to professional services, largely because they represent an excellent model for the future of all differentiated business. In the near future, all companies that have truly differentiated offerings will in essence be professional service firms.

PROFESSIONAL SERVICES AND KNOWLEDGE SPECIALIZATION

Professional services is defined by knowledge specialization. Corporate clients can perform many functions with their own capabilities and expertise, but increasingly need to access highly specialized knowledge from outside, both in outsourcing functions, and enhancing their own processes. Professionals have the scope to focus their resources on very narrow fields of expertise, gain experience across a diverse range of clients, and innovate in the course of their engagements. As both individuals and organizations they are able to develop a far greater depth of knowledge and expertise within highly specialized areas than their clients can. As such, most corporations and institutions usually find that the most effective use of their resources is to seek out professional service firms when they require highly specialized expertise. Clearly, large professional service firms are able to bring together many experts in diverse fields in order to become in some sense "knowledge generalists" to their clients, though this capability is built on a legion of specialists.

Learning from Other Industries

Until recently, each of the professional service industries thought of itself as distinct from others, and so looked primarily to its direct peers and competitors in learning how to confront key business challenges. Law firms studied other law firms, advertising agencies tried to implement best practices in advertising, and engineering firms looked within their own field for ideas and innovation.

This pattern is rapidly changing as professional service firms realize not only that the fundamental nature of their businesses is the same as those in other professional industries; but also that they are facing essentially the same competitive pressures, and sometimes even the same competitors. Given their common foundation, each professional service industry has a tremendous opportunity to learn from the methods of all other professional fields. From now on the greatest innovation in professional service firms will come from that cross-pollination, by adapting and implementing excellent practice from what are fundamentally similar businesses working in different industries.

This book treats the sphere of professional services as a unity, in order to assist practitioners in each industry to learn not only from commonalities across professional services, but also from specific practices in other industries that can be applied in their own fields. Throughout the book we will draw on a wide variety of professional service industries for examples of innovative, excellent practice; most of these provide lessons that can be adapted or directly implemented in other professional service companies. I strongly recommend that in reading each of the examples and case studies you endeavor to adapt and relate the approaches to the circumstances of your own industry.

All Organizations Are Becoming Professional Service Firms

All organizations are becoming professional service firms, as Tom Peters contends.[2] His point is that not just services, but also manufacturing, retailing, and indeed all other industries are rapidly becoming knowledge-based, and as such they are naturally evolving toward the organizational approaches that the professional service industries have pioneered. So in discovering what is relevant to professional service firms, we are also learning what is becoming applicable to almost any organization. Indeed, the principles of knowledge transfer can be applied not only in business-to-business services, but also in product sales, individual services, and certainly government and nonprofit organizations. Certainly any organization deliberately making its clients more knowledgeable is in effect a professional service firm.

As we saw in Chapter 1, client offerings in all industries comprise product, black-box service, and knowledge transfer components. In many product-based industries the knowledge transfer component is small; however, if developed into a larger part of the overall offering, or performed better than competitors, this component can become a vital source of differentiation.

Our focus on corporate and institutional clients in no way suggests that knowledge transfer is not important for individual and retail clients. Certainly the degree of client sophistication impacts the most effective approaches to transferring knowledge, although many individuals make buying decisions based on the knowledge transfer component of offerings. An obvious example of this tendency is found in financial services, ranging across banking, insurance, and stockbroking. While individuals are not usually as sophisticated as institutional clients, they have a strong desire to increase personal control by developing their knowledge underlying the financial decisions they make, and will tend to favor vendors who assist them in making educated decisions. Investors who choose to buy and sell shares through a full-service stockbroker rather than on the Internet are effectively doing so on the basis of the knowledge transfer involved. In product sales, retail customers tend to value highly any genuine efforts to impart knowledge that enables them to make better buying decisions.

Product Companies Become Professional Service Firms

This tendency for organizations to become professional service firms has in fact been very visible, with product-based companies in particular leaping to establish professional service and consulting divisions. The key driver here is that businesses across the board are recognizing that knowledge is a key element of the value they add to clients, and they are formalizing that realization in their offerings. The most obvious example is found in the computer hardware companies. IBM has transformed itself from a company that primarily sold computer hardware to an organization that receives less than half its revenue from hardware, and more than a third from pure services.

Hewlett-Packard's beginnings were in technical instrumentation, though over time computers has become its core business. The firm has now sold off the division representing its original business line. In 1997, Hewlett-Packard set up HP Consulting, which in one fell swoop established a global consulting organization with more than 5,000 employees.

In a very different industry, Continental Grain, one of the largest suppliers of grain worldwide, has established ContiTec, a consulting arm which both provides focused internal consulting services through the company, and services select clients with specialist knowledge on engineering and nutritional issues in their grain processing.

FORCES OF CHANGE IN PROFESSIONAL SERVICES

The field of professional services has become subject to powerful forces, which have already had a substantial impact, but are likely to result in far more dramatic change in the coming years. One of the most fundamental forces is deregulation, which has gradually removed the legal constraints that previously delineated many industries. The influence of deregulation has played a key role in the changing landscape of business over recent decades; telecommunications and banking are two obvious examples of industries affected.

Only more recently has the trend toward deregulation started to impact professional services. Now that the artificial boundaries and constraints of industry regulation are disappearing, more fundamental forces are allowed to come into play. Two key trends are driving change in professional services: *convergence* and *unbundling*. These forces, combined with other factors, are leading to a powerful, accelerating trend to *commoditization*, making it increasingly difficult for professional service firms to differentiate their offerings.

Convergence

The industries that constitute the field of professional services are rapidly converging, with the boundaries between each becoming less distinct, and each industry increasingly encroaching on others' territory. What were formerly quite distinct professions are now gradually merging into a broader single field of professional services. The most striking example is that of the top tier accounting firms. In the period from 1989 to 1998 the Big Eight global accounting firms became the Big Five, all proclaiming themselves to be no longer just accounting firms, but integrated professional service firms. This shift in emphasis reflects the fact that a large proportion of their business has become consulting across a wide variety of disciplines, with a major emerging thrust into legal services and other new disciplines.

Another illustration is found in the arena of corporate finance and mergers and acquisitions (M&A). The roles of investment bankers, lawyers, and accountants in structuring and carrying out these transactions were once fairly distinct. However, each of these professional groups has endeavored to take larger roles in the overall transaction, frequently making them direct competitors for the same business. The Big Five professional service firms are now often competing directly with large investment banks, while law firms are finding that investment banks are now performing work that traditionally would have been viewed as their territory.

In the advertising industry, cries of horror have been raised for several years now at the encroachment of the management consulting firms. These firms have begun to work with major corporations on their branding and market positioning, traditionally one of the most lucrative businesses of the advertising agencies. Advertising conferences and magazines commonly refer to this incursion as a major threat to the business of agencies.[3]

These instances, and many more, illustrate how the field of professional services is gradually converging, with fewer clear distinctions between industries. This trend is resulting in ever more new entrants to each market. While these new entrants often do not have extensive experience in the industry itself, they bring a high degree of competitiveness through existing relationships with the major clients, knowledge of the common methodologies of professional services, and often extensive resources.

Multidisciplinary practices, which bring together professionals in a range of disciplines within a single partnership, are rapidly emerging as a powerful force as regulatory constraints dissolve. Law firms around the world are anxiously tracking the development of the legal services divisions of the major professional service firms, such as Andersen Legal and KPMG Legal. The nature of convergence in professional services, in which there is increasing overlap and direct competition between what used to be fairly distinct industries, is represented in Figure 2–1. The actual professions named in the diagram are simply for

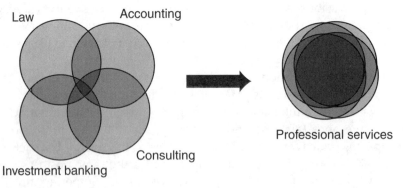

FIGURE 2–1   Convergence in professional services industries.

illustrative purposes, rather than indicating the specifics of how convergence is unfolding.

Unbundling

The rise of new market entrants in each professional service industry has been closely related to unbundling, a trend observed in various forms in almost all industries today. In the older, more comfortable days, companies often bundled all their offerings together into a single package. This way of doing business meant that clients could choose either to take the entire package or nothing, leaving them with no knowledge of the relative value or pricing of the offering's components.

In virtually all industries new competitors, rather than competing head-to-head with existing suppliers for the full range of services offered, have selected a single aspect of those services in which to offer specialized competition. These focused guerilla attacks have left established service providers with little choice but to unbundle their offerings. These pressures have come just as much from the client side, however, with clients seeking more specialized knowledge, greater value, and the ability to compare more directly the pricing and value of the offering's various elements. This has been particularly apparent in separating the knowledge-based and other components of client offerings. Figure 2–2 illustrates the common experience in professional services as to how a single bundled service traditionally offered to clients has now been broken into several components. While Figure 2–1 shows the convergence of the territory encompassed by each professional service industry, Figure 2–2 denotes how actual client offerings are becoming more specifically targeted; this relates in part to how competition between different professions has been engaged.

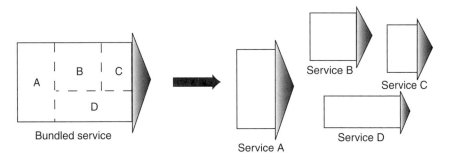

FIGURE 2–2   Unbundling of professional services.

Recent developments in the advertising industry exemplify this trend. Until the early 1990s, advertising agencies in the United States and the United Kingdom provided a broad range of services to their clients, including branding and positioning, media buying, and advertisement creation. The fees for this eclectic range of services were set as a proportion of the costs of media placement. Since then, key client offerings aside from advertisement creation have been offered as stand-alone services by new entrants. As noted before, management consulting firms have made major inroads into the market for branding and positioning consulting, while media planning and buying has effectively become a separate industry, consisting of divisions of the major advertising and media groups and start-up companies that have entered the fray.

Another example is that of retail stockbroker commissions. A typical full-service stockbroker offers highly customized service, market research, account information, and the execution of buy and sell orders, with the price for this overall package determined by a commission on transactions. The advent of Internet stockbroking has stripped out the execution component, which is now available along with research at very low cost. These changes have left full-service brokers struggling to justify their far more expensive brokerage commissions to their clients; this is essentially possible only with knowledge transfer, as opposed to simple information provision.

In a similar vein, when consulting firms in the course of client engagements used to uncover opportunities for further work, they would get that follow-on business fairly automatically. It is becoming far more common for any new projects to be tendered out to a panel of service providers, with little advantage to the firm that originally identified the potential business.

Globalization and One-Stop Shopping

While strong underlying forces are driving unbundling in professional services, these are being met with countervailing forces, some specifically engineered to combat this trend. The Big Five professional services firms, a handful of the global investment banks, the major strategy consulting firms, and the top advertising and media conglomerates, most notably, are actively presenting themselves as "one-stop shops" for their clients.[4]

This positioning is designed to allow clients to focus all their business with one service provider, based on the advantages of deep client knowledge and more effective communication. More importantly, significant advantages exist for global organizations in being able to work with a single supplier across their worldwide business units. Large corporate clients have had mixed responses. Some focusing of relationships has occurred, particularly in the more generic services such as auditing, where there are clear advantages to using a single auditor globally. Other clients prefer to maintain multiple relationships; we will discuss this matter later in the chapter.

The issue remains one of knowledge specialization. Corporate clients are demanding the greatest level of expertise, especially in new and emerging fields, and are increasingly comfortable selecting from a moving array of providers for the professional services they require. Almost all investment banks have given up trying to cover all the global financial markets, and even the giants are presenting themselves as "multi-niche" providers.

Commoditization

All professional services are experiencing a powerful trend toward commoditization. The twin forces of convergence and unbundling are the main factors, but by no means are the only ones at work. Other forces include the increasing digitization of information, the greater availability of information to clients, more rapid communication leading to faster diffusion of innovations, and lower barriers to entry to industries, among others. These forces are applicable in different forms across all industries, resulting in a common experience of a rapidly increasing trend to commoditization. The way these forces are reflected across the spectrum of services is shown in Figure 2–3.

A commoditized market is one in which clients perceive little or no difference between product or service offerings—they have become indistinguishable commodities. In this case the market becomes price and cost-driven: price is the only way clients differentiate between offerings, and sustainable price competition, in turn, depends on achieving lower costs in producing the offering. In light of these market changes, the industry usually becomes largely driven by technology—and sometimes by international production and sourcing—as a means of controlling production costs.

The shape of the business world has changed dramatically since Michael Porter first propounded that essentially two business strategies exist: price-based competition and value-based competition; but if anything this distinction is becoming more evident in the marketplace.[5] This is

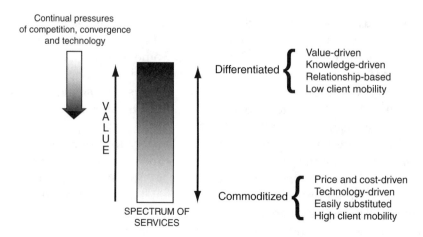

Continual pressures
of competition, convergence
and technology

V
A
L
U
E

SPECTRUM OF
SERVICES

Differentiated {
Value-driven
Knowledge-driven
Relationship-based
Low client mobility

Commoditized {
Price and cost-driven
Technology-driven
Easily substituted
High client mobility

FIGURE 2–3   Commoditization and differentiation across the spectrum of services.

the same distinction as that between commoditized and differentiated markets. In commoditized markets price is the primary means of distinguishing between vendors, while in differentiated markets vendors command premium pricing by adding value to clients in ways other than price.

When client offerings were bundled together, any element of the offering could differentiate the entire package. Much of the process of unbundling across all industries has happened specifically by the actions of new entrants in separating out one part of the overall package in which they can make an equivalent or better offering, and competing directly on price for that component. Once this competition has begun, more entrants step in, and the new market segment becomes purely price and cost driven—a commoditized market.

The middle management executive placement industry exemplifies a professional service that is becoming increasingly commoditized. Perhaps the primary pressure is that of new entrants—it is one of the easiest possible businesses to set up, so many white-collar workers leaving the workforce have established themselves as recruitment consultants. There is continual downward pressure on fees and undercutting by competitors, and differentiation through relationships and excellent service is usually the only factor enabling firms to win business over others at these lower fees, rather than achieving premium pricing.

The Acceleration of Commoditization

The emerging dynamics of increased competition, digitization, and diffusion of information are resulting in an acceleration of the trend toward commoditization. The time cycle for industries to move from value-based (differentiated) to price-based (commoditized) is growing ever shorter. The pressures being experienced by professional service firms will not ease, but rather will intensify over time.

Differentiation

In the face of rapid and accelerating commoditization, how do professional service firms differentiate themselves from their competitors? What are the products and services that are not as strongly subject to these forces of commoditization, and that allow sustainable premium pricing? The answers ultimately lie in the quality of the knowledge held in firms, their ability to apply that knowledge, and the ability to learn and generate new knowledge. This perspective is reflected in Arie de Geus' well-known statement: "the ability to learn faster than your competitors may be the only sustainable advantage."[6] This observation holds true for all industries, but particularly in professional services, the quintessential knowledge business.

Technology will always be an important source of differentiation, but this differentiation is subject to extremely rapid decay as competitors implement similar technology. It is particularly important to identify where diminishing returns on incremental investment set in, and to compare the potential return on investment in technology with other approaches to achieving differentiation. For many information technology-intensive organizations, higher marginal returns are yielded from investment in knowledge and skill development than from incremental investment in technology.

I identify three strongly interrelated sources of sustainable differentiation in professional services:

- Greater specialist knowledge and expertise effectively embedded into products and services. The traditional view of professionals is that their key source of differentiation is greater expertise in their chosen field. This is indeed vital, and the recent flurry of books on knowledge management contains excellent analysis and prescriptions for how to leverage organizational knowledge and embed it into products and services.[7]
- Closer and deeper client relationships. Closer relationships are always a source of differentiation. This includes the personal aspects of relationships, the ability to better understand and service the

client's requirements, and to identify mutually beneficial business opportunities and transactions. For many professional service firms, organizational and personal relationships are the primary ways of winning business over their competitors.

- Greater knowledge transfer, resulting in enhanced client decision-making and business capabilities. This is already an extremely important source of differentiation, and its relevance is increasing. The ability to add value to clients through knowledge transfer relates both to depth of content and process knowledge, as well as organizational capabilities in transferring that knowledge to achieve real benefits for clients.

This book focuses on the interaction of the last two of these three major sources of differentiation. Developing and leveraging internal knowledge is clearly critical to professional service firms, and intrinsic to efforts to transfer knowledge. However, we will not attempt to duplicate existing work in these areas, and will only examine internal issues as they relate to knowledge transfer and client relationships.

UNDERSTANDING PROFESSIONAL SERVICE FIRMS

Having recognized the existence of many important common elements and issues across all professional service industries, identifying and exploring these elements will help us develop a detailed understanding of the field. In addition, it will give us further insight into each professional service industry by revealing which elements differ from those in other industries. This approach enables us to determine what practices in one professional service firm are likely to succeed when applied or adapted to other related industries. Throughout our discussion, we will develop the theme of professional service firms as organizations based on specialist knowledge. We will look at the resources, inputs, functions, and the nature of relationships in professional service firms, and how they add value to their clients' functions. These elements are summarized in Figure 2–4.

Resources of Professional Service Firms

The key resources of professional service firms are certainly not fixed assets such as plants and machinery. Trying to understand knowledge-intensive companies has driven the development of the new field of

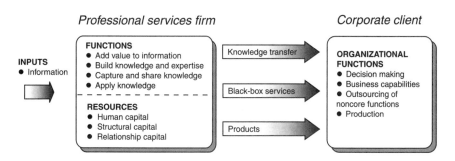

FIGURE 2–4   A general model of professional service firms.

intellectual capital, which has provided us with frameworks for managing and beginning to measure the intangible assets of organizations. Of course, professional service firms as prototypical knowledge-based organizations provide an excellent illustration of the tenets of intellectual capital.

Frameworks for intellectual capital have been proposed by, among others, Sveiby,[8] Stewart,[9] Edvinsson and Malone,[10] Roos et al.,[11] and Brooking.[12] These frameworks all build on the original work of Sveiby; as such their basic structure and composition are very similar, with a few differences between authors over terminology and distinctions between the major categories of intellectual capital.

We will present our preferred framework for categorizing intangible assets, which is based on the work of all of the authors above, and uses definitions relevant to our purposes. The intangible assets of organizations can be separated into three categories:

- Human capital
- Structural capital
- Relationship capital

Human capital refers to the people who work for an organization, and their skills and abilities in creating value for the organization and its clients. *Structural capital* includes systems, processes, legally protected intellectual property such as patents, and organizational culture. *Relationship capital* includes relationships with clients, suppliers, alliance members, regulators, and other parties, as well as image and reputation.

Looking at this framework from the perspective of knowledge generation and transfer, human capital—essentially the people in an organization—is ultimately the key resource of professional service firms, and where the most valuable knowledge resides. Increasingly, organizations are attempting to capture that knowledge in documents, databases and processes—that is, to make it part of their structural capital. Nevertheless, the ability to apply that knowledge to generate profitable business depends on the quality of the organization's relationship capital, notably its client relationships.

Inputs of Professional Service Firms

The traditional inputs of industrial companies are basic commodities and low-level manufactured goods. What are the inputs of professional services firms? Information is the primary raw commodity used by knowledge organizations in performing their functions. These firms take information from external sources, and using their resources, including the knowledge held by their people, process that information in order to create value for their clients.

Financial markets are a clear example of a world completely driven by information and its interpretation by market participants. Financial market brokers and traders must have access to all major information sources, and their daily work is completely based around analyzing and making decisions based on that information. Walter Wriston, former chairman of Citibank, writes about how information flows through the nervous system of global financial markets to determine how money and prices move.[13] Similarly, lawyers can only perform their work on the basis of complete information about relevant legal cases, together with information and knowledge about their clients and the business environment.

Functions of Professional Service Firms

Professional service firms, when seen as knowledge-based organizations that add value to their clients through the execution of services, perform four key functions which draw on their resources and inputs. These are:

- Adding value to information
- Developing knowledge and expertise
- Capturing and sharing knowledge
- Applying knowledge

Adding value to information is a key process in professional firms, which we will cover in detail in Chapter 3. It is a particularly critical function when knowledge transfer is an important issue, as much of the process of adding value to information lies in making it easy to internalize as knowledge, and readily usable in decision making.

Developing knowledge and expertise is an ongoing task for professional firms. The existing knowledge of their partners and staff is a base on which they must continually develop and build. The staff must not only keep pace with knowledge development in their fields by reading journals, going to conferences, and keeping an open dialogue with their peers, but also continually generate new knowledge by building on what they have learned, and applying the experience gained in working on client projects.

Capturing and sharing knowledge is at the heart of what is commonly called knowledge management. Particularly in larger firms, developing individual knowledge and expertise is less important than getting the most useful, valuable knowledge to be made available and used as widely as possible across the firm. To the extent that knowledge can be captured (i.e., made explicit), it can become part of the permanent structural capital of the organization rather than simply existing in one key individual's mind. As we saw in Chapter 1, sharing knowledge can happen directly or indirectly; both rich social interaction and the effective implementation of technology are essential.

Applying knowledge is the final step that makes the knowledge valuable. This application can be in product development, marketing, strategic decision making, performing services for clients, or any of the many activities that generate revenue and profitable business. Developing and sharing knowledge are only meaningful and useful if that knowledge leads to better business results through its application to the critical operations and functions of an organization.

Adding Value to Client Functions

Adding value to clients is ultimately about enabling them to add greater value to their own clients and customers. We saw in Chapter 1 that client offerings can be broken down into three intertwined components: products, black-box services, and knowledge transfer. These are the means available to add value to clients. We will briefly review the key client functions that these components impact in creating value.

The value added through products includes increased efficiency and production capabilities for client organizations. Black-box services enable clients to outsource specialist functions that can be performed more effectively or at lower cost than if handled in-house. This strategy adds value by achieving better outcomes at lower cost in noncore functions, and allowing management to focus on their core capabilities and competencies. As we have seen, knowledge transfer essentially adds value by resulting in either better decision making or enhanced business capabilities, or in both results.

THE NATURE OF PROFESSIONAL SERVICE RELATIONSHIPS

The relationships of professional service firms with their clients differ from relationships in many other industries primarily in the richness of interaction. The heart of professional services is in providing high-level knowledge-based services, which requires a high degree of client contact. Many other industries do not require that degree of interaction. Maister proposes that the two distinguishing characteristics of professional services are the high degree of customization of services, and the emphasis on face-to-face interaction.[14]

The structure of professional service relationships with clients is guided by the nature of professional services—which applies specialized knowledge when it is required—and the way competition has developed in these industries. Here we will examine several important aspects of how professional service relationships are structured. Practical approaches to structuring client contact are examined in detail in Chapter 7.

Project-Based and Ongoing Relationships

Since professional service firms provide specialist knowledge resources, they are often only brought in by their clients when situations arise in which these resources are required. Usually the client has a specific objective in mind, and achieving that outcome constitutes the project or engagement for the service provider. For example, lawyers are engaged for particular cases or transactions, consulting firms are hired to address specific challenges, and investment bankers work on deals to raise capital.

On the other hand, particularly when services constitute an outsourcing of knowledge-based functions, relationships can also be ongoing in nature. Public relations firms might manage their clients' images on an ongoing basis, the financial market arms of investment banks and stockbrokers help their clients manage their portfolios on a day-to-day basis, and large corporations usually appoint a single advertising agency to develop and manage all their advertising campaigns.

In many cases these two relationship models are combined; this is perhaps the most accurate characterization of professional service relationships. Service providers are engaged for specific projects or transactions, but within the context of an ongoing relationship. Different industries, or usually even different services within each industry, are more transaction-oriented or ongoing, though most have aspects of both models. One of the challenges of professional service relationship management is managing individual transactions or projects within the scope of an ongoing relationship.

Multiple Service Provider Relationships and Panels

A critical issue inherent in many professional service industries is that major corporations and institutions have relationships simultaneously with a number of competitive vendors. Depending on the industry, this situation can result in the selection of a service provider for any specific project from among the chosen few with whom the client has an ongoing relationship, often through direct competition with the others.[15]

One implication is that the client must ensure that it does not spread its business too thinly, or it will not receive focused attention from its service providers. This potential pitfall is often addressed by nominating a panel of service firms. If the services are project-based, providers for specific engagements will be selected from the panel; whereas if the relationships are ongoing, as in portfolio management, business is allocated among the panel members. The panel arrangement limits the number of firms to which business is allocated, and allows many of the advantages of close relationships, as well as access to a range of suppliers.

Prime Contracting and Controlling the Relationship

Increasing client demand for specialized knowledge has helped to drive unbundling, with small professional firms springing up in highly focused fields or areas of expertise. The Big Five's response has been to grow bigger and to encompass as many of their clients' requirements as possible, but they can never be all things to all people. However, clients do not want to incur the expense and effort of individually selecting each professional service firm they require, and then managing the resulting medley of organizations.

This situation has presented an excellent opportunity for prime contracting or project management roles to develop, in which the client contracts to a single firm which undertakes to identify, bring together, and manage all the "best-of-class" service firms in each field. This strategy is indeed becoming more common, with broad alliances allowing these kinds of networks to develop as true competitors to the largest professional service firms.

The key issue here is to identify who controls the client relationship. While these networks are a good opportunity for small, highly specialized firms to acquire ongoing business, the value they create—and the fees they receive—are limited to their defined scope of operation. The only firm in this arrangement able to build it into an ongoing virtuous circle of value creation is the one that controls that relationship with the client. This will be the prized role in the emergent professional service networks, which again emphasizes the critical value of relationships and relationship development.

ANALYSIS OF KNOWLEDGE TRANSFER IN PROFESSIONAL SERVICES

To put the issues of knowledge transfer in professional services into perspective, it is valuable to examine in greater detail how they apply in several industries. We will study strategy consulting, institutional stockbroking, and corporate legal services, to bring out some of the commonalities and differences among a range of professional service industries. For each one we will look briefly at what distinguishes the black-box service and knowledge transfer components of the client offering, what value is added to clients in decision-making and enhancing capabilities, the nature of client contact, and pricing models. Additional information about these issues are given in Chapters 1, 4, 5, 7, and 9 respectively.

Each industry examined encompasses great diversity, with individual firms in the industry categories often taking very different approaches to business. Thus, only general statements can be made about many aspects of those industries. Because of this diversity, any brief analyses such as the following will be fairly simplistic, but are nevertheless useful in getting a flavor for the real-world application and relevance of knowledge transfer in professional services.

Strategy Consulting

Here we look at consulting firms which specialize in assisting their clients in establishing top-level organizational strategy. This is the core service offered by most of the top global management consulting firms.

Components of the Client Offering

Strategy consulting is often open-ended in that clients themselves do not know precisely the questions they want answered or the outcomes they seek—consultants are commonly asked to define issues at stake as well as an optimal course of action. A typical consulting engagement (if there is such a thing) involves defining outcomes with top management, gathering and analyzing information both internal and external to the client organization, making recommendations for action, and sometimes assisting in implementing the recommendations.

There are several different schools of thought within strategy consulting, which can most easily be distinguished by where they fall on the spectrum between black-box services and knowledge transfer. In the former case, consultants get a briefing, gather information inside and outside the organization, and eventually return with a report giving the results of research and subsequent recommendations. On the other end of the scale, projects involve combined teams from the consulting firm and client, and the client is essentially facilitated in coming to its own conclusions. The nature of the consulting engagement, and the preferences and style of both the client and consulting firm will determine the style of engagement. However, over the past two decades there has been a clear shift to more knowledge transfer in strategy consulting projects.

Decision Making

The outcome from strategy consulting is explicitly better strategic decisions by the client. In the case of the black-box consulting style, the firm presents recommendations for action, and while justification for these is given, the process by which the conclusion is reached is often not clear; clients can either accept or reject the recommendations. In this case the decision is effectively made by the consultant, with the client only required to endorse it. In the knowledge transfer approach, key decision makers on the client side are led to understand the issues at stake in the decision, how to deal effectively with them, and to make optimal decisions. Strategy consulting clearly deals specifically with strategic decision making, with few implications at the line management level, unless they are relevant to the implementation of strategy.

Enhanced Capabilities

Much of the consulting relating to enhancing client capabilities is essentially not strategy consulting, but more process consulting. The implementation of recommendations from strategy projects can involve this style of consulting. Within the field of strategy consulting, some styles focus on facilitating the client in developing more effective decision-making processes. This approach results in helping the client to have greater strategic decision-making capabilities beyond the scope of the consulting project.

Nature of Client Contact

A wide variety of approaches are utilized in client contact. Generally the senior members of the consulting team are briefed by the client's top management, and lead the presentation of the findings, while much of the work underlying the project is usually done by more junior consultants. Consultants will either work off-site for more analytical projects, or in the case of interactive projects may work as part of a joint client-consultant team, or be based at the client organization.

Pricing Models

Strategy consulting, while traditionally charged on an hourly or daily rate, or on the basis of project fees usually reflecting the expected time required by consulting staff, has begun to implement more innovative approaches to pricing. More and more, strategy consulting firms are seeking to link the value created by their engagements, in terms of impact on costs, profitability, or even share price, to the revenue they receive from projects.

Institutional Stockbroking

Here we examine the global stockbroking industry servicing institutional fund managers. With financial services industry consolidation, institutional stockbroking is often a division within investment banks, although some independent stockbrokers remain.

Components of the Client Offering

Almost all the black-box service components of institutional stockbroking can be considered to be the execution of trades—quickly and efficiently buying and selling often large blocks of equities in a rapidly moving and sometimes illiquid market. A number of factors contribute to these capabilities, including the skill of the broker's traders, the size of its balance sheet, its willingness to use the balance sheet in taking large market positions to facilitate trades, and its relationships with major investors.

The remainder of the service—and by far the bulk of the value—provided is in knowledge transfer. This consists of high-value information, research, and advice on issues ranging from the flow of trades in the market to strategic portfolio positioning.

Decision Making

Fund managers live and die by their decisions—adding value to their ability to make profitable investment decisions holds the greatest value for them. This represents a classic example of portfolio decision making.

Fund managers generally have access to similar commercially-available (commoditized) data and information as stockbrokers—value is provided both in high-value short-term information such as detailed market activity, and in comprehensive research on macroeconomics and specific stocks. Fund managers almost always make their own decisions, although they can both be guided to specific opportunities by the brokers, and given input into their own decision-making processes. This is one of the purest examples of value being attributed to knowledge communication and elicitation.

Enhanced Capabilities

Fund managers do not generally look to stockbrokers to enhance their overall capabilities as part of their relationship. Some leading stockbrokers provide analytical models and tools which clients can apply for themselves; arguably, however, these are "products" in the sense that they encapsulate but do not transfer knowledge.

Nature of Client Contact

The nature of client contact is rapidly evolving. Equity salespeople originally had most of the contact with fund managers, channeling the appropriate research from their research team, with most contact on the telephone, supplemented by occasional research analyst visits. It is now increasingly difficult for equity salespeople to speak directly with a fund manager—contact is often handled mainly by voice-mail and e-mail.[16] Research analysts are spending an increasing proportion of their time in direct contact and discussion with clients, and less time on producing generic published research.

Pricing Models

Revenue was originally based on commissions on share transactions, with commission levels regulated in most countries, although these have now been deregulated with spectacular consequences. Fund managers traditionally rewarded stockbrokers for good ideas or service by executing transactions through them. More recently, allocation of revenue to stockbrokers has become commonly based on systems in which fund managers vote on which stockbrokers have added the most value to them. This subject is examined in more detail in Chapter 9.

Corporate Legal Services

Here we examine services provided by law firms to corporations. We will limit ourselves to nonlitigation services, which nevertheless will cover a very broad range of services.

Components of the Client Offering

Lawyers until recently have tended to think of themselves as subject experts performing services within their field of specialization for clients, usually with little or no knowledge transfer. This is a classic model of black-box services. In most instances clients indeed choose to outsource this specialist expertise, and have services performed for them. Lawyers often describe themselves as "advisors," although this still most commonly means recommending to the client the single best decision or approach rather than providing input to decision making.

Many law firms run seminars for their clients, however, these usually result in limited knowledge transfer. Client newsletters are increasingly common, though are often intended more to impress clients with the firm's knowledge than to result in effective knowledge transfer. It is fairly common for law firms to temporarily post their lawyers at key clients, which is a far more effective means of adding real value.

The legal industry is making a concerted effort to "productize" its services, increasingly by establishing wholly owned or joint venture companies. Products are still usually a small part of the client offering, however.

Decision Making

As mentioned above, law firms tend to provide advice to their clients on major decisions and transactions, though the advice is usually framed as a set of recommendations rather than input to their clients' decision-making processes. The better law firms use their close relationships with top management at their client organizations to maintain a dialogue on strategic issues, which means that they can provide input on legal, regulatory, and broader business issues relevant to their clients' strategic thinking.

There is often a significant element of knowledge transfer to line decision makers by law firms, though the lawyers consider it a low-value service. This knowledge transfer is commonly implemented in briefings and training courses for line managers on issues such as health and safety, human resource practices, and other subjects. Some of the higher-value services in this area include knowledge relevant to product development, such as issues of intellectual property and product liability.

Enhanced Capabilities

Lawyers are usually very reluctant to enable their clients to take over any of their own functions. While the size of in-house corporate legal functions has fluctuated over time, they have recently tended to grow larger, making the role of enhancing capabilities more relevant. It is increasingly common for corporate counsel to specifically request knowledge transfer from their legal firms.

Nature of Client Contact

Most client contact tends to be concentrated on senior partners at the law firms, partially as much of the work performed by junior staff can often be done with little client contact. The results of engagements are almost always communicated in written reports—the traditional form of legal communication. There is a greater degree of client interaction, and the black-box model is slowly eroding.

Pricing Models

The legal industry works largely on a per-hour billings basis, which is usually transparent to clients. Contingency fees have always been part of the legal landscape in the United States, but have only recently been introduced in the United Kingdom and Australia. They are still most common in litigation, but are beginning to be used more often in other fields.

SUMMARY: PROFESSIONAL SERVICES AND KNOWLEDGE-BASED RELATIONSHIPS

Professional services are business services based on the application of highly specialized knowledge. This definition includes a wide variety of industries, including not just the traditional professional service practices such as consulting, investment banking, and law, but a far more diverse range of organizations. The common theme of knowledge specialization which underlies professional services means that all industries within the field have much to learn from each other, and the fundamental importance of knowledge in the economy means that indeed almost all organizations can use their approaches as a model.

There are powerful forces at play throughout the field of professional services, however, such as convergence and unbundling, which are resulting in accelerating commoditization. It is increasingly difficult for firms to differentiate themselves from their competitors, and knowledge transfer is a vital source of that differentiation.

The field of intellectual capital informs us that the primary resources of knowledge-based organizations are human capital, structural capital, and relationship capital. The primary input of professional service firms is information, while its functions include adding value to information, as well as developing, sharing, and applying knowledge.

The structure of professional service relationships is guided by the nature of professional services as based on specialist knowledge. Depending on the industry and situation, they will be based on some blend of specific projects with clear objectives and parameters, and ongoing relationships. This often leads to situations where clients work with a panel of service providers, or sometimes a prime contractor that coordinates a network of firms.

In Part I we have covered some of the fundamental issues of knowledge, knowledge-based relationships, and the professional service firms to which these subjects are most relevant. The next step is to understand how knowledge is used in adding value to clients. The three chapters in the next section address adding value to information, client decision making, and client capabilities. They develop further some of the principles we have introduced, and start to become more pragmatic in suggesting practical approaches which professional service firms can implement to address these issues, drawing on examples of excellent practice. The nuts and bolts of implementation will be covered in the third section of the book.

NOTES

1. David H. Maister, *Managing the Professional Service Firm* (New York: The Free Press, 1997): xvi.
2. Peters, op. cit., 11.
3. For example, "Management Consultants: What's Their Agenda? How Should Advertising Agencies Respond?" Account Planning Group Conference, London, June 11, 1997.
4. Bresnahan looks at some of the pros and cons of one-stop shopping, as well as issues of knowledge transfer in IT consulting. See Jennifer Bresnahan, "The Latest in Suits," *CIO Enterprise* (October 15, 1998).
5. Michael E. Porter, *Competitive Advantage: Creating and Sustaining Superior Performance* (New York: The Free Press, 1985).
6. Arie P. de Geus, "Planning as Learning," *Harvard Business Review* 66, no. 2 (March-April 1988): 70–74.
7. See for example Davenport and Prusak; or James Brian Quinn, *Intelligent Enterprise: A Knowledge and Service Based Paradigm for Industry* (New York: The Free Press, 1992).
8. Sveiby, op. cit.
9. Stewart (1997).
10. Leif Edvinsson and Michael S. Malone, *Intellectual Capital: Realizing Your Company's True Value by Finding Its Hidden Roots* (New York: HarperBusiness, 1997).
11. Johan Roos, Göran Roos, Leif Edvinsson, and Nicola Dragnetti, *Intellectual Capital* (Basingstoke, UK: Macmillan Press, 1997).
12. Annie Brooking, *Intellectual Capital: Core Asset for the Third Milennium Enterprise* (London: International Thomson Business Press, 1996).
13. Walter B. Wriston, "Dumb Networks and Smart Capital," *The Cato Journal* 17, no. 3 (Winter 1998).
14. Maister, xv.
15. Eccles and Crane have done an analysis of multiple service provider relationships in investment banking. See Chapter 3 of Robert G. Eccles and Dwight B. Crane, *Doing Deals: Investment Banks at Work* (Cambridge, MA: Harvard Business School Press, 1988).
16. Stephen Irvine, "The Year of Retrenchment," *Euromoney* (September 1998).

Part II

Adding Value with Knowledge

Chapter 3

Adding Value to Information
From Information to Knowledge

Professional service firms can add value to clients through performing black-box services, providing information, and enhancing clients' decision-making and business capabilities. Information now plays a central role in the global economy, however, information only creates value for clients when it is applied.

The essential distinction between information and knowledge is that information can be digitized, while knowledge is intrinsic to people. Knowledge can be transferred either directly between people through socialization, or indirectly by delivering information which people can internalize as their personal knowledge. Both means of transferring knowledge are fundamental to professional services, and while direct interpersonal contact is critical for rich knowledge sharing and relationship development, the dynamics of technology and markets mean that information is playing an increasingly dominant role in shaping the world of business. In this chapter, we examine the dynamics of adding value to information in serving professional service clients.

INFORMATION AND DIGITIZATION

Probably the best way of understanding the nature of information is that it is something which is or can be digitized.[1] The digitization of information allows it to be stored indefinitely, duplicated at will, communicated almost instantly anywhere in the world, analyzed and compared with other information, and accessed easily from vast databases. These are fabulous benefits, which leads to a very strong motivation to digitize information wherever possible. Digitization is driving the tremendous growth in the information technology industry, which now attracts over half of US capital investment. Simultaneously, digitization has rapidly become more possible and pervasive through the exponential improvement of the price/performance ratios of both computing power and communications, combined with its increasing scope, which has extended from simple data and text to pictures, sound, video, and beyond.

While there are many advantages to digitized information, it also has very real limitations as a means of interpersonal communication and knowledge transfer. In other words, technology will never completely replace face-to-face meetings and interaction. The major limitation of digitized information is found in its inability to communicate subtleties.

The visual aspect of meetings can be digitized, although the restricted bandwidth of videoconferencing means that important social and other cues are missed, substantially reducing the effectiveness of interaction. Moreover, the relative formality (and cost) of these situations means that the more tangential yet often more productive conversations usually just don't happen. As the term "socialization" implies, much useful knowledge transfer happens informally and by osmosis, which requires being in the same location. I, for one, do not look forward to a day when I share a virtual beer with a virtual colleague or client after a day of virtual work—and those who attempt to work solely in that way will be significantly disadvantaged over those who have rich ongoing informal interaction.

So while face-to-face interaction and knowledge transfer will never be fully supplanted in high-value situations such as professional services, it remains that the role of information in adding value to clients is critically important. This role will become even more important as the dynamics of the digital economy make information cheaper and more effective as a rich communication medium. In implementing knowledge transfer to clients, we need to understand how to add the greatest value to information, how to transform raw data into high-value information, and how that information can become valuable knowledge for our clients.

INFORMATION OVERLOAD!

Perhaps the most obvious feature of the Information Age is the overwhelming flood of information in which we are swimming (or drowning!). We are deluged with articles, quotes, and data that tell us how much information we are receiving and how fast the information flow is growing, with commentators wailing that humans were never meant to swim in these turbulent waters, and that this kind of society is not sustainable.[2]

This information overload is driven not only by the availability of information, but by the fact that almost all managers find they need more information about more topics than ever before. Professionals need to keep up-to-date and informed not only in their own fields of specialization, but also on their clients' industries, as well as on broader changes in the business environment, including the rapidly developing impact of technology. In a study commissioned by Reuters, 85 percent of middle managers agreed that they need as much information as possible in order to keep abreast of their customers and competitors.[3]

The Attention Economy

Information overload is a critical factor in the productivity of all knowledge workers, and is in many ways at the heart of the knowledge economy. One of its most important consequences is the competition for people's attention. Some argue that there is now no shortage of primary resources, capital, or information, and that attention is the only true scarce resource today—and thus that which drives the economy.[4] In the "attention economy" those who can attract and keep people's attention are kings and queens.

Seeing attention as the key economic resource helps us to understand many of the changing dynamics in the business environment. It has driven the shift of emphasis from product marketing to customer relationships, which in turn has been an important factor behind global consolidation in financial services and other industries. The rise of "one-to-one marketing," which focuses on customizing products and services to individual customers, also reflects this trend.[5] Perhaps most obvious, the business models of most Internet companies are based on attracting visitors with services, entertainment, and cheap goods; and then exploiting their valuable attention through advertising or gathering customer information.

The same principles apply in sophisticated professional services, in which clients are often overwhelmed with high-value information from service providers and would-be providers. Information must be able to cut through the massive information overload clients experience to capture their attention. This critical ability underscores both the vital roles of relationships, which are often essential in getting even the first glance at your information, and the importance of designing information that captures and keeps attention.

The Democratization of Information

The increasing availability and access to information which are driving spiralling information overload are also having a major impact on the economics of information. Once information is created, it can be duplicated at virtually no cost, resulting in constant downward pressure on the market value of information.[6] Most information is now commoditized, and in fact an enormous amount of information is being made available for free. The swift development of the Internet has allowed anyone who so wishes to make information easily and broadly available; this is helping to accelerate the pace of commoditization.

The nature of the media industry is fundamentally changing in that customers now have access to much of the same raw information as it does. Customers are no longer forced to go to newspapers, magazines, and television for their news, but can often get it directly from the same sources as the media. People will choose to go through media only if value is added to the original information. This is just as true in business—clients usually have access to the same general information as their service providers, and will only pay for information to which high value has been added.

These trends have substantially changed how professional firms add value to clients with information. Access to information used to be a significant differentiator, but that is far less the case today—clients can find much of the information they need for free on the Internet or for a small fee from databases. The emphasis is increasingly on adding value to information, providing context, and applying it in the client's situation. This has always been the case, of course, but now that clients have very similar information available to them as their service providers have, professional service firms are being driven to add increased value to information.

Internal and External Orientation

Effective information management systems must address the issues of information overload, striving for the delicate balance between delivering and giving access to the most vital information people require in performing their functions, without overloading them. To date these systems, however, have been primarily oriented to internal use in organizations. The dynamics of adding value to information with an external orientation—that is, for clients—are substantially different. Most importantly, there is far less control over information dissemination, and in contrast to internal systems, which hold a quasi-monopoly of their users' attention, external suppliers must compete with a host of other information sources.

THE VALUE OF INFORMATION

For professional service firms, the most relevant and useful way of thinking about the value of information is the practice of how to add value to it from a client perspective. We will address this question in some detail later in this chapter. But what *is* the value of information, and how can we measure it? It is difficult and in some ways almost meaningless to try to attribute an absolute "value" to information. However, in order to be most effective in adding value to information, it is worth briefly examining the nature of the value of information.

Value Depends on Context

The value of information and knowledge is entirely dependent on the context in which they are made available. A report on best practice in implementing e-commerce could be worth millions of dollars in savings to a large company planning to embark on such a project, substantially less to a smaller company or one already well down the track on implementation, and nothing to an individual or company with no plans for e-commerce. For information to be valuable to an organization, the organization must be in a position to act on it, and the profitability of the resulting action will suggest the information's value.

In addition, the way any information adds value to an organization depends substantially on the context of all other information it receives and to which it has access. If a client has little knowledge of a specific field, then the most valuable information will be an overview of the situation. More often clients already have access to fairly rich information on any given topic, meaning general information is likely to be of lesser value, and what will be most valuable is specific intelligence and recommendations for action that build on the client's existing knowledge.

High, Low, and Negative Value Information

While the value of information varies with context, it can also be seen across contexts in its capacity to create value. Information that will affect the valuation of a company in a multibillion dollar takeover can easily be worth hundreds of millions of dollars, while knowing how many ice cream cones the corner shop sold yesterday will never be worth a fortune to anyone. We can certainly begin to distinguish between high-value information and low-value information.

What is less obvious is that information can have negative value, as Karl-Erik Sveiby points out.[7] This point becomes clearer when we understand that the value of anything equals the benefits from using it, minus the costs of using it. In a world of information overload, the cost of "using" information in terms of the time and effort required to read or otherwise internalize it is often more than the benefit gained from that information. When people send you a glut of information that is not highly valuable to you, they are in fact subtracting value from you. Time and attention are extremely valuable; for example, the value of your time and attention in reading this book is many times greater than the price you paid for it.

The objective of professional service firms, or indeed any organizations that disseminate information, is to take low-value information and use it to create high-value information. As we saw in Chapter 2, the primary input of professional firms is information, however, this is mainly low or negative value information. One of the key functions of these firms is to add value to this information by using it to create high-value information for their clients, as well as for use in their own operations. We will examine this process in detail in a moment.

Knowledge and High-Value Information

Having seen that information can have high, low, or negative value within a given context, it is useful to revisit the distinction between information and knowledge. Many people state or imply that high-value information is knowledge, while low-value information is information. Using these definitions, it is impossible to say what distinguishes information and knowledge. At what point does information become valuable enough to call it knowledge? This issue emphasizes the importance of differentiating between information and knowledge by understanding that knowledge is intrinsic to people. Having made that distinction, we can then better understand the domain of information by distinguishing between different levels of value.

While we can talk about the value of information, the value of knowledge can only be regarded as a general concept. Knowledge as the capacity to act effectively cannot be subdivided into components—it is an integral whole. Yes, knowledge is valuable, having perhaps the greatest value there is, but since it is intrinsic to a person only the sum of his or her knowledge could be effectively valued, and not any discrete part of the total. For information to have a very high value it must be easy to internalize as knowledge; as we will see, the ease of assimilating or internalizing information is a key factor in determining its value.

The question frequently also arises as to the distinction between data and information. This is less clear-cut than the distinction between information and knowledge, however, we will use the term "data" to refer to low or negative-value information. This tallies with the definition of information as "data that makes a difference," which suggests that data in itself doesn't make a difference.[8]

ADDING VALUE TO INFORMATION

The rapidly developing importance of information means that adding value to information represents a substantial, growing proportion of the process of creating value in the economy. The steps and processes in making information more valuable to clients are at the heart of value creation, and are core professional service activities. Implementing and continually improving these processes within an organization are vital to its success.

The business of providing data or low-value information will remain important, and certainly many clients are prepared to purchase information for input into their own value-adding processes. The nature of this business, however, is commoditized and low-margin, and we will choose to focus on the delivery of high-value information as a source of differentiation, significant client value, and premium pricing.

The Role of People

The processes that add the most value to information are those performed by people and that cannot be computerized or automated. This is certainly true at the moment. Over time computers will be able to perform more and more of the processes that add value to information;

however, people will still add the greatest value. There are two key reasons for this observation. Knowledge is about combining and synthesizing information based on meaning and context, which cannot be done without understanding; computers are a long way from being capable of understanding. And anything that can be automated will become commoditized in fairly short order, meaning that differentiation will continue to depend on the abilities of intelligent people.

In order for people to add value to information, they must first internalize it as knowledge. This means integrating it into their existing knowledge, adding value to that knowledge—which often happens in the process of internalization, as well as through subsequent analysis and synthesis—and then externalizing it as value-added information. This process is illustrated in Figure 3–1.

How Information Is Used

Information can be used in a wide variety of contexts and situations. Decision making is the most obvious application of information; this topic will be covered in detail in Chapter 4. Information may not be destined for use in specific decisions; however, it may be intended simply to keep managers informed of what is relevant and important in their business environment, and to help build the knowledge that provides a broad backdrop to decision-making and business activity. In most cases managers do not acquire knowledge to address a specific situation, but draw on their existing knowledge to act effectively, and seek to develop their working knowledge on an ongoing basis.

Information is not always used by people, of course—it is now often used as raw input into computer systems and models which either perform specific analysis, or sometimes look for patterns or generate

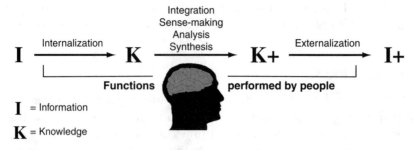

FIGURE 3–1   How people add value to information.

rules for behavior, as with neural networks. Most of the raw information used by these systems is commoditized, and the major issues in information delivery in this situation are in data validation and formatting. We will not examine these issues in detail, as this creates little value compared with providing information for use by people.

THE PROCESS OF ADDING VALUE TO INFORMATION

There are seven key processes in adding value to information. Our focus here is adding value to information users outside the organization, although the same principles apply to adding value to information for use within an organization. These seven processes are:

- Filtering
- Validation
- Analysis
- Synthesis
- Presentation
- Ease of access and use
- Customization

We have seen that the value of information depends on the context in which it is used, and most of these processes can be performed effectively only if the context is specified. Customization can actually be considered to be part of each of the other processes. We have chosen to distinguish it as a separate process, however, as a critical aspect of adding value to information.

Filtering

Filtering is a process of reducing the quantity of information by assessing its relevance and value. In most cases this can only be determined relative to the intended audience. The narrower the audience, and thus the greater the specificity of assessing relevance and value, the greater the value of the filtering process.

Technology can help with low-level filtering, for example, by selecting documents that contain specified key words. Agent software takes this a step further by learning user preferences over time on the basis of feedback. Still, computers may be good at processing information, but remain very poor at assessing its relevance and usefulness.

Collaborative filtering technology works by getting people to grade the relevance and value of all documents they read, and pools those assessments to provide recommendations to other people with related job and interest profiles. This means that all levels of executives can input their evaluations of the documents they read, leading to far more useful assessments of the documents' value than would be achieved by dedicated administrative staff.

Nicholas Negroponte writes of the importance of serendipity in information searches: stumbling across unexpected and unsought valuable discoveries.[9] Receiving information that is too highly filtered reduces the chances of coming across other useful information. While focused information sources, such as legal technology newsletters, should be filtered within tight parameters, when providing a larger proportion of your clients' overall information requirements it is best to strive for a balance between a high degree of filtering and allowing for serendipitous discoveries.

Validation

The reliability and trustworthiness of information from the client's perspective is a key element of value. The first aspect of validating information is ensuring that the information provided is indeed correct, or instead assessing and rating its reliability. The second aspect is making your clients confident that your validation is itself reliable. If they have faith that information you supply is accurate and correct, it can save them substantial time and effort in checking and cross-referencing, and allows for instant action.

The reputation of newspapers, magazines, and wire services is largely dependent on the perception that the information they provide is accurate. Elaborate checking procedures are usually in place to ensure that incorrect information does not go out, often at the cost of timeliness. Companies are prepared to pay substantially more for information provided by Reuters or Bloomberg, for example, than for the same information on the Internet, in part because they can be confident the information is correct. The reputation of these firms for information quality has been built up over time.

Information validation is to a significant degree a manual process. Some of its elements can be automated, especially those providing an alert to potential spurious data; however, human judgment and supervision are required. Fortunately, much of the information validation process can be performed by fairly low-level, inexpensive staff. Organizations may choose to establish centralized information validation functions; alternatively, teams can set up quality systems to cross check each other's work, which is usually the practice in major consulting firms.

Analysis

Analysis includes a wide variety of approaches and techniques for manipulating, categorizing, and correlating information. In many cases, analysis is performed with computers; however, selecting the type of analysis to be performed usually remains a human task.

Categorizing is a type of analysis, as it gives a context—and thus some meaning—to information. Identifying correlations in data adds substantial value, as it reveals trends that can lead directly to profitable action, or at least a deeper understanding of the business environment. This is a prime task for number-crunching machines, though people still play an important role. An example of this kind of analysis is found in visual data mining software, which shows visual representations of the patterns underlying enormous bodies of data, and in turn enables people to pick out relevant correlations and trends.

Analysis includes the use of many quantitative tools and models. Proprietary analytical approaches, in particular, can turn data into information directly relevant to decision making. An example is found in credit rating agencies such as Moody's and Standard & Poor's. Their detailed access to many companies' accounts over an extended period has enabled them to assess the relative importance of different data in determining credit quality. This evaluation has produced proprietary models that assess credit risk for each industry, and can be used to analyze data in ways that add substantial value. It is important to note, however, that these quantitative analytics form only a part of the rating agencies' assessments, and human judgment is a major component of their rating processes.

Synthesis

Synthesis of a wide array of disparate information in a meaningful way can create massive value. For the purposes of this discussion, we will treat synthesis as an ability that—for the present time, at least—can be performed only by people. Only people can leap between different levels of logic and categorization in order to draw meaning or sense from a world of information. Internalizing information requires it to be related to existing knowledge, so simply understanding new information or experience is already an act of synthesis.

The ability to recognize patterns in one's business environment and organization is one of the most fundamental and valuable skills in management, as the doyen of strategic planning, Henry Mintzberg, and others have pointed out.[10] Pattern recognition, which discovers the hidden relationships within information and puts them into a useful framework, is a very powerful form of synthesis. Recognizing patterns creates enormous value, and the ability to do it well can command extremely high fees. In a similar vein, all creation and innovation can be said to be based on synthesizing different perspectives, as suggested by Arthur Koestler.[11]

Synthesis is generally a senior-level function, since to be most valuable it must draw on very broad experience and knowledge. It is a role commonly performed by the most senior team members, who are generally only brought in to provide the "big picture" as to how all the strands are woven together. While the ability to synthesize information and recognize patterns is founded on broad experience, there are also skills involved that can be developed and improved. Traditional courses on creativity address some of the required skills, but rarely cover more fundamental issues such as broadening perceptual filters and developing approaches to structuring patterns.

Presentation

The fact that information's primary value is found in being internalized by people as knowledge means that presentation is one of the most important parts of adding value to information. If information had intrinsic value, its presentation would be irrelevant. As it is, the presentation of information must be designed very specifically with the intention of making it as easy as possible for the intended audience to internalize or assimilate as useful knowledge.

In the first instance, we want to minimize the "cost" of using information in terms of the time and effort required; in a world of information overload, only information that is extremely easy to use and internalize will capture limited attention. Furthermore, we want to help our audiences to get the most value from the information by integrating it deeply and easily into their knowledge frameworks.

There are many key elements involved in the effective presentation of information, including effective writing and structuring, and the use of visual representations. Readability has a major impact on value; if a document is written in an easy-to-follow style and format it will be far more valuable than if it is written in jargon such as legalese. Simple quantity of information can be a critical factor: an effective one-page summary is often far more valuable than a 100-page document, simply because of the relative time investment required.

Immense amounts have been written on these fundamental communication skills. However, very little specific attention has been paid to the communication of knowledge, and the customization of communication for different audiences. These are extremely important issues in the knowledge economy; a detailed background is given in the Appendix, and some useful approaches are covered in Chapter 10.

Ease of Access and Use

There is a critical distinction in information management between information push—in which information is "pushed" to users automatically—and information pull, in which users actively seek information ("pull" it) for themselves. Achieving an effective balance between information push and pull is at the heart of a good information management system. In a world of information overload, however, users increasingly prefer to access information themselves rather than being presented with prespecified information. The most important issues are the ability to access relevant information with minimal time and effort, flexibility in accessing that information, and subsequently being able to manipulate it easily.

User access issues include providing facilities to search for information based on keywords and other criteria, structuring information in hierarchies of detail, and providing alerts to notify users that new information is available. In addition, how information is presented or formatted can strongly impact its value. For example, providing data in spreadsheet format can be far more valuable than simply presenting a chart of the data, as clients may wish to manipulate the data themselves rather than just see the outputs. These are primarily technology issues; much of the current focus of information and document management relates to how to improve ease of use and accessibility of information.

Customization

Customization is intrinsic to almost every aspect of adding value to information, as well as to all knowledge transfer. Information's potential value is limited by the breadth of its intended audience. Information targeted to a broad cross-section of business executives, such as that in national business magazines, can never command a high price. However, information produced for a very narrowly targeted audience can sometimes justify a very high price.

Customization can be considered to be a process in its own right. It begins from understanding the client's situation, and processes information specifically to add maximum value in that context. In effect, customization consists mainly of filtering, analysis, synthesis, and presentation, with each of these processes performed within a very specific context. Each of these can be performed without a specific audience in mind, but this approach will strongly limit the value created. Validation and ease of access can generally be implemented effectively without customizing for a specific client or user.

One important aspect of customization is translation, which involves framing information or messages in the language or format that will be best understood by the client. On a basic level, this can refer to the actual language in which the message is written. However, just as important are the language and style of communication favored by the culture of the target individual or group. The way in which engineers like information to be presented is very different to the preferences of human resource managers or bond traders, for example, and each group uses different language and specialized terminology in its communication.

We will now examine how people take in information, including a discussion of how we can customize its presentation. We will return to the theme of customization, especially in Chapter 7 on designing client contact in firm-wide relationships; customization is a fundamental theme in the implementation of effective knowledge transfer.

INTERNALIZATION OF INFORMATION AS KNOWLEDGE

Internalization is the process by which people make information part of their personal knowledge. The essence of this process is found in establishing new connections and associations to and within existing knowledge, which happens through perceiving associations and similarities to prior experiences, thoughts, and mental structures.

The Appendix examines in detail the nature of knowledge, how experience and ideas are internalized as understanding, and how to communicate knowledge more effectively. Here we will introduce these topics, as they are fundamental to the issues of effective knowledge transfer.

Generic and Customized Knowledge Communication

How can we design and present information so that our clients can easily internalize it as knowledge they find useful and valuable? This objective can be accomplished on two levels: first, in making it easy for people in general to understand your communication; and second, in designing the communication specifically for one person or a small group, based on their preferences and approaches to taking in information.

In order to maximize the value added to broad audiences, we need to understand how people take in and think about information. The field of cognitive psychology provides us with many useful lessons. What most interests us is how people take in conceptual information and think about complex situations, rather than low-level functions such as how they perceive objects or comprehend spoken words.

Cognitive Styles

In tailoring our presentation of information for specific individuals or small groups, we need to understand the *differences* in how individuals take in information, analyze it, and make decisions. We can learn useful distinctions by drawing on the study of *cognitive style*, which examines the range of preferences people express in their cognition and personality. There can be dramatic differences in how people go about making decisions, and if we do not understand that diversity and the particular cognitive styles of the people involved, it is far harder to communicate in ways that create value.

Far too often, professionals unwittingly design client communication in line with their own cognitive style, which is fine when the styles mesh, but will mean that real knowledge transfer is limited when clients have different preferences. In addition, in the case of communication to a large group, then there is certain to be sufficient diversity of cognitive styles to ensure that any presentation designed within one style will be poorly understood by a significant proportion of the audience. It is a fundamental rule that effective knowledge transfer to large groups must be designed to cater to a range of cognitive styles. As such, an understanding of cognitive styles should be a core skill of all professionals who communicate with clients.

When interaction is focused on an individual or a small group, then understanding their cognitive styles can allow the tailored design of communication for maximum impact and client value. Failing to consider these issues can result in miscomprehension or worse.

Visual Representations

One of the most useful ways of improving the internalization of knowledge from information is the use of visual representations. The use of visuals is a very powerful tool in the effective presentation of information, as well as in actually enhancing people's understanding and knowledge. This theme is developed in more detail in Chapter 10, together with practical examples, while supporting evidence for the benefits of visual approaches is presented in the Appendix.

DEVELOPING INFORMATION AND KNOWLEDGE CAPABILITIES

Having created an understanding of the processes of adding value to information for clients, we need to achieve improved organizational performance of these processes. We will accomplish this objective by presenting a framework for developing the information and knowledge capabilities of professional service firms, which is applicable both internally in their own operations, and externally in adding value to clients. Since knowledge and adding value to information are dynamic in nature, it makes far more sense to think in terms of developing capabilities in these areas rather than "managing" knowledge; focusing on capabilities inherently recognizes that these can always be developed and improved.

Domains and Means

We must consider two key domains in developing information and knowledge capabilities: the individual and the organization. As we have seen, people are intrinsic to the processes that add the most value to information: it is crucial to focus on developing the capabilities of individuals in dealing with information. Individuals, however, work within an organizational context, which brings people together in useful ways and provides direction and coherence to their efforts. We must also address the organizational level in enhancing capabilities, particularly in developing the flow of knowledge.

Technology is an essential means of enhancing information and knowledge capabilities at both the individual and organizational levels, and thus massive investment goes into information technology. The use of information technology is not sufficient in its own right, however. Developing skills and behaviors is also a vital means of achieving enhanced capabilities, but is often neglected relative to technology, partially due to the difficulty of implementing initiatives, and in measuring their success. However, the return on investment in developing skills and behaviors is greater than incremental investment in technology; in any case, technology is worthless unless people have the skills and behaviors to use it effectively.

Fields for Developing Capabilities

In developing information and knowledge capabilities, a matrix is formed by intersecting the two domains—the individual and the organization; with the two primary developmental means—technology, and skills and behaviors, as shown in Table 3–1. The four quadrants mapped by the matrix represent the key areas for developing information and knowledge capabilities. Since the matrix covers each of the most important fields in developing information and knowledge capabilities, it can be used to assess whether existing knowledge initiatives are broad enough in their scope to achieve success. Many so-called "knowledge

TABLE 3–1   Developing Organizational Information and Knowledge Capabilities

	Individual Use of Information and Knowledge	*Organizational Flow of Information and Knowledge*
Technology	• Search engines • E-mail filters • Intelligent agents • Information visualization • Push technology, etc.	• E-mail • Intranets and groupware • Electronic bulletin boards • Knowledge yellow pages • Videoconferencing, etc.
Skills and Behaviors	• Filtering information overload • Reading and note-taking • Analysis and synthesis • Making effective decisions • Knowledge communication skills, etc.	• Organizational culture • Propensity to share • Teamwork and team objectives • Group processes • Facilitation skills, etc.

Source: Advanced Human Technologies. Used with permission.

management" initiatives address just one or two of these four fields, which greatly limits their potential effectiveness.

Individual Technology

How can technology assist individual knowledge workers in the process of adding value to information? Examples include the effective filtering of "push" information, as in collaborative filtering; e-mail filters; and being able to "pull" the information that workers require using search engines. Intelligent agents acting on behalf of the user, in this case searching for relevant information as well as learning the user's interests and inclinations, are likely to play an increasingly important role. Another valuable tool is information visualization software, which assists in making sense of and finding patterns in large amounts of data, and for communicating information usefully to others.

Organizational Technology

This quadrant covers the technological tools that assist in the organizational flow of information and technology. Many practitioners of "knowledge management" seem to think that addressing this field is all that is required. The tools start with e-mail, and include intranets, groupware, electronic bulletin boards, videoconferencing, and knowledge yellow pages, which are databases to help identify who within the organization has expertise on specific topics. These initiatives are absolutely essential in providing the means for large distributed organizations to leverage their internal knowledge; however, in and of themselves they function far more as enablers than as a source of value creation.

Individual Skills and Behaviors

This quadrant focuses on the absolutely vital field of information and knowledge skills. Professionals are the quintessential knowledge workers—their entire function is managing knowledge, whether using it to achieve results, or transferring it internally or to clients. Very few knowledge workers, however, have had any specific training and development for the skill sets on which much of their role is based: dealing with and adding value to information and knowledge. Some core skills in which professionals are usually already proficient, but can always develop with substantial improvements in productivity, include setting information objectives, filtering information overload, reading and note-taking, analysis, synthesis, using information and knowledge to make decisions, and particularly, the ability to communicate knowledge effectively to others.

Organizational Skills and Behaviors

Very little can happen in developing an organization's information and knowledge capabilities without the skills and behaviors that support knowledge flow in the organization. Much of this process is based on organizational culture, and ultimately the propensity to share knowledge with others. The motivation for skill development can stem partially from remuneration and recognition structures that explicitly reward knowledge-sharing, but these must be supported by congruent signals from management with leadership and example.[12] Specific skills and activities for development include building teams around information flow, establishing group processes for sharing knowledge within and across teams, and facilitating rich two-way communication of knowledge.

Developing Capabilities

Since professional services firms are by definition based on specialized knowledge, developing their information and knowledge capabilities must be fundamental to their competitiveness and sustainability. All firms are investing in the development of their internal capabilities in some ways, though few are effectively addressing all four quadrants of the matrix presented above. To do so requires not only implementing projects and efforts within the spheres of technology and human resources, but also coordinating these to produce results both for the individual knowledge worker and the organization as a whole.

SUMMARY: ADDING VALUE TO INFORMATION

Since knowledge is the capacity to act effectively, it is an attribute unique to people. Information is defined as what is or can be digitized, and thus stored, duplicated, processed, and communicated; but its real value emerges when internalized by people as their own personal knowledge, and resulting capacity to act more effectively. Increasing information overload is changing the dynamics and value of information, making attention the scarce resource, and democratizing access to information. Information can have a high, low, or even negative value, depending on the context. A primary function of professional service firms is adding value to information from the perspective of their clients.

The key steps in the process of adding value to information include filtering, validation, analysis, synthesis, presentation, facilitating ease of access and use, and customization. Each of these steps can be performed at least partially with the help of technology; however, the greatest added value almost always involves people.

In order to add the greatest value to information, organizations must develop their information and knowledge capabilities. The two key domains that must be developed are the individual and organizational levels, while the two primary means for developing capabilities are technology, and skills and behaviors. These form a matrix covering the critical areas that need to be addressed in any comprehensive information and knowledge initiatives.

The acceleration of digitization has resulted in an increasing emphasis on information in business communication, so it is critical to understand how information adds value. Adding value to information can be seen as the first stage of the process, but the real value is created in the application of information in the client. In the next two chapters, we will examine adding value in client decision making and client capabilities. Both of these depend strongly on high-value information generated in the ways we have discussed, but also require rich personal interaction in order to be effective.

NOTES

1. This tallies with the definition of information given by Carl Shapiro and Hal Varian, *Information Rules: A Strategic Guide to the Network Economy* (Boston: Harvard Business School Press, 1998): 3.
2. I disagree that information overload is necessarily a liability. See Ross Dawson, "Information Overload—Problem or Opportunity?" *Company Director* (October 1997): 44–45.
3. Reuters, *Dying for Information?* (London: Reuters, 1996).
4. See Michael H. Goldhaber, "Attention Shoppers!" *Wired* (December 1997). He goes so far as to suggest that attention will replace money as the unit of exchange.
5. See Don Peppers and Martha Rogers, *The One to One Future: Building Relationships One Customer at a Time* (New York: Currency Doubleday, 1993); and *Enterprise One to One: Tools for Competing in the Interactive Age* (New York: Currency Doubleday, 1997).
6. Shapiro and Varian.
7. Sveiby, 108–111.
8. Davenport and Prusak, 3.
9. Nicholas Negroponte, *Being Digital* (New York: Knopf, 1995).

10. See for example Henry Mintzberg, *Mintzberg on Management: Inside Our Strange World of Organizations* (New York: Free Press, 1989): 38.

11. Koestler coined the term "bisociation" to describe this; he proposed that creation always stems from operating on more than one plane of thinking. See Arthur Koestler, *The Act of Creation* (London: Hutchinson, 1964).

12. See Ross Dawson, "Performance Management Strategies for Knowledge Organisations," *Reward Management Bulletin* #2, no. 3 (February/March 1998): 183–186.

Chapter 4

Adding Value to Client Decision Making

Better Strategic, Line, and Portfolio Decisions

The final outcome from information and knowledge, that which provides intrinsic value to an organization, is decisions. Indeed, economics Nobel Prize winner Herbert Simon contends that management *is* decision making.[1] The greatest value added to clients through transferring knowledge is ultimately found in better business decisions: those resulting in better outcomes for companies in terms of profitability, shareholder value, or other measures applied to gauge their success.

We have stated previously that knowledge is the capacity to act, or more explicitly, the capacity to act effectively to achieve desired results. Focusing on decision making helps to bring this idea to life. Useful knowledge results in better decisions; this is where the true value of knowledge resides. Of course, action and implementation must follow decisions if they are to have value. Effective implementation, however, is itself a sequence of decisions and actions based on knowledge.

In order to help clients make better decisions for themselves, we must understand the processes they use to make those decisions. Knowing how your clients make decisions enables you to assist them in enhancing their decision-making processes, and to tailor the way you communicate information and knowledge so it can be effectively and usefully integrated into these decisions.

TYPES OF DECISIONS

As introduced in Chapter 1, organizational decisions can be divided into strategic, line, and portfolio decisions. We will revisit these distinctions and look a bit more closely at the relevance of these three categories. These distinctions are made specifically within the context of professionals transferring knowledge to clients—they allow us to refine our interaction with clients depending on the decision-making situation. Each type of decision requires different approaches in order to add the greatest value.

Strategic Decisions

To review, strategic decisions are those which determine the direction and positioning of the organization, usually within unlimited or very broad boundaries. Strategic decisions are normally made by top management, though there may be input from across the organization. They are based on the decision makers' understanding of the organization, its environment, and the relationship between them.

Strategy consulting firms explicitly target this area. The value of better strategic decision making is obvious, and premium pricing is available for those firms that can convince their clients of their ability to add real value in this area. As noted in Chapter 2, a variety of styles exist in strategy consulting, including some models which are determinedly black-box in nature (e.g., "trust us—we'll go away and come back with the answer"), as well as those strongly based on eliciting knowledge and decisions from the client. These issues will be covered in more detail later in this chapter.

Line Decisions

Line decisions are those made within a defined scope, usually at line management or staff level. All knowledge workers make line decisions in performing their functions. Since line decisions are individually less important than strategic decisions, it is usually not cost-effective to engage a professional service firm to assist with specific issues. To add value to line decisions, a service provider must develop the ability of knowledge workers to make better decisions within an organizational framework.

In this situation again, the distinction between information and knowledge is clear. Giving managers information in the form of documents is next to useless; they are usually placed on a shelf and left there. What managers need is knowledge they can readily incorporate into the thinking behind all their decisions. A good example of adding value to line decisions is found in risk reduction—getting all decisions and actions to be implemented in full consideration of critical potential risks.

Blake Dawson Waldron, a 650 lawyer-strong Australian legal firm, has established a technology group to market "preventive lawyering" solutions; among these is what it terms self-administered legal training. This program comprises computer-based training courses for staff and line managers on issues such as trade practices compliance, sexual harassment, and other important risk issues. The courses are tailored for clients to represent scenarios directly relevant to their staff members.

This example illustrates the stark difference between delivering legal information—often in the form of hefty procedures manuals—and transferring knowledge. The interactive nature of computer-based training, which involves presenting relevant information and stories and has users answering content questions, means that real knowledge acquisition and understanding are far more likely to happen in ways the staff can use in day-to-day decision making. The courses can be set up on the clients' intranets so that each staff member's performance can be monitored, minimum pass marks established, and areas for further development identified. Although line managers may not be highly motivated to learn about these issues, effectively imparting this knowledge to them can have a major impact on avoiding potential legal liabilities, resulting in substantial value to clients.

Portfolio Decisions

Portfolio decisions refer to the ongoing management of a portfolio of assets, liabilities, or risks. This concept most obviously applies to financial markets in fields such as funds management, corporate treasuries, and bank lending. However, it is also relevant to a host of corporate functions, including risk management, property management, and research and development. In addition, the advent of management based on venture capital principles is resulting in many organizations being managed specifically as a portfolio of businesses and opportunities.

The essence of portfolio decisions is that they are made on a continual basis, reflecting changing conditions in the market or business environment, as well as evolving parameters for the portfolio objectives. These decisions must be made on the basis of interpretation of all information as it becomes available. While computer models are increasingly used across the full range of portfolio management situations, they remain tools that can only be used with human guidance and judgment. High-level portfolio decisions are made by individuals or groups based on their experience, and knowledge of the current environment and context. As we will see, that knowledge is based on how these managers organize and structure information into frameworks and perspectives as it becomes available.

MENTAL MODELS

All of our decisions are based completely on our *mental models* of the world or the situation within which we are working. A mental model is the representation we hold in our minds about the way we believe the world or some part of it works. People can only think and make decisions about their environment based on their understanding of it; that understanding is represented in their mental models.

From the time we are born, we start to build models and have ideas about the way our world works, and how we can usefully interact with it. When we observe a consistent pattern in our environment we start to build an implicit model of how it behaves, and act on the basis of that model. Early in life we build models of simple mechanical and interpersonal interactions; later we build conceptual models of how the world we live in works. People's mental models about simple mechanical interactions are usually very similar, however, in more complex areas such as business, society, and interpersonal relationships we find an amazing diversity of mental models.

The term "mental models" has been popularized in the business community by Peter Senge with his influential book, *The Fifth Discipline*,[2] but the concept has been used by cognitive psychologists for decades, and applied extensively in many contexts. Among many others, Kenneth Craik wrote about mental models in 1943;[3] Henry Mintzberg referred to mental models in a management context in 1973;[4] and Chris Argyris has proposed the very similar idea of "theories-in-use."[5]

Since all decisions are made on the basis of the decision maker's mental models, professionals must understand their clients' mental models in order to be effective in adding value to their decisions. Throughout this chapter we will be covering the concept of mental models and how to use a better understanding of them to add greater value to our clients. Because of the critical importance of mental models in all knowledge acquisition and transfer, we have provided detailed coverage of their nature and structure in the Appendix.

Rich and Impoverished Mental Models

The mental models people use to make decisions in their business and personal lives can be rich in taking into account many issues and allowing diverse perspectives, or they can be impoverished in being locked into a single simple way of looking at things. In a simple world, simple mental models can be very effective; in the highly complex and dynamic business environment we work in we need similarly rich and diverse mental models. A related perspective is how flexible or rigid a person's mental models are. Flexibility means the ability to change not only our views and opinions, but also the very basis of those views. Rigidity is the inability to change views and opinions, even when these prove to be less than useful.[6]

The law of requisite variety states that a system must display at least as much variety as its environment to be successful. In other words, you are completely subject to changes in your environment—that is, you effectively have no choices—unless you have at least the same degree of flexibility and complexity as the system in which you operate.[7] What this means is that our mental models must be at least as rich, diverse, and flexible as our environment. In our increasingly complex world, rich and flexible mental models are essential for business survival.[8]

In the context of dealing with clients, we can add immense value if we can assist our clients in developing richer, more flexible mental models. This represents the highest level of adding value to client decision making, and one closely tied to developing intimate and profitable client relationships. On another level, if our clients have impoverished, rigid mental models, it is extremely difficult for us to add value. If we can help to enrich their mental models, we are both adding immense value, and paving the way for ongoing further added value and business within the context of an intimate relationship.

Risk Management and Risk Awareness

In practical terms, constructing and effectively utilizing richer mental models means taking a broader range of factors—and their interrelationships—into account in all decisions. One very important implication of this process is that people with impoverished mental models simply fail to recognize many potential sources of risk. Helping our clients build richer mental models is central to effective risk as well as opportunity management.

Risk management can never be fully computerized, because it is about perceiving risk, which is unbounded in nature. One of the greatest risks in business is that of *model risk*—that the implicit and explicit models we build and use do not cover the full spectrum of what is possible or even plausible. Computerized risk valuation techniques are extremely valuable; however, the heart of effective risk management is about ensuring that senior managers have the richest possible mental models of what could impact their business. Scenario planning, described later in this chapter, is a valuable tool in qualitative and quantitative risk management, and particularly in helping executives perceive the broadest possible scope of risk.[9]

Mental Models and Decision Making

We use our experience to build mental models of the world, so that we can then use them to understand and predict what will happen in the future. We think through and assess possible courses of action by applying them to our mental models of the situation, and seeing what results are likely based on our understanding. In this way all decision making is based on our mental models.

Figure 4–1 illustrates how mental models guide our decision making. Our mental models form the framework within which all of our thinking and decision-making take place—they are in fact all we have available to us. New information and experience can be interpreted within our mental models in two ways: either in being filtered by what our mental models allow us to perceive, or in actually changing the mental models. People's mental models dictate their perceptual filters, which determine what they actually sense in their environment, and how it is interpreted. The degree to which people use new information to adapt and enhance their mental models as opposed to interpreting it on the basis of their existing models is a measure of the flexibility or rigidity of their mental models.[10]

Traditional decision-making theory is based on establishing criteria and assessing options for action relative to those criteria. Real-life decision making by people is rarely so straightforward. However, the two phases of analyzing and thinking about the situation, and generating and assessing options for action, are central aspects of the decision

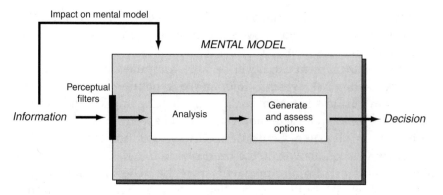

FIGURE 4–1   Mental models in decision making.

making process. Both of these processes are subject to the constraints of the mental models of the decision maker. From these a decision will be made, which should reflect what is most likely to result in the desired outcome of the decision maker given his or her mental models.

DECISION MAKING IN ORGANIZATIONS

In adding value to decision making in our clients, we need to understand the realities of how decisions are actually made in organizations, in a way which can usefully guide our interaction with them. Much decision-making theory is difficult to apply in practice, although there are some frameworks and perspectives that can help us be more effective in working with the processes of organizational decision making.

Decision-Making Theory

Decision making has been a focus of management theory for many decades. The operational term has mostly been "theory"—developing idealized models of how decisions should be made rather than examining the reality of how decisions are actually made in organizations. Much of the early research—and still a considerable proportion of current practice—revolves around "rational" decision making, and is prescriptive in describing how decisions should be made to optimize outcomes given input criteria. The main downfall of this school of decision making is simply that the criteria in all but the most trivial situations are too complex to yield to ready quantification or use in rule-based models.

Herbert Simon, together with colleagues James March, Richard Cyert, and others, helped to focus the debate on the more practical issues of how decisions are actually made in real business situations. They introduced the concept of "bounded rationality," which suggests that people are not rational in their decisions, but work within the limits of their attention, comprehension, and the availability of information. One key consequence is that managers "satisfice," that is make satisfactory rather than optimal decisions.[11]

One interesting offshoot of this approach is the "garbage can" model of organizational decision making. This model by no means suggests how best to make decisions, but rather describes how decisions are often made in organizations, particularly by committees. It suggests that rather than being addressed by importance or priority in a structured fashion, decisions and issues are tossed into an organizational garbage can where they are addressed in a haphazard fashion as and when they catch managers' attention. Solutions will be matched with problems if they happen to arise at a similar time. This model and other developments are helping to bring theory more in line with actual practice, which makes it more useful in working with clients' decision-making processes.

Individual and Group Decision Making

In understanding how to create value, we must distinguish between individual and group decision making. Individuals make decisions based on their mental models, whereas group decisions are derived both from a composite of the mental models of individuals that comprise them, as well as the dynamics and politics of group interaction.

It is possible to think in terms of a group's composite mental model, which reflects the way a group thinks about the world, and determines the decisions it takes. The relationship between an individual's mental models and his or her decision making is different from how a group's mental models relate to its decisions. There is some debate as to whether it is appropriate to apply the concept of mental models to groups; we explore these issues in more detail in the Appendix. However, I have found that it is relevant and useful to think in terms of a group's mental models in assisting decision making. Certainly all decisions made by groups, whether boards of directors, executive committees, or working teams, reflect an implicit group mental model.

There are four key elements to consider in influencing or adding value to group decisions:

- Group mental models
- Integration of individual mental models within the group
- Political factors
- Structure of the decision-making process

The first level to consider in providing input to group decision making is the group's mental model of the situation at hand. This includes the content of the mental model—which reveals the assumptions and causality underlying the model—as well as the associated perceptual filters and degree of flexibility. This element provides a broad-brush framework for guiding interaction with the client.

The degree of integration of the mental models of the individuals comprising the group—meaning the extent of common ground—will have a major impact on how to work most effectively with the group. From the service provider's perspective, the issue is understanding how the group mental model is formed, and tailoring its interaction with the group to achieve the best results. Very fragmented mental models within the group can lead to dysfunctional behavior. However, if too much similarity exists, there is a real danger of "groupthink," which could be considered as rigidity at the group mental model level. Either scenario can prove an opportunity for service providers, however there are, of course, real challenges in dealing with groups whose members' mental models are both fundamentally different and rigid.

Internal political factors will always be critical in determining the functioning and decision making of groups. From the perspective of what Bolman and Deal call the "political frame," what happens within organizations and groups can be likened to the political process, with conflict, power, bargaining, jockeying for position, and coalitions the key issues in how decisions are made.[12] These factors may affect which mental model prevails within the group, and what motives and influences may be guiding decisions. Understanding these issues to the fullest degree possible is fundamental in being able to add value to decision making, and to develop and maintain strong relationships.

Understanding clients' formal and informal decision making processes is vital in being able to provide effective input to them. Many relationship managers at professional service firms even fail to map out the key committees at their client organizations, including information such as committee responsibilities and meeting dates, let alone the detailed decision-making processes the committees follow.

Decision-Making Content and Process

It is useful to distinguish between the *content* and *process* of decision making. The content of decisions consists of the information that goes into them, the recommendations considered, the content of the mental models of decision makers, and the actual final decisions themselves. The process of decisions consists of the steps and manner in which they are actually made. This process includes how information is gathered; the players involved and their relative roles; the communication to, within, and from the decision-making team; and other factors.

Most professional service providers focus on the content of decision making, and mainly on the information input to that content, not the client's current structure and way of thinking, which is at least as important in producing decisions and action. Just to be able to provide content to decisions in a valuable way, the process aspects of decisions must be considered. And adding value to the process of decisions itself has greater impact on the client. Wherever possible, professional service providers should endeavor to add value to both the content and process of decisions.

ADDING VALUE TO DECISION MAKING

As we have seen, all decisions are made within the context of the mental models of decision makers. New information and experience are filtered by mental models for use in decisions, and can also impact the models themselves. The filtered information is then analyzed and considered, and then (or more usually, concurrently) options are generated, developed, and selected in order to produce decisions. In this section we will study how value can be added to decision making within the context of existing mental models, while in the next section we will look at how we can add value to the mental models themselves.

The three major stages of decision making in our model include taking in information, analysis, and generating and assessing alternatives. Since most input to decision making takes the form of providing options and recommendations, we will look at these issues before we examine the stage of analysis. This results in three phases of adding value to decision making:

- Providing key information
- Providing options and recommendations
- Analysis and thinking

Providing Key Information

One of the most obvious ways of adding value to decision making is in providing information that is highly relevant to the decision at hand, and not currently available to the decision makers. These issues have been fully addressed in Chapter 3; the value of information rests mainly in its application in making better business decisions, which is achieved by customizing information for the specific decisions the client must make. Customization includes providing all information necessary to make the decision at hand, filtering out everything else, and presenting the information in a format that is easy to understand and relevant for the specific decision.

As information becomes increasingly commoditized, high-value information must be geared toward being directly relevant to client decision making. Companies that are able to command premium prices for business information are those deliberately focusing on providing input to executive decisions, such as the Economist Intelligence Unit, credit rating agencies such as Moody's, and industry-specific market research companies.

Options and Recommendations

All decisions—both in formal processes and in quick informal situations—depend in some way on generating options or alternatives, which are then evaluated to choose a path of action. Generating decision options, assessing these, and presenting recommendations for action is a key role performed by professional service firms in many industries. Much of the advisory work in the legal and consulting industries, for example, consists of these functions.

We have seen that generating and assessing options takes place within the scope of the client's mental models. As such, any options or recommendations must make sense within the context of their mental models; if not they will be rejected out of hand. This emphasizes the importance of understanding the client's mental models, even when clear recommendations are being made.

In some situations clients may be actively looking for ideas that fit their world view. An example is the case of portfolio managers, who have distinct mental models of the financial markets or whatever portfolios they are running, and will reward any salesperson who can provide them well thought-out actionable ideas which take advantage of their views and opinions. The portfolio managers implicitly understand that they have their own mental models of the markets, and want professionals who can understand these models and provide recommendations consistent with them.

We have repeatedly brought out the distinction between black-box service providers, who present recommendations as an outcome; and knowledge transfer, in which clients are helped to generate and assess options for themselves in a facilitated process. Knowledge transfer can often be effectively complemented with providing additional alternatives and insights to ensure that the broadest range of considerations is used in producing decisions.

The investment consulting industry provides services primarily to the trustees and executives of superannuation and pension funds. The trustees have the responsibility to make considered decisions in structuring portfolios and selecting asset managers; the investment consultant's role is to assist trustees in those decisions. In some cases pension funds effectively outsource the decisions to the consultants, simply rubber-stamping their recommendations. In other situations, consultants provide useful input to the trustees' decisions. The highly dynamic nature of regulation and developments in the investment world mean that education is always an important part of the consulting function.

New York-based William M. Mercer, a member of the Marsh & McLennan group of companies, provides human resource strategy consulting, and within that, is the largest investment consulting firm worldwide. Mercer maintains a broad range of relationships with its clients, from individual projects through to ongoing retainers, and fully implemented consulting through to broad input to decision making. Information and recommendations are provided through regular reports, supplemented with presentations to trustees. Often the way these are presented will be developed in consultation with the trustees' chairperson, and individual meetings with board members may be scheduled where significant education on critical issues is required, or a range of opinion is represented. In situations where clients more actively make their own decisions, Mercer will present three or four reasonable positions, with full cost/benefit analysis of each. In order to emphasize that none of these is suggested as a preferred option, they may be presented in alphabetical order in the report.

Analysis—The Thinking Behind Recommendations

As we have suggested, the presentation of recommendations to clients is often performed as a black-box function—it is opaque to the client how these recommendations were generated. In this case, any decision generated is not so much one made by the client as one made by the consultant and endorsed by the client. There are situations in which the client only wants this type of recommendation; however, clients increasingly want to make their own decisions, and to use the thinking behind the generation of options and the final recommendations in future decisions.

One important reason why black-box recommendations generally yield less value than providing the content and process behind them is that they "collapse" the richness of the thinking that went into the recommendations down to a single outcome. An excellent example of this phenomenon is economic research in whatever field it is applied. Economists go through a detailed process of examining all the issues and uncertainties in looking ahead. When they collapse or condense all that thinking into a single set of figures representing their economic forecast and the justification for that most-likely outcome, however, the richness of the thinking that went into developing the forecast largely disappears for the client. While many clients simply want some numbers to slot into their budgets without much discussion (a dangerous but common approach), economists are inherently limiting the potential value of their work to clients by leaving out the breadth of the analysis behind their views.

On a related front, investment bank Morgan Stanley Dean Witter, in its financial market research, rather than giving "house" opinions on what will happen in global economic and financial markets, occasionally publishes lively debates between its senior analysts, sometimes expressing very different views. These published debates allow clients to take on the richness and diversity of thinking behind the issues for integration into their own thinking, rather than being given a single perspective. Similarly, Goldman Sachs has published a range of possible global economic scenarios and the thinking behind each, and has encouraged clients to allocate their own weightings to these scenarios and to explore their implications.[13]

ADDING VALUE TO MENTAL MODELS

Because decision making can only be done within the framework of mental models of decision makers, usually the area in which the most value can be added to client decision making is in impacting the mental models themselves.

This can be done in three ways:

- Making mental models explicit
- Integrating mental models
- Enriching mental models

Making Mental Models Explicit

An important part of adding value to clients' mental models is helping to make them explicit. Mental models are almost invariably beyond the awareness of the individual or group, and depending on the situation they can either be useful, or a barrier to success. In either case, making the mental models explicit and clear will be valuable in assisting clients to make better decisions. Helping a client's senior managers understand the way they are currently thinking about their business, and their underlying assumptions, is itself extremely valuable and paves the way to help them take on new perspectives.

Kees van der Heijden, Professor of General and Strategic Management at Strathclyde University, UK, and former head of Royal Dutch/Shell's Group Business Environment Division, uses the concept of the "Business Idea," which he describes as "the organisation's [sic] mental model of the forces behind its current and future success."[14] He emphasizes the importance of articulating managers' Business Ideas in building shared understanding in the management team, and focusing the dialogue that must take place to develop the organization's distinctive competencies.

More and more consulting firms are offering services that are designed to make the mental models of their clients explicit, often as part of a broader process of facilitating strategic decision making. The methodologies usually involve developing a visual representation of the group's mental model, using principles based on systems dynamics. *Cognitive mapping*, which is used to build maps for individuals or organizations of the way they understand their business situations, has developed as a prominent field in the 1990s, supported by considerable academic research, and use by management consultants. The basis of these approaches is explained in the Appendix.

Clearly, deep trust of service providers by clients is required for engagement in working with them at the level of their mental models.[15] Equally, the degree of intimacy inherent in the process will help to develop far deeper relationships and trust.

Integrating Mental Models

Integrating the mental models of individuals on decision-making teams at client organizations, especially around broad themes such as the business or investment environment, is one of the most valuable services possible. The idea is certainly not to make people's mental models the same; differences and divergence in individual ways of thinking within a group is invaluable. Integrating mental models is about developing a common framework that allows team members to share the ways in which their mental models are different. Integration also provides a basis for constructive communication, and builds a richer mental model that incorporates a wide variety of perspectives, as represented in Figure 4–2. The importance of integrated or shared mental models in organizations has been emphasized by a number of practitioners, especially those associated with the learning organization movement, such as Peter Senge and Ray Stata.[16]

Effective decision making depends on the group mental models on which it is based, drawing fully on the richness and diversity of individual members' mental models. Difference of opinion within groups is often reconciled through hierarchy, status, and personality rather than looking for the richer perspectives possible through synthesizing the mental models behind the different opinions. Anyone who has attended any committee meeting will recognize this phenomenon.

Making a team or organization's mental models explicit is an important means of integrating the mental models of individuals within the group; it allows people to understand how they are thinking, how that differs from others, and provides a foundation for meaningful dialogue. More generally, skillful facilitation is about finding a common ground for productive discussion, which often draws on similar approaches. These are vital foundation skills for professionals who are seeking to add value to their clients' decision making.

Enriching Mental Models

We have already seen the importance and value of richer mental models. Any service provider that can effectively enrich the mental models

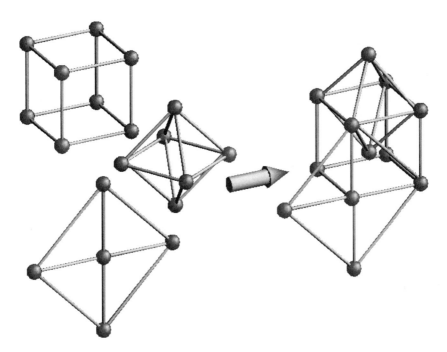

FIGURE 4–2   Integrating a range of individual mental models produces richer group mental models, and the basis for constructive communication.

of its clients, and link that enrichment to better decisions, will add immense value. All client interactions have the potential to help them to gain richer and more useful perspectives, and this should be a core intention behind all conversations and meetings. If, however, clients explicitly give "permission" to formally help enrich their ways of thinking, the potential impact can be far greater, and clients are far more aware of its value.

One approach is simply challenging clients by presenting alternative views that require them to think beyond their current mental models. Doing this poorly can easily result in the clients rejecting those views and becoming alienated; ideally the alternative views will take into account the clients' cognitive styles, existing mental models, and how these can best be developed. A key aspect of enriching mental models is bringing assumptions to light. People's assumptions are their blind spots. Often people don't perceive certain issues because they are taken for granted, so bringing these issues into their field of perception is extremely valuable.

There are any number of more formal techniques and methods for enriching mental models. Some of the most effective approaches are methodologies such as scenario planning and war gaming, which are covered below. One approach which is explicitly focused on enriching mental models is what Global Business Network (GBN) calls "learning journeys." This is described in the box on GBN.

FACILITATING DECISION MAKING

In general, it is more valuable to help clients make decisions for themselves than to go through part or all of the process for them and provide recommendations. Facilitating clients in their own decisions is a good example of knowledge elicitation—the assumption is that the client has most of the knowledge required to make the best decision, but can be assisted in drawing that out and working with it so as to result in the desired outcomes. Indeed it is hard for a professional service firm to suggest that it knows the client's organization better than the client does; however, it can certainly provide expertise in decision making and the business environment, which adds substantial value that results in better decisions for the client. In most cases facilitating decision making not only contributes value to the decision at hand, but also enriches the client's mental models and ability to make better decisions in future situations.

Here we will present two structured approaches to facilitating client decision making which have gained currency over the last few years: scenario planning and war gaming. While other approaches are also used, these two are representative, and probably have the longest pedigrees of success.

Scenario Planning

Scenario planning is a well-established approach to strategic decision making. It first became widely known in the business community when Shell had developed a scenario for a sharp rise in oil prices before the onset of the 1974 oil crisis, and as a result was better positioned than its competitors to respond effectively. Since then, scenario planning has become broadly used across a variety of industries, with a resurgence of interest in the wake of the "Asia crisis" and ensuing financial market volatility, as businesspeople were forcibly reminded that the future is unpredictable.

Scenario planning is a process of developing a number of scenarios or stories for the future which are plausible to the decision makers, complementary in that together they cover the broadest possible scope of uncertainty in the organization's environment, and relevant to the key decisions the organization faces. The methodology usually involves getting broad participation in uncovering the underlying trends and critical uncertainties in the organization's environment; building these into engaging narratives which form the scenarios; and using these to generate, explore, and refine a cohesive and robust strategy in the face of uncertainty.

The history of scenario planning has seen it applied mainly to making major decisions and developing organizational strategies. However it is increasingly also used as a tool for developing the ongoing interactions and processes within the organization that result in effective decision making. Even today, all major investment decisions at Shell must be assessed against a set of scenarios. Scenario planning is increasingly being implemented in-house as an intrinsic part of the strategic planning process in many of the largest corporations worldwide. Most commonly external organizations are involved, because of their value in introducing fresh perspectives as part of projecting beyond what scenario planners call "the official future," which is essentially the organization's mental model of its future.

Pierre Wack, considered the guiding light behind the development of scenario planning and the writer of two seminal *Harvard Business Review* articles on the topic,[17] introduced the concept of "remarkable people" to the practice of scenario planning.[18] Since building scenarios useful for strategic decision making requires examining and challenging existing mental models, the role of these people is quite simply to present very different ways of thinking in order to shake up decision makers.[19] This is a primary role of Global Business Network's individual members (see box on p. 98), who are often used in GBN's scenario planning engagements with its clients.

War Gaming

War gaming has gained currency recently as a powerful approach for adding value to strategic decision making. As the name suggests, its genesis was in the simulations that have been used extensively by the military for centuries. In the context of organizational management, it

Global Business Network

Global Business Network (GBN), of Emeryville, California, was established in 1988 by five founding members, most of whom had been involved in scenario planning in Royal Dutch/Shell over the previous 15 years. While it has 55 full-time staff, GBN describes itself as a network linking its corporate and individual members, who represent an eclectic range of expertise in the arts, literature, sciences, social sciences, government, and business.

Its core service is corporate membership in its Worldview services. An annual membership fee gives its clients access to the resources of GBN. This includes regular publications of GBN research; membership in the GBN book club; access to their website and online forums; attendance at GBN's meetings and conferences, which examine key issues affecting organizations now and in the future; and access to GBN's consulting services. GBN generally only provides consulting services to members, as its principals believe that isolated consulting engagements do not result in lasting changes, and that consulting projects must be implemented as part of an ongoing commitment from the client.

GBN also provides training services, which are open to all parties. While GBN provides extensive content knowledge on the issues facing different industries and on the future of business and society, its focus is perhaps more oriented to process, such as how to conduct an effective scenario planning project. It does not attempt to hold on to that process knowledge, but actively teaches its clients how to do it for themselves. Furthermore, it has quite happily welcomed to its training courses representatives of many organizations that could be considered competitors, such as the major professional service firms.

The entire philosophy of GBN, and the basis on which it was designed, is about enabling interactions and learning from others in unstructured and chaotic ways, often across traditional boundaries, reports Nancy Murphy, head of communications at GBN. The network structure and nature of the interaction between network members is designed to bring together different knowledge, experience, and perspectives to create new understanding, with GBN playing the role of leader and facilitator as well as participant in the resulting discussions.

An illustration of the approaches used by GBN to elicit useful knowledge and broaden mental models is what it calls "learning journeys." These are experiential tours that take executives to visit places and have experiences relevant to their industries and decisions at hand, though often in tangential and unexpected ways. GBN usually designs scenario planning exercises to include learning journeys, and has also designed week-long learning journeys to achieve specific learning outcomes with groups of executives.

provides an intense simulation of real-world business environments and decision making.

One of the professional service firms which uses war gaming extensively is strategy consultant Booz•Allen & Hamilton, though others including PricewaterhouseCoopers are adopting similar services. Typically Booz•Allen involves 60–80 senior managers from its client organization over about three days.[20] The managers divide into teams which play their own company, a selection of their major competitors, and the marketplace for their products or services. Each team is given critical background information, with the team playing the marketplace given detailed customer research to guide its response to the developing range of offerings available through the game.

The game proceeds through a sequence of moves by each team, which can be measured in months or years. Each move is based on the outcomes of the previous move, resulting in a dynamic and evolving competitive marketplace. External discontinuities in the market such as deregulation can be designed into the game, or strategic innovations introduced by the teams.

Similarly to scenario planning, war gaming challenges the implicit assumptions of managers about the dynamics of their industry and how it will evolve, and helps them to think through how they will respond to previously unforeseen circumstances. The highly experiential nature of the game and the approach of forming teams for different players in the industry results in powerful learning opportunities for participants, and the dynamic nature of war gaming can bring new issues to light. However, it generally does not cover the scope of uncertainties that is the essence of scenario planning.

SUMMARY: ADDING VALUE TO CLIENT DECISION MAKING

Arguably, management *is* decision making. As such, adding value to our clients' ability to make better business decisions can create immense value. For the purposes of adding value to clients, we can distinguish between strategic, line, and portfolio decisions; each of these requires different approaches in order to add value effectively.

People make decisions on the basis of their mental models, or ways of thinking about the world they live in. By understanding group and individual decision-making processes, we can add value to those decisions, and the mental models clients use in their decisions. The greatest, longest-term value is created by enriching clients' mental models, which allows clients to incorporate a broader perception of issues into their thinking and decision making.

A range of specific methodologies is available to facilitate clients in making better decisions. One example is scenario planning, in which clients develop a number of plausible scenarios for the future of their business environment as a tool for making better strategic decisions. War gaming immerses clients in a simulation of their business played against their competitors, to give them a better understanding of the potential issues they face.

While business is about decision making, this only happens within the context of the organization. Organizations are defined by the competencies and capabilities that enable them to create value for their customers or clients, and will survive only if these remain superior and distinctive. Knowledge is at the heart of those capabilities, and a fundamental role of professional service firms is adding value to the capabilities of clients. This is the subject of Chapter 5.

NOTES

1. As pointed out by Chun Wei Choo, *The Knowing Organization: How Organizations Use Information to Construct Meaning, Create Knowledge, and Make Decisions* (New York: Oxford University Press, 1998). See for example Herbert A. Simon, *Administrative Behavior: A Study of Decision-Making Processes in Administrative Organizations* 4th ed. (New York: The Free Press, 1997): 305.

2. Peter M. Senge, *The Fifth Discipline: The Art and Practice of the Learning Organization* (New York: Currency/Doubleday, 1994).

3. Kenneth Craik, *The Nature of Explanation* (Cambridge, UK: Cambridge University Press, 1943).

4. Henry Mintzberg, *The Nature of Managerial Work* (New York: Harper & Row, 1973).

5. Chris Argyris, "Single-Loop and Double-Loop Models in Research on Decision Making," *Administrative Science Quarterly* 21 (September 1976): 363–375.

6. Markides notes that "very strong mental models can hinder active thinking and the adoption of new ideas . . . we tend to hear what already supports our existing beliefs and ways of operating, while any new information that does not support what we believe we discard as wrong and not applicable." See Constantinos Markides, "Strategic Innovation," *Sloan Management Review* (Spring 1997): 9–23.

7. Originally proposed in W. Ross Ashby, *An Introduction to Cybernetics.* (London: Chapman & Hall, 1956). The law of requisite variety originated from the

field of cybernetics, but has been very influential, recurring across a wide range of disciplines, including anthropology and social ecology (see for example Gregory Bateson, *Steps to an Ecology of Mind* [London: Paladin, 1973]); management (Nonaka and Takeuchi nominate it as one of the five enabling conditions of organizational knowledge creation); and neurolinguistic programming (NLP), in which it is one of the basic presuppositions of the field.

8. Paradigms can be considered to be the highest level of shared mental model, which are the hardest to shift. See Thomas S. Kuhn, *The Structure of Scientific Revolutions* (Chicago: University of Chicago Press, 1970); and Thomas Clarke and Stewart Clegg, *Changing Paradigms: The Transformation of Management Knowledge for the 21st Century* (London: HarperBusiness, 1998).

9. See for example Ron S. Dembo and Andrew Freeman, *Seeing Tomorrow: Rewriting the Rules of Risk* (New York: John Wiley & Sons, 1998): 38–45. For a coverage of applying scenario planning to financial risk management, see Ross Dawson, "Did You Forecast Asia? Scenario Planning in Portfolio and Risk Management," *The Australian Corporate Treasurer* (August 1998).

10. Isenberg suggests that good managers continually test and revise their mental map of the problems and issues facing them. See Daniel J. Isenberg, "How Senior Managers Think," *Harvard Business Review* (November-December, 1984).

11. For an excellent review of this approach, see James March, *A Primer on Decision Making: How Decisions Happen* (New York: Harvard Business School Press, 1994).

12. Lee Bolman and Terrence Deal, *Reframing Organizations: Artistry, Choice and Leadership* 2nd ed. (San Francisco: Jossey-Bass, 1997).

13. An example is from Goldman Sachs' global equity research—see Neil Williams, "Global Strategy—Equities and Economic Shocks," *The Global Economic and Strategy Weekly* no. 99/03 (Goldman Sachs International: January 20, 1999).

14. Kees van der Heijden, *Scenarios: The Art of Strategic Conversation* (London: John Wiley & Sons, 1996): 59.

15. In the context of articulating the Business Idea, van der Heijden notes that the "choice of the facilitator is important, and will normally be limited to team members or well-trusted outsiders," van der Heijden, op. cit.

16. Stata explicitly writes about shared mental models. See Ray Stata, "Organizational Learning—The Key to Management Innovation," *Sloan Management Review* (Spring 1989): 63–74. Senge refers to the related concept of "shared vision."

17. Pierre Wack, "Scenarios: Uncharted Waters Ahead," *Harvard Business Review* 63, no. 5 (September-October 1985): 73–90; and "Scenarios: Shooting

the Rapids," *Harvard Business Review* 63, no. 6 (November-December 1985): 131–142.

18. Schwartz, Peter. *The Art of the Long View: Planning the Future in an Uncertain World*. (New York: Doubleday Currency, 1991): 10.

19. Janis, in examining the highly relevant issues of "groupthink," suggests that outside experts should be invited in to challenge the views of core team members. Irving L. Janis, *Groupthink: Psychological Studies of Policy Decisions and Fiascoes*. (Boston: Houghton-Mifflin, 1982): 266–267.

20. The description of the Booz•Allen & Hamilton war gaming process is drawn from John E. Treat, George E. Thibault, and Amy Asin, "Dynamic Competitive Simulation: Wargaming as a Strategic Tool," *Strategy & Business* (2nd Quarter, 1996).

Chapter 5

Adding Value to Client Capabilities

Enhancing Processes and Skills

Any company's competitiveness—and raison d'être—is based on its competencies and capabilities, and their relevance to its business environment. Ultimately a company will survive and thrive only if it has valuable competencies and capabilities that allow it to meet consumer or business needs, and develops these capabilities in response to changes in its environment.

Organizations must draw on both internal and external resources in order to develop and evolve the competencies and capabilities on which their future depends. Harvard Business School's Dorothy Leonard notes that most or all companies must import knowledge from beyond their boundaries in order to build core capabilities.[1] The sources for that knowledge include customers, alliances, universities, and other organizations.

Any organization adding value to others by transferring knowledge and enhancing capabilities, whether it can be categorized as a product vendor, research organization, alliance partner, consultant, government body, or anything else, is playing the role of a professional service firm. And any firm assisting its clients or partners to enhance their competencies and capabilities is adding immense and often irreplaceable value.

COMPETENCIES AND CAPABILITIES

For the sake of clarity we will distinguish between competencies and capabilities; both terms have been used in a variety of ways in the business literature. Competencies, as authoritatively defined by Hamel and Prahalad, refer to fields of often technological knowledge and expertise that can be combined and applied to the provision of a broad range of products or services; examples include miniaturization, precision optics, or building alliances.[2] Knowledge transfer could equally constitute a core competence which would be applied in enhancing competitiveness across an organization's complete range of products and services.

Capabilities are the abilities underlying performance in specific spheres of business; these could include activities such as attracting and retaining staff, manufacturing with consistent quality and at low cost, or marketing to high-income consumers. Stalk, Evans, and Shulman, writing in *Harvard Business Review*, state that strategic capabilities are transformed from the building blocks of key business processes.[3] Verna Allee refers to "knowledge competencies" and "performance capabilities" to help distinguish between the two terms.[4]

Together, competencies and capabilities form the source of competitive advantage for an organization. As such, it is critical that they be continually reinforced by investment and management attention, and adapted in line with changes and anticipated developments in the business environment. Competencies are based on organizational knowledge and expertise, while capabilities are primarily based on processes and skills. In both cases external service providers can play a critical role in building relevant knowledge for their clients, and enhancing the processes and skills on which their capabilities are based. Throughout this chapter we will refer to enhancing client capabilities, although the same principles are almost always applicable in working with competencies.

Processes and Skills

The two essential components of business capabilities are processes and skills. Processes in organizations are knowledge that is encapsulated in methodologies, or systematic sequences of actions. These processes can be formal or explicit in that they are clear, documented, and replicable. However, more often they are informal or implicit, in that they are embedded in "the way things are done," and their efficacy is not understood in detail.[5] Business systems of all kinds, including accounting systems, work flows, and reporting systems, can all be considered to be processes.

Skills, in the same manner as knowledge, are unique to people. Skills are a vital component of knowledge—they usually refer to tacit knowledge, they must be used in the context of an individual's overall knowledge and experience, and they are a significant component of the action in the "capacity to act effectively."

From an intellectual capital perspective, as introduced in Chapter 2, processes and systems are part of structural capital, and skills part of human capital. Structural capital, by definition, remains whether the people are there or not. Certainly formal processes, which are documented or embedded in technology, are part of structural capital. Many informal processes, which are built into the way teams work, will survive people leaving and being replaced by others who learn the processes on the job; in this case they are also part of structural capital. If, however, the processes are so informal that they do not survive the departure of key staff then they are effectively part of human capital.

Capabilities are in practice a fusion of both processes and skills. A process alone is not valuable without the skills to perform the process effectively, while skills in themselves are of limited use unless they are applied within an effective process. As such the processes and skills on which capabilities are built are an inseparable system—each depends on the other for it to have value. In developing our clients' capabilities, we must focus not only on both processes and skills individually, but deal with them as an interdependent system.

Capabilities and Meta-Capabilities

As we have seen, capabilities are the ability to achieve high performance in a specific sphere of business. Capabilities in areas such as attracting and retaining high-quality staff, total quality manufacturing, or efficient back-office processing are primary sources of competitive advantage. Organizations place a very high value on firms that can assist them to develop and enhance those capabilities.

Perhaps the most valuable capabilities of all are those that contribute to developing and enhancing other business capabilities. These can be called *meta-capabilities*, as they act on other capabilities.[6] The relationship of meta-capabilities to capabilities is illustrated in Figure 5–1. Some of the capabilities that can be considered to be meta-capabilities or to support them include:

- Rapidly learning new processes and skills
- Open communication throughout the organization
- Sharing and leveraging knowledge internally

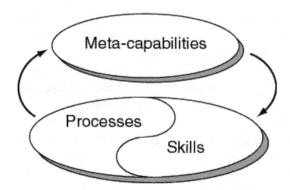

FIGURE 5–1   Capabilities are a fusion of processes and skills; meta-capabilities contribute to developing and enhancing other business capabilities.

- Taking in knowledge from outside the organization
- Flexibility and adaptability of organizational structure

Clearly, enhancing clients' capabilities at this level is more valuable than working with capabilities that apply only to a limited range of functions. Developing client meta-capabilities is potentially immensely valuable, but more difficult to achieve than with other capabilities. In the first instance, the client must recognize the value of these initiatives, which is not easy when there is a short-term result orientation. In addition, it can be a major challenge to identify or quantify the results of programs that act at this level.

Organizational Learning

Organizational learning has been one of the most influential management trends in the 1990s. John Browne, CEO of BP-Ampol, says that "to generate extraordinary value for shareholders, a company has to learn better than its competitors and apply that knowledge throughout its businesses faster and more widely than they do."[7]

The concept of organizational learning in fact encompasses the ongoing development of all meta-capabilities within an organization. Organizational learning is the process by which organizations and the individuals within them continually develop their ability to further develop their own capabilities. This has to be implemented in processes and skills, particularly those that involve observing results achieved by current processes and actively experimenting with new approaches. In practice, organizational learning is reflected more in attitudes than anything else, which makes it particularly difficult to influence from outside the organization.

Chris Argyris of Harvard University has proposed a distinction between what he calls single-loop and double-loop learning.[8] Single-loop learning refers to learning processes and skills within the context of established norms of the organization, looking mainly externally; while double-loop learning requires individuals to question their own and the organization's assumptions and norms by looking inside, as represented in Figure 5–2. This is very similar to the distinction between working within the scope of an individual's or group's existing mental models, and actually changing or enriching those mental models, as described in Chapter 4. As such the lessons learned in adding value to decision making can also be applied in assisting organizations to develop organizational learning.

The fact remains that it is very difficult to add value to clients at the level of developing organizational learning without already having a very close relationship. To be effective, organizational learning initiatives must be ongoing and embedded into the organization's leadership, culture, and projects, with results assessed primarily at a group

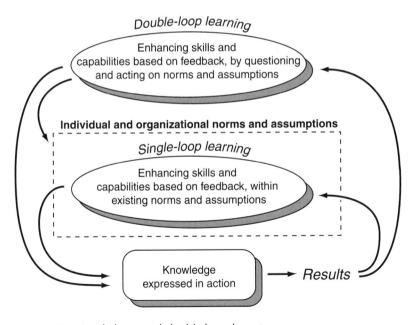

FIGURE 5–2   Single-loop and double-loop learning.

level. As such, the existence of a top-level commitment within the client organization will be a key success factor.

Approaches to Enhancing Client Capabilities

As we have seen, enhancing organizational capabilities depends on the development of both processes and skills in a coordinated fashion. The primary focus of the service provider may be on either processes or skills; however, both fields will always have to be considered if the goal is to achieve an impact at the level of clients' business capabilities.

Throughout this chapter we will examine both process-oriented and skills-oriented approaches to developing client capabilities, as well as approaches that integrate both aspects in a more holistic manner. The objectives behind initiatives should always be framed at the highest possible level; this can transform, for example, a training initiative into a program that develops organization-wide business capabilities and generates substantially greater value.

We are interested in how to develop both specific business capabilities as well as meta-capabilities. Since meta-capabilities are in fact a type of capability, in general the same principles will apply. However, as we have seen, we need to focus on the level of attitudes and mental models in addition to the basic processes and skills involved in continual learning and improvement. One of the most important aspects of developing meta-capabilities is that they are generative, in the sense of acting as a foundation for further development of capabilities beyond the time frame and scope of the professional service firm's engagement.

PROCESS IMPLEMENTATION AND ENHANCEMENT

One of the most straightforward means of developing client capabilities is in implementing effective business processes. This is a core element of many professional service offerings. In selling or implementing processes, there are two possible situations: the client doesn't have a formal process in place to achieve the desired results or is willing to discard its existing process; or it wishes to develop and enhance the processes it is currently using.

In some situations implementing a new process can be relatively straightforward in simply giving the client a series of actions to follow. However, in many cases processes need to be adapted to the client's culture, or the organizational context in which the new process will be embedded. In order to enhance existing processes a deeply interactive approach is required, starting from studying those processes, designing enhancements, and helping to implement those changes to the existing process.

Process Documentation

Processes are often provided to clients in the form of written documentation, which details all the steps in the process or its implementation. There are clearly substantial limitations to the effectiveness with which process knowledge can be transferred through documents. Simpler processes such as software registration procedures or immigration compliance for new staff are clearly far more amenable to transfer through documentation than complex and diverse processes, such as replicating best practice or implementing enterprise-wide software.

There are, however, advantages to both providers and clients in that once documentation has been produced it can be sold and resold without requiring any additional professional time, and is relatively inexpensive for clients. Process documentation as a stand-alone means of knowledge transfer can be very useful for smaller clients who cannot afford or do not justify the dedicated time of expensive professionals.

Naturally, process documentation is most valuable when combined with other means of knowledge transfer, so it provides a complement to more experiential approaches, as well as an easy and accessible reference source when required. When used in isolation it is of limited value and impact in knowledge transfer.

Software

Software offers many advantages over documentation for process implementation, partially in that the business process can be embedded in the way the software works and is used. As such, it is increasingly used as a means to encapsulate and transfer processes. This is perhaps most obvious in workflow-based software, which in its usage actually dictates a specific sequence of actions by people with nominated functions in the organization, and coordinates communication flow between them.

The implementation of process software must be accompanied with training and specialist advice in order to add maximum value to clients. Ultimately, implementing software in itself is unlikely to provide a competitive advantage. One reason for this is that in general, software embeds knowledge implicitly, and thus that knowledge is far less available to the client to work with, adapt, and use. In addition, purchasing a commercially available software package can never provide differentiation from competitors. It is only in combining it with the development of skills or enhancement of processes that the potential exists for major value creation. This is illustrated by the massive consulting projects involved in the implementation of enterprise resource planning (ERP) software such as SAP or PeopleSoft—the value resides more in the customization, adaptation of processes, and training than in the software itself.

Business Process Reengineering

Business Process Reengineering, affectionately known to many as BPR, reached its zenith about 1995, when it was estimated corporations spent $51 billion on these initiatives.[9] The basic principle of BPR involves looking at organizations from a process and work flow basis, and reengineering those processes to achieve greater efficiencies. While it is no longer as popular, in part because many BPR initiatives inadvertently cut out valuable intellectual capital from organizations, the principles are still practiced extensively on a lower-key basis.

BPR is itself a process, and can be performed either as a black-box service, or as a knowledge transfer project that enables the client to perform BPR for itself. When BPR was extremely popular in the early to mid-1990s, Ernst & Young chose to offer it only as a package which included a single implementation of BPR within the client organization, combined with training and licensing the client to implement the process for itself whenever it was subsequently required. Ernst & Young implicitly recognized that the client would in any case learn the process to a substantial degree in the implementation, so made that part of the offering and pricing structure. Since BPR is about enhancing existing processes, teaching clients to implement BPR can certainly be considered to be developing a meta-capability.

Technology Transfer and Technocultures

Technology transfer is clearly a central aspect of enhancing client capabilities. Most people recognize that the effective transfer of technology means far more than just delivering a piece of equipment or its specifications—it is also based on knowledge transfer, which results from

The RiskMetrics Group

J.P. Morgan spun off its risk products group in 1998 as The RiskMetrics Group (RMG), with Reuters and the employees of the new company joining the bank as shareholders. RMG provides methodologies, software, data, and training for financial institutions and corporations to enable them to better manage financial risk.

Two of the company's core products—the RiskMetrics® and CreditMetrics® methodologies—are actually provided free of charge; documents specifying these methodologies can be downloaded from its website. The data sets required by the methodologies can also be downloaded daily. The original product— RiskMetrics®—was released in 1994, when sophisticated financial risk management was in its infancy. The release helped establish it as an industry standard, promoted greater transparency in the market, and helped reduce overall risk in the financial system.

RMG also licenses software that implements these risk management methodologies. Since the methodologies are publicly available, other software vendors have implemented them in their offerings, although RMG clearly has an advantage in selling software based on its own methodologies. In line with the philosophy behind openly releasing the methodologies, all calculations performed in the software are fully documented and accessible to clients. The software is licensed on an annual basis, including installation and training, and full ongoing support on implementation, methodologies, and general risk management issues. This ensures that processes are implemented effectively, and that associated skills are developed in the client organization.

Training on financial risk management is provided as a separate function to give client executives across a broad range of functions an understanding of the fundamental concepts. It is provided using computer-based training approaches, including interactive exercises and simulations. These are supplemented with support from tutors, who grade exercises and projects and are available to answer questions.

interaction between people. When installing high-technology equipment, most manufacturers understand they have to provide skilled personnel on-site at the client organization for a period of time in order for the equipment to be implemented effectively. The equipment provides the process or a framework for the process, although people must have the skills and knowledge to translate that into a capability.

Bill Ford, former head of the department of organizational behaviour at the University of New South Wales in Sydney, Australia, emphasizes that technology must be considered within its cultural context; and that technology transfer requires an understanding of the different "technocultures" of the exporting and importing organizations and nations.[10] These technocultures develop from the relations between technology, skill development, and work organization, and lead to different assumptions about how technology is used and integrated into organizational processes. The implications are particularly pronounced when suppliers from different countries or technocultures provide joint solutions. Ford has worked successfully in facilitating disparate groups of suppliers and their clients in uncovering gaps in technocultures. He has also helped to facilitate the implementation of technology in ways which mesh with the importing organization's culture to result in enhanced capabilities, for example, at Carlton United Breweries, a division of one of the world's largest brewers—Foster's Brewing Group.

CLIENT SKILL DEVELOPMENT

Developing the skills of client staff is critical to enhancing the organization's overall capabilities, both in its own right, and as a complement to the implementation of processes. Skill development is often separated from other aspects of organizational development and knowledge transfer when engaging professional service firms. Many organizations treat skill development as purely a training issue, and they bring in training companies to address specific development needs, often without placing these needs in an overall strategic context.

Skill development needs to be treated as a far broader issue by service providers and their clients, both in terms of addressing skills as a source of organizational capabilities and sustainable competitiveness, and in applying the full range of approaches which result in effective development. Classroom training and workshops are just some of the ways of developing skills and knowledge. Practical knowledge is most effectively gained through experience, however, which emphasizes the importance of experiential learning in client interaction. Other valuable means of developing client skills include client coaching and mentoring.

Training as a Component of the Professional Service Offering

At their best, training companies are engaged in a very pure form of knowledge transfer, as the outcome of effective training is very explicitly skills, knowledge, and the capacity to act effectively. Certainly training companies are professional service firms. Here, however, we will choose to concentrate on how training is used within broader professional service relationships in order to transfer knowledge and add value to clients. In any situation in which knowledge transfer is important there are many lessons to learn from the training industry, as it focuses explicitly on knowledge and skill development, and best practice within the industry is based on extensive research and experience regarding what is most effective in achieving those outcomes.

In Chapter 6 we will examine some of the differences between seminars, training, and workshops, and their respective roles in knowledge transfer. Here we will look in more detail at training in general, and especially its role in enhancing client capabilities. Developing client skills through training is valuable on many levels, as it adds substantial value, builds closer relationships, and develops more sophisticated clients who can gain greater value from high-level professional services.

Client Training

Training can add value to clients within broader professional relationships in a wide variety of ways. Sometimes training is even required for the client to understand the value of the offering; this is notably the case in e-commerce, new media, and other technology-based developments, in which clients may not fully understand the relevance and impact to their businesses. In other cases training helps clients to be able to derive the greatest value from joint projects; this "project induction" training is discussed later in the chapter. Formal training is often an integral part of process implementation and other consulting projects.

The advertising industry has traditionally offered training courses as part of its suite of services. These are sometimes packaged as part of the overall relationship, or are made available separately for an additional price. The basic intention of the training courses is to develop the client's ability to use advertising effectively; they usually include topics such as the advertisement development process and media placement. The intention is that the client and advertising agency are able to work together more smoothly, and better results are achieved. The agencies have a strong interest in seeing their clients achieve value for the cost of their advertising.

BMP DDB, an advertising agency based in London, UK, has been running a "Creative Role-Reversal Course" since 1970. It is designed to place its clients in the role of an advertising agency so they can better understand the process of how advertising is developed, though the course is now open to any young marketer or brand manager who deals with advertising agencies. Over an intensive five days, participants break into syndicates that play the roles of agencies pitching for business. The subject is usually a real-world situation in the agency, and the syndicate presentations at the end of the week are judged by a panel, including a senior representative of the relevant client and the top management of BMP. Each syndicate is assigned a tutor who acts as a mentor and sounding board for the group as they work. While there are instructional talks and exercises throughout the course, the primary emphasis is on developing advertising ideas in a realistic situation.

CIBC Global Markets, the investment banking arm of Canadian Imperial Bank of Commerce, in 1995 established the School of Financial Products, which provides structured training programs in the use of financial derivatives for its clients and prospects. The spectacular losses in derivatives during the mid-1990s of Orange County, Procter & Gamble and other organizations led to a tendency for corporations to shy away from using complex financial instruments, despite their value in portfolio and risk management. CIBC Global Markets chose to establish formal training programs for its clients, examining not only the practicalities of dealing with financial derivatives, including risk management, but also broader strategic issues such as establishing policies and procedures for managing sophisticated financial products. The School of Financial Products runs more than 30 formal programs in its New York offices, as well as in other locations in North America and worldwide. These are provided free of charge to any organization introduced by CIBC Global Market's front-line sales staff and relationship managers.

EXPERIENTIAL LEARNING

For the majority of people, the most effective way to learn a process or skill is by doing it. Book or classroom learning is usually not sufficient in itself to enable a person or team to develop skills effectively, or learn how to implement or run a business process. Knowledge acquisition is almost always substantially more effective if it is based on practical experience. Over the last couple of decades the training industry has taken into account the clear evidence that experiential learning yields the best results, and training is now usually strongly oriented toward activities, simulation of real work environments, and learning by doing. Action learning—which embodies the same principles—has emerged as a key framework for internal development initiatives.

While the principle of experiential learning often guides the design of training programs, it should also be implicit in the design of all client interaction that is intended to facilitate knowledge transfer. This principle in fact directs how many professional service firms implement knowledge transfer—by taking clients through a real-life process in such a way that they can then implement the process unassisted. This was the case with Ernst & Young's provision of business process reengineering services. Ernst & Young trained the client to do BPR by actually performing the process in one of its business units or operations, and worked with key client staff at all stages, so they had experienced how to resolve major challenges throughout the process.

The reality is that any time an organization engages an outside consultant to perform a process for it, the hiring organization learns many essential components of how to do that process. This is true whether the consultant explicitly attempts to transfer that knowledge, and even whether or not the client deliberately tries to learn as much as possible from the interaction. Since the client will in any case learn substantively how to perform the process for itself, it is often worth formalizing the knowledge transfer, doing it effectively, and specifically charging the client for it or gaining recognition for the value added. Attempting to hang on to this knowledge is not as profitable in the long run as explicitly selling it.

Joint Client/Service Provider Teams

If experiential learning is about doing, then the design of client projects should be based on getting clients to work through the processes for themselves. The black-box style of professional services is closely related to all the work on a project being performed by the service provider, while knowledge transfer-based projects are often founded on teams comprised of staff from both the service provider and the client. Implementing project teams which substantially involve client staff not only results in strong experiential learning, but also provides the ongoing rich interaction between professionals and client staff which results in socialized knowledge transfer, and closer personal and organizational relationships.

Choosing whether and how to build joint client/service provider project teams is a fundamental element of project design. Whether it is appropriate in a given instance depends on the nature of the project and the client culture, as well as the usual approach and stance of the professional service firm. Certainly joint project teams are increasingly the norm in many professional service industries. Having chosen a high level of involvement in conjunction with the client, the issue becomes how to design interaction throughout the project to optimize useful knowledge transfer.

Consulting firm ksbr Brand Planning, based in Hertfordshire, UK, uses intensive consumer research as the basis of brand planning for its clients. Rather than doing the research, developing a theoretical framework to understand it, and then presenting that to the client, ksbr encourages its clients to become involved from the very beginning of the process. Moving beyond the practice of simply having clients attend several focus groups and interviews central to the research, the firm offers to assist clients in running the focus groups themselves. For each project it works on, ksbr helps establish a range of focused teams within its client organization, with responsibilities including managing the project, generating ideas, and approving the internal recommendations. The firm participates in the client teams to assist them in creating a rich variety of output from their ideas and work, including physical objects and videos which can be presented to senior management, in the process often challenging and debating with teams on the value of their findings. Its approaches are based on the belief that to achieve change in the large service businesses that represent many of its clients, the internal project team itself must be influential; team formation and internal communication from the project are all designed to achieve a lasting impact.

Project Induction Training

One of the most critical milestones in running joint projects is the launch, which establishes common ground between the client and professional service firm. This is often addressed in formal project induction training. This training is not intended to provide the ultimate desired outcome in its own right, but rather to pave the way for effective interaction and learning by the client in the process of the consulting engagement.

At global consulting firm McKinsey & Co., for all projects that involve a joint McKinsey/client team, the client team members attend a one to three-day induction session, in order to establish ground rules, as well as the basic approaches, thinking, and methodologies to be used in the project. This forms a reference point for the thinking processes that the joint teams use throughout the project. As such, it enhances the experiential learning of applying these processes and approaches throughout the project, and maximizes the clients' ability to use them for themselves in subsequent situations.

Similarly, Strategic Decisions Group, a decision quality consulting firm based in Menlo Park, California, takes its new clients through a two-week training course which is essentially the same as that used for the induction of its own new consultants. This training course is intensive and highly interactive, with participants leading workshops and coming up with recommendations in the course of running simulated consulting projects.

Simulations

One of the best ways of providing focused experiential learning is through simulations of business environments. War gaming, as described in Chapter 4, is a form of simulation focused on developing capabilities in strategic decision making. Other simulations are focused on specific and technical skills.

KPMG has established what it calls a Client Mentoring Center in Radnor, Pennsylvania, which provides clients with a week-long immersion in data warehousing tools and technologies. Client executives get hands-on experience with the products and approaches they will be using to develop their own systems in-house. Samples of their own corporate data are loaded on the databases at the center beforehand, so clients can model and work with the technologies in ways which are directly relevant to them.

CLIENT COACHING AND MENTORING

Coaching and *mentoring* are rapidly gaining currency across a very broad range of organizations as valuable tools in internal skill development and knowledge transfer. Coaching is an approach to skill and knowledge development that encourages and guides people in their own knowledge acquisition, especially by providing focused, constructive

Celemi

Celemi, based in Malmö, Sweden, with North American headquarters in Simsbury, Connecticut, offers what it calls "learning tools" to facilitate learning for its clients. These are structured processes that are run interactively around actual models of companies or similar materials; these can last between one-half day to several days. One of its tools, named "Apples and Oranges," takes employees at all levels in an organization through an understanding of the company's key financial indicators, and how their individual actions contribute to these indicators. Another tool, "Tango," simulates several years in the life of a knowledge-based organization, with teams playing rival firms who must compete for clients, talented staff, and challenging projects.[11]

Complementing these packaged products, about half of Celemi's business is the customized development of learning tools for specific client situations. One example is its work with Sainsbury's, the United Kingdom's largest food retailer, which had identified a need to enhance its customer service. Celemi developed a series of learning tools that simulated real-life situations in the stores, which employees used in discussion groups to establish their own approaches to improving service.

Celemi's clients have gone on to use its products to develop the learning and capabilities of their own clients. Pfizer Pharmaceutical Sweden was seeking to add value to the medical community through education programs, but was finding that traditional-style lectures were not resulting in any changes in behavior. It established the DAISY program, which is intended to enable practitioners to diagnose illnesses faster and more accurately, and recognize the benefits of new drugs and treatment programs so they would feel comfortable prescribing them.

The program usually involves an initial two-day session that takes participants through a specific illness in the context of the human system, its causes and effects, and the pros and cons of available treatments. Celemi develops for Pfizer interactive learning tools for each targeted illness, including visual diagrams and case studies. Participants usually meet again several weeks after the workshop to review and discuss what they have learned in a practical context. The DAISY program has reached 70 percent of Pfizer's target group of primary care physicians in Sweden.

feedback. Mentoring is usually implemented as a one-to-one relationship maintained over an extended time period, in which an experienced person assists a more junior colleague in his or her career and personal development; this process can cover a very broad range of work and other issues. The popularity of these approaches is based on their success in achieving personal development, which is largely a result of the richness of interaction allowed by the relatively unstructured approach.

Coaching and mentoring are most obviously applicable within a single organization, partially due to confidentiality issues, and also as these relationships are most useful when they are open-ended rather than defined within the time and resource constraints of a contract or external relationship. Still, there are many opportunities across a broad range of industries for companies to engage in a coaching or mentoring-based style of interaction with their clients in order to maximize knowledge transfer and added value.

The flexibility and "bandwidth" of effective coaching or mentoring relationships mean they can be exceptionally effective at knowledge transfer. In addition, the closeness implicit in these relationships again demonstrates the deep ties between knowledge transfer and client relationships.

"Coaching" is usually a better term in client relationships, as clients may not be comfortable with the implications of seniority or greater experience suggested by "mentoring." Interactive marketing agency Giant Step, described in Chapter 7, sometimes refers to "co-mentoring" with its clients, to imply that each has knowledge that it needs to transfer to the other, while emphasizing that this transfer is achieved through an ongoing highly interactive relationship. Whatever words are used, formalizing client contact so that the broadest experience of the professional can be applied in a fairly unstructured way to the issues facing the client results in substantial benefits to both parties.

Implementing Client Mentoring

Mentoring is commonly referred to and used in the field of software development. When organizations have their own software development teams, their productivity and effectiveness can be greatly enhanced by having regular access to people who have had substantial experience with similar challenges in development and project management. Object International of Raleigh, North Carolina, commonly allocates an executive to work together with the client team for two to four weeks for the initial project design, and then spends a week every two to four weeks with the client to assist in resolving ongoing issues. Mentoring executives have had development in team facilitation and group dynamics to complement their software and project expertise.

A number of high-level software and programming training companies offer a package whereby trainees in advanced programming languages such as C++ initially undergo a multiday training program. This training program is followed by a period of several months in which trainees have access to a mentor to guide them in the on-the-job application of the principles they have learned.

Mentoring-based approaches have become widely accepted in the field of software development due to their obvious applicability, and similar approaches can readily be adapted to other industries and situations. As discussed, mentoring may not always be the best description for marketing the services, but the underlying principles and philosophies are among the most effective in achieving knowledge transfer and adding substantial value in skill development.

Providing Unstructured Advice

Providing unstructured advice is an excellent means to add value and develop and broaden client relationships. In essence, this is a specialist coaching relationship, which allows professional expertise to be available when required. Being in a position to provide ad-hoc advice depends on a high degree of trust and is usually built from an existing relationship. This kind of relationship, which can arise spontaneously or be suggested by the professional, is an excellent vehicle for knowledge transfer, helps to develop close personal relationships, positions the professional as an advisor and sounding board, and very importantly starts to broaden the perceived expertise of the professional.

Many senior lawyers, accountants, consultants, bankers, and other professionals sit on company boards, reflecting the scope of their relevant business experience. Establishing mentoring-style relationships enables professionals to broaden their relationships beyond their nominal field of specialization to encompass far more of their general business experience and expertise.

It is important to recognize that many "soft" and interpersonal skills are required in effective coaching and mentoring, which are not part of the core expertise or repertoire of many professionals. These include strong questioning and listening skills, giving feedback effectively, demonstrating respect, and letting people explore their own learning opportunities. Whenever possible, professionals who are entering a coaching-style relationship with a client should be given at least introductory training and development in some of these foundation skills.

SUMMARY: ADDING VALUE TO CLIENT CAPABILITIES

A company's competitiveness is based on its competencies and capabilities; these stem from a fusion of effective business processes and skills. The greatest value, however, is in developing "meta-capabilities," which enable clients to continually improve their own capabilities. There are a variety of approaches to implementing and enhancing business processes, including implementing process documentation, software-based methodologies, business process reengineering, and technology transfer. Client skill development is intrinsic to developing effective capabilities, and should be built into all professional service relationships.

The processes and skills that form capabilities are best developed through experiential learning, which means implementing project teams involving both the client and service provider; project inductions and simulations are useful tools within that framework. Coaching and mentoring represent excellent models for the sorts of ongoing and highly interactive relationships that result in real development of capabilities, and greater client intimacy.

Over the past three chapters we have looked in detail at how value is added to clients with knowledge. Adding value to information is a primary function of professional service firms, and increasingly important to clients as the scope of digitization develops. Clients' ability to make better decisions at all levels of their organizations is central to their success, and one of the most valuable outcomes of effective knowledge transfer. Enhancing the processes and skills that constitute clients' business capabilities can result in powerful and lasting value creation.

In the third and final section we will examine the practical issues of implementation—what professional service firms must do to achieve greater added value to clients with knowledge, and stronger and more profitable client relationships. These issues include managing communication channels, structuring relationship management, co-creating knowledge with clients, pricing knowledge, and pulling all these together with enhanced knowledge communication skills to yield superior business performance.

NOTES

1. Dorothy Leonard, *Wellsprings of Knowledge: Building and Sustaining the Sources of Innovation* (Boston: Harvard Business School Press, 1995): 135.

2. Prahalad and Hamel.

3. George Stalk, Philip Evans, and Lawrence E. Shulman, "Competing on Capabilities: The New Rules of Corporate Strategy," *Harvard Business Review* (March-April 1992).

4. Verna Allee, *The Knowledge Evolution: Expanding Organizational Intelligence* (Boston: Butterworth–Heinemann, 1997): 20–26.

5. Badarraco distinguishes between "migratory knowledge," which can move readily and quickly between organizations and across national boundaries; and "embedded knowledge," which resides in relationships between individuals and groups, and affects the way information flows and decisions are made. Embedded knowledge, while essential to the success of the firm, cannot be easily understood and captured and so can only move slowly between organizations. See Joseph L. Badarraco, *The Knowledge Link: How Firms Compete through Strategic Alliances* (Boston: Harvard Business School Press, 1991).

6. The term "meta-capability" has been used by Jeanne M. Liedtka and John W. Rosenblum, "Shaping Conversations: Making Strategy, Managing Change," *California Management Review* 39, no. 1 (Fall 1996): 141–157.

7. Prokesh.

8. Argyris.

9. Thomas H. Davenport, "The Fad that Forgot People," *Fast Company* no. 1 (November 1995): 70.

10. G. W. (Bill) Ford, "Technology Transfer, Technocultures, and Skill Formation: Learning from Australian Experience," *Asia Pacific Human Resource Management* (Summer 1991): 67–73.

11. See Thomas A. Stewart, "The Dance Steps Get Trickier All the Time," *Fortune* (May 26, 1997).

Part III

Implementation

Chapter 6

Channels for Knowledge Transfer
Managing Communication Portfolios

Knowledge transfer clearly depends on communication. There are many channels available for that communication, including meetings, documents, extranets, and others. Each channel has different characteristics in how it facilitates and enables knowledge transfer. These features must be considered in order to build communication strategies that maximize knowledge transfer, the value added to clients, and the depth of relationships.

MANAGING COMMUNICATION CHANNELS

Some communication channels are far better suited to certain projects and situations than others. However, in client relationships the issue is not choosing the best single channel or channels, but managing the overall *portfolio* of channels to achieve the greatest impact. The issues of managing client contact from the perspective of relationship development will be covered more in Chapter 7. In this chapter we will focus on how to use the communication channels available to maximize knowledge transfer, though the issues are closely linked.

Information Richness and Media Richness

The concepts of *information richness* and *media richness* in organizational communication were first introduced by Daft and Lengel.[1] They defined information richness as the "ability of information to change understanding within a time interval," and noted that communication media vary in their capacity to process rich information. The idea of "changed under-standing" is clearly that of knowledge, or changed mental models.

The researchers reported that the richest medium is face-to-face meetings, because it provides multiple cues via body language, facial expression, and tone of voice, and provides immediate feedback so interpretation can be checked. They also noted that as the complexity of management challenges increases, richer information and media must be used in order to reduce uncertainty and clarify ambiguity.[2] This early research has spawned whole schools of study on information and media richness in organizations, which recently have begun to focus more and more on computer-mediated communication, and its richness in achieving "changed understanding."[3]

ENABLERS OF KNOWLEDGE TRANSFER

Given the broad array of communication channels available to us, we need criteria to guide us in assessing their effectiveness in enabling knowledge transfer. These criteria will allow us to design a strategy for communicating with our clients in a way that maximizes knowledge transfer. The four key characteristics or enablers of knowledge transfer in communication are:

- Interactivity
- Bandwidth
- Structure
- Reusability

Of these, interactivity and bandwidth are the most critical, al-though structure and permanence are also important considerations.[4] We will now examine each of these in more detail.

Interactivity

Interactivity is one of the prime buzzwords of the information age. How does this relate to knowledge transfer? Most importantly, it defines the degree to which the flow of information between people or organiza-tions is two-way as opposed to one-way. Documents and television, for example, have essentially no interactivity. While you can choose what you read or watch, usually no information about your reactions or anything else is communicated back to the organization that initiated the communication.

The greatest value creation for both clients and service providers stems from rich two-way knowledge flow, although flow back from clients is often limited. For example, information about client usage patterns of websites can be captured and used to enhance the design of knowledge transfer processes. This is a form of interactivity, but in this case only limited information about a narrow range of behaviors flows from the client, which is far less powerful than if rich knowledge is flowing in both directions. Some media—most obviously face-to-face meetings—enable this rich two-way interactivity, while others limit the richness of flow in one or both directions.

The best and most basic model of interactivity is simply dialogue. Throughout the ages knowledge has always been developed through discussion and interaction with others, which is still true today. Technology increasingly allows us to interact in new ways; however, the closer the interaction is to an actual discussion, which enables people to question, probe, and elaborate their understanding, the greater its effectiveness.

The dynamics of interactivity depend on the number of people involved. Interaction between two people is already very high, although the potential benefits of interactivity increase with the number of people involved. There can, of course, be decreasing returns in adding more people, depending on the quality of facilitation within the group.

A different type of interactivity results when a person interacts with a machine, but the information is not necessarily captured. For example, interactive video games respond to users, but their input does not usually flow back to the manufacturer. Computer-based training can be very effective for knowledge transfer because it forces users to answer questions and provide input that guides the information presented. Even if the users' responses aren't captured, this kind of interaction with the computer results in far more effective internalization of knowledge than by simply reading a document.

Bandwidth

We introduced the concept of bandwidth in Chapter 1 as one of the most fundamental issues in knowledge transfer, and defined it as the amount of information that can be communicated over a given period. Clearly bandwidth is an essential element to media richness, certainly in terms of its ability to achieve changed understanding, or in other words knowledge transfer. The more communication channels used within a client relationship, the broader the total bandwidth.

The effective bandwidth of a text document, for example, is quite narrow in terms of possible information transfer in a given period. The value of multimedia can be viewed as tapping greater bandwidth, by using sound, moving pictures, and other media to achieve richer communication. The sound and image resolution of even high-quality video, however, is still significantly limited compared with face-to-face meetings, in which the real flow of information is many orders of magnitude greater.

Structure

The concept of structure in communication channels groups together two related ideas. The first is how easily the relationships within and between ideas and information can be communicated. Greater structure means less ambiguity, and more clarity in implementation or further communication. Information customized for a specific client can be structured in a way to make it clear and usable in formulating action plans. The second idea is the ability to structure information so as to be aligned with the structure of your clients' mental models, which allows it to be most easily internalized as knowledge. This concept is developed in the Appendix.

While communication channels have varying capacities to convey structure, the importance of structure will also change depending on the type of knowledge to be communicated. For example, if knowledge is procedural in nature, such as how to implement software or report on a breach of safety regulations, then the communication needs to be highly structured. In the case of developing strategic responsiveness to unforeseen developments, an unstructured approach is likely to be more effective. Global Business Network very deliberately designs conferences for its members so that valuable unstructured conversations take place, which enables new and unexpected perspectives and insights to come to light. Generally knowledge communication—teaching existing knowledge—requires structured communication, while knowledge elicitation—drawing out the capacity to act effectively—favors unstructured approaches.

Reusability

The ability to reuse communication for other people or in other situations depends first on its permanence, which can be seen as the ability to capture the communication in a useful form, almost always digitally. This allows the communication—and the knowledge embedded in it—to be referred to again by the same or other people in the client organization, which can substantially increase its value.

Some media, however, while allowing content to be captured, do not lend themselves to easy reuse. For example, while a document can quickly and easily be accessed and utilized by many people, a video of a presentation is time-consuming to watch and hard to reference by content, making it unlikely to be used again unless it is extremely relevant to the issues at hand. Technology is beginning to make this easier. Voice recognition software is enabling automated conversation transcription, and more ready access and reference to specific parts of conversations, as well as "conversation mining," in which patterns in conversations can be identified, as in a call center. The same technology can be used to provide indexes to videos, though this is still usually done manually.

The degree to which communication has been customized for a specific person, group, or situation will influence how valuable it is in other situations. We have seen how customization adds substantial value within a specific context, but by the same token this can make it less valuable in other situations. Recording a conversation which clarifies a client executive's concerns about a project is likely to be of limited value to anyone else; however, a presentation about the impact of e-commerce on the client's industry could well be valuable to many other people in the organization.

COMMUNICATION CHANNELS

We will distinguish as communication channels each of the approaches and technologies available for communication that have significantly different characteristics in knowledge transfer to clients. Some of these channels represent ways of structuring face-to-face communication that have always been available, while others represent the use of recent technological developments.

Since digital technology has already encompassed the communication of data, sound, and moving pictures, in a business context the most likely impact of future technological developments will be the increase in bandwidth and potential interactivity of existing approaches. The fundamental knowledge transfer characteristics of technology-based communication channels will not change, but will be improved over time. There will be an increasing opportunity for these to replace face-to-face communication, although the time will never come when meetings will be entirely supplanted by interactions intermediated by technology.

Naturally, each of the communication channels we will examine are commonly used whether or not knowledge transfer is intended. However, we will focus here on studying these with regard to how well they enable knowledge transfer, as summarized in Table 6–1. It is important to note that the table indicates the potential of each communication channel to enable knowledge transfer, although this potential is not always used. From there we will examine the roles of each available communication channel in designing an overall knowledge transfer strategy.

TABLE 6–1   Knowledge Transfer Capabilities of Different Communication Channels

	Interactivity	Bandwidth	Structure	Reusability
Documents	Nil	Low	High	High
E-mail and fax	Medium	Low-Medium	High	High
Telephone	High	Medium	Low	Low
Meetings	Very High	Very High	Low-Medium	Low
Presentations and seminars	Medium	High	High	Low-Medium
Multimedia presentations	Low-Medium	Medium-High	High	High
Facilitated workshops	Very High	Very High	Medium	Low
Training	Medium	High	High	Medium
Computer-based training	Medium	Low-Medium	High	High
Coaching	Very High	Very High	Low	Very Low

Documents

Documents—whether in paper or electronic format—are the basic means of capturing and communicating information. As such, the lessons learned in Chapter 3 are directly relevant in maximizing their value in knowledge transfer. The main limitations of documents are that they are not interactive and have relatively low bandwidth. This gives them limited impact in rich knowledge transfer; documents need to be used in conjunction with other channels to be most effective.

The main advantages of documents include their easy storage and retrieval, and their ability to be highly organized, presenting logic and structure very effectively. The ability to use visual representations to complement text is a particular strength of documents. Documents will always be used for more formal communication, such as recommendations resulting from projects, although more informal modes of communication such as e-mail are replacing the traditional role of documents. We will discuss some of the specific characteristics of digital documents in the section on digital channels.

E-mail and Fax

The primary characteristic of e-mail and fax is that they allow rapid communication of text and documents. This speed of communication starts to allow a level of interactivity, with e-mails or faxes being sent back and forth as a form of dialogue. This process can be fairly slow and stilted, but allows clear exposition of ideas in text, and the use of diagrams. As such the advantages of documents are supplemented by greater interactivity, as well as easy reusability.

While faxes can only communicate text and diagrams, e-mail is increasingly being used to send software files, including not just documents but also richer communication such as spreadsheets or architectural designs. This results in both a broader bandwidth for communication, and a rich level of interactivity in terms of the client's ability to modify or notate the file, then send it back to the service provider. Clearly e-mail will play an increasingly important role in the future, though one limitation is its perceived informality.

An increasing number of institutional fund managers are no longer taking telephone calls from their stockbrokers, essentially denying them the possibility of rich interactivity. This leaves e-mail, fax, and voice mail as the most effective means for brokers to communicate high-value information to their clients. In fact, some financial market sales training courses deal specifically with how best to use these channels to service clients.

Telephone and Voice-Mail

Telephone usage provides the first level at which the richness and degree of interactivity allows knowledge transfer through socialization. Being able to hear the tone and inflection of voice, as well as to interrupt and clarify at will, provides far richer information and communication than that which can be conveyed through documents or e-mail. The bandwidth of telephone communication is itself very limited compared to that of face-to-face meetings. However, one of the key benefits of a telephone is that you only need to pick it up in order to interact; getting to meetings and participating in them can be very time-consuming. The major limitations of telephone conversations are that they do not allow highly structured communication, making it hard to convey complex information, and that they are not readily stored or reusable. In knowledge transfer, telephone conversation enables easy and quick discussion, dialogue, sharing of views, responses to questions, or clarification of specific points. Telephone allows relatively rich communication within tight time parameters.

Meetings

Face-to-face meetings in a wide variety of formats are the fundamental channel for most knowledge transfer. Much knowledge transfer in professional situations is informal, and often occurs in one-on-one or small meetings which ostensibly have other objectives such as to define the assignment, discuss issues, or present results informally. The rich interactivity and bandwidth of communication in meetings enable complex and subtle knowledge transfer. Well-run meetings can have good structure, and there can be some element of permanence and reusability if minutes or notes are taken and transcribed.

Presentations and Seminars

Presentations tend to be more structured and less interactive than most meetings—they are primarily designed for one-way communication. Bandwidth can be high, as there is usually not only oral communication, but also visual or documented presentation. Very importantly, presentations (hopefully!) command the audience's attention, in contrast to documents, which are most often scanned briefly and thrown aside.

While presentations are commonly used in sales situations, they also serve as an important tool in knowledge transfer. This includes adding value to clients through knowledge transfer in the sales process itself, as a way of demonstrating value and the intended style in the project. In addition, presentations are commonly used for the more overt knowledge transfer processes in client engagements, for example in communicating the results or conclusions from a project.

Seminars are a common tool to add value to clients in many areas of professional services. They are a useful complement to documents, however, the one-way dynamic of seminars can result in mere information dumping. Visuals, if used effectively, good handouts to complement the talk, and a dynamic presentation style (not always seen in professional services!) help to make seminars more useful to clients. Nevertheless, seminars have significant limitations as a medium for rich knowledge transfer.

Training

Training is the most formalized approach to knowledge transfer and skill development, and as such, it will often be important in achieving knowledge transfer outcomes. As discussed in Chapter 5, it is usually carried out in a classroom-type environment. While it has traditionally been offered in a lecture format, increasingly it is undertaken in a very interactive and experiential style, to the degree that that is possible in a classroom.

Training carries a very high potential bandwidth, as people are on location with the trainer, and all media can be used if needed as part of the training process. The material can be structured as much as useful for a particular topic, and training programs can usually be repeated fairly readily. There is ample opportunity for high interactivity, however, training tends to be focused on a defined knowledge curriculum.

Facilitated Workshops

What distinguishes facilitated workshops from training is that they are primarily oriented toward knowledge elicitation rather than knowledge communication—the intended result is usually for clients to develop their own new and useful understanding. Their fundamental premise is interaction, and gaining the greatest value possible from bringing together a group of people who have different and complementary knowledge, experience, and perspectives.

The knowledge content in workshops may come solely from client staff, who together share and build knowledge; in this case, the often very high value added by service providers stems purely from their expertise in the facilitation process. More often than not, service providers also provide knowledge content, which together with the client's knowledge helps to develop new knowledge. These issues are covered in more detail in Chapter 8 on the co-creation of knowledge.

Clearly, the important issues here are the degree and richness of interactivity; a well-facilitated workshop is usually about getting the type of interaction that will result in significant useful knowledge creation. Although its structure is flexible, a workshop is not intended to be "reused" or recreated. Its value lies both in the explicit deliverables from the session, and the enhanced knowledge of workshop participants.

Coaching and Mentoring

We have already discussed coaching and mentoring in Chapter 5; here we will assess it against the key knowledge transfer enablers as a comparison with other communication channels. Arguably the bandwidth and interactivity of coaching and mentoring relationships is unmatched by any other channel. The richness of interaction applied over an extended period in an informal context, together with access to structured approaches where they are useful, is more likely to achieve real knowledge transfer than almost any other single approach. Nevertheless, it demands a serious time commitment from senior staff, and since the benefits are in the participation, the interaction cannot be reused. While it can be difficult to implement mentoring-style relationships with clients, they form a very powerful model on which to base and design knowledge-based interactions.

DIGITAL CHANNELS

The importance of digital channels in all aspects of business communication, including knowledge transfer, is increasing extremely rapidly. Since most information is now digitized, it is usually easier and cheaper to communicate digitally than by other means, and most clients now have access at least to the Internet as a mode of digital communication.

There are many advantages to digital channels, which means that almost all information flow is likely to happen digitally in the near future. One critical advantage is found in what John Peetz, Jr., chief knowledge officer of Ernst & Young, refers to as the "scalability" of communication.[5] This means that once digital information is captured, it can be duplicated indefinitely, communicated globally almost instantaneously, and accessed and referenced without limit, making the system almost equally usable by as small or as large a group as desired. Importantly, location becomes transparent, and videoconferencing and other tools allow easy international collaboration (though it can result in meetings at strange times for some!). In addition, the speed of communication of digital information means that interaction can encompass actual work-in-progress, including elaborate design and production work as well as simple documents.

The growing sophistication of systems will continue to allow for greater levels of interaction between computers and people, in terms of interfaces which can both recognize speech and gestures, and respond in ways that evoke thinking and learning from the user. On a related front, information technology systems can be integrated with communication structures, which will increasingly allow automated systems capable of interaction, and customization of content and interactivity for users at low cost.

Communication Access and Bandwidth

The client's access to digital communication and available bandwidth are important considerations in the implementation of digital communication. Naturally this connectivity will be used for many communication functions: here we will focus on issues relating to knowledge transfer and avoid specific technological issues, which in any case are changing rapidly.

The key issue is the communication bandwidth available to clients, used in the technological sense rather than the broader sense of communication between people. Narrow bandwidth in client relationships limits the potential for richer channels and forms of communication and interactivity. Currently the Internet can provide reasonable bandwidth; however, it is unreliable and remains inadequate for some kinds of interaction. One example is interactive computer-based training, which we will cover in more detail below. This can be delivered over the public Internet, but this type of interactive application may not be effective if clients have only narrow bandwidth access.

Some service providers have chosen to install dedicated communication lines to their clients. One major law firm has established an extranet for its clients to access background legal information and work-in-progress on their cases, and has decided to bear the cost for the lines connecting it to its major clients. Possible future enhancements include enabling clients when browsing through their case information to click on a button in order to speak to their lawyers, or even to establish a videoconferencing link. This intimacy and ease of interaction provides a solid foundation for building closer relationships with key clients.

Extranets

Extranets can be considered as intranets—internal computer systems using Internet-style technology, including browsers—which have been expanded to an extended enterprise potentially including clients, suppliers, alliance members, and other stakeholders. Just as widespread use of browsers has facilitated the development of intranets as a primary tool for knowledge-sharing within companies, extranets provide a common and easy-to-use interface for clients to access high-value information from their service providers.[6]

Investment banks were early implementers of extranet technology, in order to provide their clients with research faster and on a searchable basis, thus offering a significant improvement (or complement) to paper-based research. All the major investment banks are providing research to key clients using extranets. Rather than using extranets simply to deliver information, investment banks are more frequently delivering the analysis behind their research in an interactive format, such as spreadsheets which clients can manipulate to input their own assumptions, and to use in developing their own thinking. For example, Credit Suisse First Boston provides its institutional clients with interactive models of its Economic Value Added™ (EVA) analysis of stocks.

Other companies which are primarily providers of high-value information, such as publishers of specialist newsletters, market research firms, credit information bureaus, and so on, have been enthusiastic users of extranet technology. Most companies that provide this type of information are disseminating their publications on extranets as well as in printed form, or starting to implement this practice.

State Street Global Link^SM

State Street Bank, based in Boston, Massachusetts, specializes in serving institutional investors. Its core business has been global securities processing, with $5 trillion in assets now under custody. However, its fund manager subsidiary, State Street Global Advisors, has become one of the seven largest in the world; and its treasury division, State Street Trust & Bank, is known as a major player in the foreign exchange markets.

In 1997, State Street introduced Global Link, an electronic system for foreign exchange trading and delivery of research. In order to reach its clients, it established an alliance with Bridge Information Systems, the world's second largest financial information provider. In conjunction with Bridge, State Street offers to its clients the opportunity to install its own server at their premises, provides a dedicated connection line (if Bridge does not already have that relationship), and maintains these lines on an ongoing basis, all free of charge. More than 180 clients are connected to the system.[7]

The system has four modules: research, strategy, execution, and administration. Access to each is provided only to authorized personnel within the client organization. Part of the unique value provided by the research section is that it uses data on the portfolio flows of the $5 trillion under custody at the bank—clearly a solid foundation for value added analysis and insights into global foreign exchange flows. The execution module allows clients to trade on-screen; this method was used to execute $40 billion in business in 1998. While every client does not use all modules of the system, State Street always provides access to everything, so clients can get used to having it as part of their desktop, and gradually use more of its facilities. The system is intended to complement personal relationships, and State Street dealers will generally speak with their clients daily to provide knowledge and service that cannot be delivered effectively online.

DIGITAL CHANNELS IN KNOWLEDGE-BASED RELATIONSHIPS

The advantages of digital channels mean they are gradually becoming pervasive in all aspects of business communication, from advertising to payment to ongoing service. These developments are beginning to have a massive impact on the shape of business and society, with the fundamental business models of many companies changing to respond to the advent of electronic commerce. Our focus here is not so much on e-commerce and its broader ramifications as on how these digital channels can be used to enhance knowledge transfer. Since the business model in the case of professional services is inherently characterized by high levels of personal interaction, digital channels will primarily serve to facilitate that interaction, rather than fundamentally changing the nature of the business.

Delivery of High-Value Information

Digital channels are usually the most effective media for communicating information. As such, in a knowledge transfer context, digital channels will increasingly be predominant in the delivery of high-value information. Most of the issues covered in Chapter 3 in terms of creating high-value information apply whatever channel is used to deliver the information. The key elements affected by delivery through digital channels—rather than documents, for example—are presentation, and ease of access and use.

Ease of access and use draws strongly on the benefits of digital technology, in terms of being able to search large databases readily, and access valuable information in usable formats. Information can be structured in useful ways, for example, showing the relationships between documents or themes, while hypertext allows users to follow the links that are most useful and relevant to them.

Online Consulting

Extranet technology can be used to package and deliver less-customized consulting services to a broad market at limited cost. Ernst & Young led the fray when it introduced an online service called Ernie in 1996, aimed at the mid-sector market of firms with revenues of under $250 million. For an annual fee Ernie gives clients access to a variety of online services. At its heart is the ability to ask questions on any business issue by e-mail; Ernie channels these to the appropriate expert within Ernst & Young, guaranteeing a concise response within 48 hours. The proprietary content from the questions and answers is stripped off to build a database of previously asked questions, which not only gives quick and easy access to valuable information, but also allows clients to track the interests of their peers. Other aspects of the service include interactive modules that provide detailed and structured assistance and recommendations on issues such as software selection and supply chain diagnostics.

This online service is a good example of extranets as an effective channel for communication between people, complementing the simpler task of providing access to information and databases. The issues for Ernst & Young in making Ernie work are far more human and organizational than technological—the firm needs to provide appropriate motivation for busy professionals to respond promptly to queries. It has successfully addressed these issues, and has now embedded the solutions as part of its overall operations.

Other professional service firms have implemented similar types of services, each with slightly different philosophies and approaches, but which all use extranet-based systems to provide high-value information and interactivity in areas of specialist knowledge. PricewaterhouseCoopers has its Tax News Network online, while details of Arthur Andersen's KnowledgeSpace service are discussed in Chapter 8.

Computer-Based Training

The rise of multimedia technology has enabled the development of *computer-based training* (CBT), which allows individuals to go through interactive training courses at their own pace, and at times suitable to them. CBT is rapidly taking an increasingly large slice of business training budgets.

While CBT has thus far primarily been used in staff skill development as a substitute or complement to classroom training, the approaches and technology can equally well be used in knowledge transfer to clients across all industries. Most developers of CBT draw extensively on the field of adult learning, and design courses to result in specific knowledge outcomes for users. As such, professional service firms can use the principles of CBT in a wide variety of situations with their clients. The case of law firm Blake Dawson Waldron given in Chapter 4 is a good illustration of how CBT can be used to add value to line decision making.

Baan, a global enterprise resource planning software company with joint headquarters in Reston, Virginia and Pullen, the Netherlands, has introduced what it calls Baan Virtual Campus, an Internet-based training environment providing education for clients, partners, and distributors. It includes training courses and certification programs on its software, as well as 24-hour access to instructors and application specialists. The Virtual Campus was designed specifically for the mid-market segment, which is difficult to directly provide with full service.

New York–based games2train.com has taken the concept of computer-based training a step further to what it calls game-based learning, which marries the principles of interactive learning with the look and feel of computer games. It believes that the members of the "Nintendo Generation" need a very high level of engagement, and that the traditional training courses and approaches of presenting information followed by testing on its comprehension will not sustain the interest of these groups. Its fast-moving games use and incorporate the training content of its clients, which include firms such as Chase Manhattan, American Express, and Reuters. One client, computer-aided design software firm Think3, engaged games2train.com to develop a videogame-based tutorial for its own user base, which consists primarily of young engineers; the training product puts the learner in the role of an intergalactic space agent on a mission to save the universe.

Service and Support

Online support will quickly become the prevailing means to service both retail and corporate clients; it will be given a big boost when it becomes practicable for clients to speak directly with support staff through the same system. From the perspective of knowledge transfer, the critical issue is whether service is provided simply in order to remedy problems, or whether it is used as an opportunity to educate the client so as to avoid recurrence of these problems. Service provides an excellent illustration of the value of knowledge transfer, as it is very clearly a win-win situation. Clients can avoid problems as well as fix them quickly and more easily by themselves, and the vendor can spend less on support services.

Networking equipment manufacturer Cisco Systems has always tried to move as much of its client interaction as possible online. Most of its support is provided online; however, more recently it has made a more concerted effort to make its clients more knowledgeable in being able to support themselves, and has established a family of products which it calls Cisco Interactive Mentor. This includes a self-paced interactive CD-ROM training course which uses simulated networking labs so clients can practice and apply the lessons. In addition, clients gain access to Cisco's Knowledge Community Website, where further support is available, and users can share insights and resources.

Joint Project Management

Extranet-style systems enable easy coordination and information sharing on projects that involve a number of different organizations. One example is mergers and acquisitions, and other corporate finance projects, which involve parties such as investment banks, law firms, and accountants, as well as the client. Construction projects that involve architects, engineers, and consultants also raise the same issues of collaboration.

An extranet can provide a forum for these parties to interact, exchange critical information about the project, discuss and resolve issues, and collaborate to find solutions to problems. In addition, the extranet provides substantial additional value to clients not only by keeping them informed of progress on the transaction, but also enabling them to learn useful lessons from the successes and challenges of the project. The structure of joint project management using extranet technology is illustrated in Figure 6–1.

STRATEGIC USE OF COMMUNICATION CHANNELS

Given the array of channels available for knowledge transfer, professional service firms must establish strategies for the effective use of these channels. The nature of these strategies will vary substantially across different industries. However, organizations need to go through a conscious process of considering their objectives in knowledge trans-

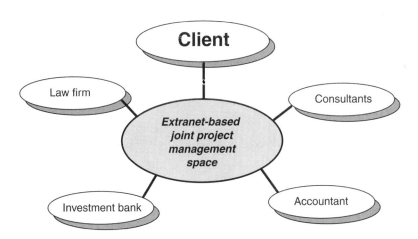

FIGURE 6–1   Using extranet technology for joint project management.

fer and relationship development, and establishing the appropriate use of a portfolio of communication channels to achieve these.

Offering Clients Choices of Channels

In some professional service industries, particularly those based on high-value information and its use in strategic decision making, it can be appropriate to offer clients a choice of channels, which can then be priced according to their value to the client and the time required by professional staff. Several of the leading information technology market research companies offer clients service delivery through a wide variety of channels in order to maximize effective knowledge transfer. For example, META Group, a market research and consulting firm based in Stamford, Connecticut, offers its retainer clients a wide range of services. This starts with written research, which can be delivered on paper, by fax, or through Internet, Lotus Notes, or CD-ROM. The next level brings in participation in teleconferences run by industry analysts on topical issues. META Group recognizes the importance of the reusability of knowledge by giving its clients for this service transcripts and audiotapes of the teleconferences.

Group meetings include META Group conferences, which cover either broad directions or specific topics in the information technology industry; and briefings, including morning seminars and roundtable discussions that allow clients to get together and share experiences. Individualized services that are part of the package of retainer service include a review of the client's strategic plan, and a customized half-day briefing, which can be used however the client wishes. To cap it off, the client receives unlimited telephone consultation with META Group analysts. This allows for knowledge transfer "on demand," and with the high interactivity of telephone conversations, specific issues can be quickly and accurately addressed.

SUMMARY: MANAGING COMMUNICATION CHANNELS

Knowledge sharing and transfer depends on communication, so we must actively manage the range of channels we use to communicate with our clients. There are four key enablers of knowledge transfer: interactivity, bandwidth, structure, and reusability. Each of the range of channels available has different characteristics in terms of facilitating knowledge transfer, which affects how these should be used and combined to build an effective portfolio of communication channels.

Digital channels are becoming increasingly important in client communication, and offer many advantages. Extranets are a primary way of implementing effective digital communication with clients, and many organizations are establishing extranets to help add value to their clients. They can be used a wide variety of ways, including many clearly aimed at knowledge transfer rather than information delivery, such as online consulting, computer-based training, service and support, and joint project management.

Having developed an understanding of the practical issues in developing a portfolio of communication channels with the client, we need to examine how best to structure contact with our clients. Chapter 7 deals with how to manage knowledge-based client relationships to result in maximum value creation and intimacy.

NOTES

1. Richard L. Daft and Robert H. Lengel, "Information Richness: A New Approach to Manager Information Processing and Organization Design," in *Research in Organizational Behaviour*, vol. 6, B. M. Staw and L. L. Cummings, eds. (Greenwich, CT: JAI Press, 1984); and "Organizational Information Requirements, Media Richness, and Structural Design," *Management Science* 32, no. 5 (May 1986): 554–571.
2. Daft and Lengel (1984): 194.
3. See for example the *Journal of Computer-Mediated Communication*, at www.ascusc.org/jcmc.
4. Wathne et al. have empirically linked rich channels of interaction, trust, and openness in achieving knowledge transfer. See Kenneth Wathne, Johan Roos, and Georg von Krogh, "Towards a Theory of Knowledge Transfer in a Cooperative Context," in *Managing Knowledge: Perspectives on Cooperation and Competition*, Georg von Krogh and Johan Roos, eds. (London: Sage Publications, 1996): 55–81.
5. Ross Dawson, "Managing Professional Knowledge," *Company Director* (March 1998): 22–23.
6. Ross Dawson, "Now, a Net for Clients Who Need That Extra Bit," *Australian Financial Review*, Special Report: Intranets and Networking (November 24, 1998): 6.
7. Part of the information on State Street Global Link can be found in Andrew Capon, "Setting Sail into the Digital Age," *Global Investor* (April 1999).

Chapter 7

Firm-Wide Relationship Management
Structuring Client Contact

Knowledge transfer to clients and developing client relationships are deeply entwined, and the success of each depends largely on how client contact is structured and managed. Effective relationship management has always been a central issue for professional service firms, as it is so obviously critical to their success. Some of the approaches currently in use, however, do not adequately address the changing dynamics of the information and knowledge economy.

We discussed the deeply interrelated nature of developing client relationships and knowledge transfer in Chapter 1; we now want to examine the issues in structuring and managing client relationships so as to maximize both knowledge transfer and the depth, breadth, and profitability of those relationships. This will build on what we have learned about adding value to clients with knowledge, and on communication channels with clients.

MAXIMIZING KNOWLEDGE TRANSFER AND RELATIONSHIP DEVELOPMENT

Our primary objective is to develop sustained and highly profitable relationships with organizational clients. Meeting this goal clearly depends on our ability to add significant value. We have already seen that knowledge transfer is pivotal in adding value to clients, and that knowledge transfer and relationship development are closely linked in a virtuous circle. These building blocks offer us some key reference points to help develop strategies for relationship management.

Some of the specific outcomes we should keep in mind in designing the structure of client contact include:

- Maximum value added to clients as perceived by key client executives
- Greatest knowledge transfer, resulting in better decisions and enhanced capabilities
- Close contact with and high "share of mind" of key decision makers
- Ongoing generation of mutually profitable business
- Learning from the client and getting high-value feedback

Clearly, other issues are involved; however, focusing on the issues of two-way knowledge transfer and relationship development, and how these together flow into ongoing profitable business, will result in a sound foundation on which to base relationship management strategies.

Industry and Client Differences in Structuring Contact

It is difficult to generalize about how to structure client contact, since what is most effective will depend on the style and capabilities of the professional service firm, the client industry, and the client's culture and organizational structure. Variables between industries and engagements with the greatest impact on the most effective structure of client contact include:

- The balance between black-box services and knowledge transfer
- The intended outcome of knowledge transfer: decision-making or capabilities enhancement
- The organizational function and level in the client where knowledge transfer takes place
- The time frame of the engagement, and of any client decisions to be made

Professionals will recognize what is most common in their industry and firm for each of these issues, and the implications in terms of modifying the design of relationships. Beyond the more general issues that determine how different firms will tend to manage their relationships, it is important to recognize when different types of engagements or clients demand variations in the usual approaches, and to maintain the flexibility to modify these easily.

Client Culture

The culture of the client organization can have a dramatic effect on the most effective approaches to relationship management and knowledge transfer, and indeed to what degree knowledge transfer will be valued. One of the most important dimensions is how autocratic or participatory the client culture is. This will have a major impact on the design of relationship management and interaction, most obviously in the degree to which contact and knowledge transfer is concentrated on top management—or sometimes even an individual—as opposed to being distributed throughout the organization. A related dimension is the degree of centralization or decentralization of the client organization, especially in decision making.

Another significant factor affecting the design of knowledge transfer is the degree to which the client culture is "expert"-based. This is usually evident in the status accorded to experts or knowledge specialists. Most professional service firms clearly fall into this category; however, client organizations may or may not mirror this. One implication of dealing with an expert-based client culture is the importance which must be placed on interacting with and getting buy-in from the experts, who are the arbiters of the value of knowledge within their organizations, and can hold sway far beyond that suggested by their titles or positions.

Taking into account national cultures is also critical in knowledge sharing and transfer; as suggested in our discussion of technocultures in Chapter 5, the relative cultures of the exporting and importing organizations or countries must be considered. A US professional service firm attempting to apply its usual approaches, for example, in Japan, Brazil, or France would likely have limited success. Knowledge is not only personal, it is also has a strong cultural basis, especially in its creation and sharing. These cultural divides to knowledge transfer can be bridged, but they require close attention and respect for cultural differences.[1]

INSTITUTIONALIZING KNOWLEDGE TRANSFER

Since knowledge is an attribute of individuals, it is a real challenge to "institutionalize" knowledge transfer, in the sense of embedding it in the client organization beyond a few key staff members. Many consultants wax lyrical about knowledge transfer in their brochures and proposals. Where most fail to deliver, however, is in truly institutionalizing the knowledge transfer, rather than providing a few documents, presentations, and workshops which make select individuals in the client organization feel they are more knowledgeable. Gary Hamel notes the crucial distinction between firms gaining access to skills from others, and actually *internalizing* those skills.[2]

To achieve this degree of knowledge transfer demands a deep understanding of organizational dynamics and knowledge flow. Knowing the client organization extremely well is just as important. People within an organization usually do not need formal training to understand what is happening internally and how to influence effectively; a similar depth of understanding is needed on the part of outside professionals in order to achieve knowledge transfer that is effective at an organizational level. Again, the strength of the relationship and the degree of knowledge of the client organization are critical in achieving this objective.

Since institutionalizing knowledge transfer depends on internal knowledge flows within the client organization, sensitivity to political factors is crucial. In closer client relationships, the service provider often starts to become part of the internal political landscape, which can be both a benefit and a hindrance. In fact, one of the very valuable roles external professionals can play is in acting as a bridge or even mediator between different client divisions and groups. There is often limited or ineffective communication within client organizations, so that the position of a professional service firm can allow them to assist and develop internal knowledge flows, which adds substantial value in itself, and is intrinsic to ensuring the institutionalization of the knowledge it offers.

Establishing Knowledge Transfer Outcomes

A key element in achieving effective knowledge transfer is establishing and agreeing on specific knowledge transfer outcomes with the client. This step is very important for four reasons. First, it establishes whether the client truly values knowledge transfer. If it doesn't, then that clarifies and simplifies the client engagement. Second, it provides a specific link, both in the formal agreement and in the client's mind, between knowledge transfer and value. Third, it provides a specific and presumably top-level endorsement of knowledge transfer, which can help overcome organizational politics. And fourth, it provides a way of charging the client on a value basis as opposed to a time basis. This theme will be developed further in Chapter 9, which covers the pricing of knowledge.

Knowledge transfer outcomes can be defined on the individual level in terms of development of personal knowledge or skills, while on the organizational level capabilities can be measured in terms of change in productivity, quality, or similar yardsticks. Most high-value knowledge transfer outcomes are difficult to assess or quantify for the purposes of formal agreements. Even so, to the degree that they can be stated as objectives, it is valuable to do so. In some cases it may be preferable not to link them to specific performance or payment targets, because of the difficulty in accurate measurement and the impact of other variables, although it is usually worth at least stating them in order to establish client recognition of value.

Managing Knowledge Gatekeepers

All organizations contain people who play the role, usually informally, of knowledge gatekeepers. In a positive context, they are often centers of influence in the organization, provide usefully filtered information and knowledge from the business environment to the organization, and greatly facilitate the impact of professional service providers. On the downside, they can use their positions of influence to control information and knowledge flow according to their own priorities and agenda.[3]

In most professional services engagements there are one or two designated contacts at the client organization, and their propensities as knowledge gatekeepers will play a key role in the success of any knowledge transfer in the project. It is rarely appropriate to "go around" the primary client contacts, even if it would result in better outcomes for the client organization.

In many cases the heart of the issue is in positioning your primary contacts as the heroes of the engagement, rather than claiming all the glory of success for yourself. If in their roles as knowledge gatekeepers they are able to provide real value to others in the organization, they will facilitate the knowledge transfer process. If, however, they want to maintain strict control over contact within their organization, the restriction on interactivity, bandwidth, participation, and flexibility will strongly impact the knowledge transfer outcomes.

Project Ownership

One of the greatest barriers to knowledge uptake is what has been called the Not-Invented-Here Syndrome.[4] Many organizational cultures, particularly in industries driven by innovation, believe that they come up with the best ideas, and if it is from outside, it is suspect and probably not as good. Addressing this is an important management issue, as in an increasingly interconnected economy no single company can compete on its own ideas alone.

From the perspective of a professional service firm, a culture in the client organization that is suspicious of outside knowledge can easily doom a project, whether or not it depends on knowledge transfer. In any engagement with limited scope it is probably unrealistic to attempt to change the corporate culture, which means that success will depend on the people who are centers of influence in the client feeling that they have ownership of the project. Getting client "buy-in" must be a key objective in all professional service engagements, however, it is particularly critical where knowledge transfer is essential to the project.

The essence of getting clients to feel and act as if they have ownership of the project is clearly in participation. All stages of the project, from setting objectives and designing the process, should include the broadest possible involvement from the client consistent with its culture. Selecting the key players who act as centers of influence in the organization to participate is critical. This strategy starts to cast the role of the professional service firm increasingly as one of knowledge elicitation rather than knowledge communication. If indeed the client perceives that its knowledge and capabilities are being enhanced rather than external knowledge delivered or imposed, the likelihood of success of the project will be greatly improved. Once this perception has been established, it provides a far greater opportunity for service providers to apply their own methodologies and content knowledge. Of course, in some client cultures the issue of ownership will not be major, and it may instead be specifically looking for an outside expert to provide knowledge leadership.

Project Handover—Leaving a Legacy

One of the most critical junctures in all professional services engagements, and especially ones in which knowledge transfer is an issue, is that of project handover. How professional services firms approach this reflects whether they truly wish to transfer knowledge, or just talk about it. Effective project handover will result in the client experiencing a large degree of completeness (and presumably satisfaction) with the project, while ineffective handover will mean the client may need to come back for more work on the same issues. This is often what is intended; while this may generate more business in the short run the client will be highly inclined to change to a new supplier when the next significant project comes up. It is increasingly common for sophisticated clients to expect and demand effective project handover specifically in order to achieve greater self-sufficiency as an outcome of engagements.

There are two essential outcomes to address in ensuring successful project handover: the knowledge of staff members, and access to codified knowledge or information. Both are essential for the client's knowledge to be usable on an ongoing basis, and neither is sufficient by itself.

In addressing the people side of project handovers, the issues that must be addressed include:

- What knowledge and skills are required by which client staff members
- Where in the organization these staff are likely to be posted
- Whether they will have the time to address ongoing project issues
- What will happen if key staff members leave the company or are transferred to new roles

A strategy must also be in place to ensure the necessary information is available to the client. This will often include documentation on methodologies, as covered in Chapter 5. Even if individuals at the client organization have learned experientially, they will still want to refer to documentation, and this can be used to develop skills in other staff members.

Information can and certainly should be provided in documents and additions to the client's knowledge base; however, far greater value can be provided by providing access to dynamic information, such as a continually-updated website. One advantage of this approach is that it helps to strengthen the relationship and the "share of mind" of the client; that is, the share of awareness and thought about the service provider by key client executives. Building in an ongoing knowledge transfer component to all significant engagements can play a major role in developing relationships.

Often a key element in successful handovers is specifically training the client to run its own internal programs to develop the skills and knowledge of a broad range of its staff after the service provider has left. This can include providing training manuals and "train the trainer" courses for specified client staff. Providing knowledge in a generative form, which means the client can develop skills further on its own, allows the use of licensing fees, which can be a healthy complement to the usual fee structures. This subject will be covered in more detail in Chapter 9.

Particularly where knowledge transfer is a key objective, project handover should be formalized, rather than just letting the engagement end. In addition to the issues of staff skills and codified knowledge, other issues that should be addressed include circumstances in which the supplier may need to be called back in to work on or further develop the same project or issue. Establishing that contingency clearly in advance means that if further work is necessary the service provider will not be seen to be "freeloading."

HP Consulting often runs what it calls a "project snapshot" with clients. This began as a way of identifying lessons for itself from projects it had run, though it is now extended to be run as a similar process with clients. It can be done at any time in the project, though it usually occurs at the conclusion. HP Consulting allocates to every project what it calls "knowledge consultants," who are responsible for designing the process for the engagement by drawing on the firm's previous experience, and derive lessons from the current project. Part of their responsibility is to facilitate the project snapshot workshop, which is commonly run over a few hours. The team seeks to identify what has worked in the project, what hasn't worked, what useful knowledge has been created, and what lessons are applicable in other parts of the client organization. It also identifies what documents or other materials are needed for the client to reuse the lessons from the project in other ways and places. HP Consulting also uses a process it calls "knowledge mapping," which involves drawing a map of knowledge at the firm and at its client. The map traces what knowledge needs to flow to which people at the client group and in what form; this is used as a basis for planning effective knowledge transfer to the client.

KNOWLEDGE RELATIONSHIP ROLES

Several distinct roles are played in professional service firms in achieving knowledge outcomes for clients. Managing and coordinating these roles and the way they work together is at the heart of developing an effective structure for client contact and relationship management. This requires understanding the roles, the skills they require, and the ways in which they interact and complement each other in building client relationships.

In the traditional style of professional services, partners were selected from those that demonstrated the ability to cover the full spectrum of professional activities, including business generation, client relationship management, specialist knowledge, and staff management. Now there is far more flexibility in the roles that need to be fulfilled, and the overall relationship is commonly run by teams rather than a single individual.

The primary knowledge relationship roles are senior representative, relationship coordinator, knowledge specialist, and knowledge customizer. Clearly any one individual can play all or any combination of these roles; however, it is unusual to find the necessary skills for all of these roles in one person, and it is increasingly common for the roles to be separated. As we will see, the essence of what distinguishes different models for relationship management in knowledge-based relationships is the configurations in which these roles are combined and applied.

Senior Representative

In most relationships, the professional service firm has a senior representative who acts as the face of the firm in top-level client contacts, and sometimes though not always assumes overall responsibility and supervision of the account. The function of the role is essentially to establish credibility with the client, often in the selling phase, and also at critical junctures in the project and relationship, particularly when access to the top client level is required. This role does not play an important part in knowledge transfer per se, however is often central in the initial framing of the relationship between the companies, and its ongoing development.

Relationship Coordinator

The person who assumes the role of relationship coordinator is often called a relationship manager, account manager, or project manager. However, we have avoided these terms to more clearly distinguish the role of coordinator from the other knowledge relationship roles. A relationship coordinator is responsible for orchestrating the resources of the service provider to achieve the desired outcomes for the client.

This is often fundamentally a project management task, which includes defining the project objectives with the client, and establishing and guiding a process that achieves those. This is particularly the case where there is a specific engagement, when the relationship coordinator is most commonly called a project manager.

More generally, particularly in ongoing relationships, the function involves furnishing access to the relevant resources of the service provider. Effectiveness as a relationship coordinator depends on rich knowledge of both the client and the service firm. The coordinator must not only know what resources are available within the service provider and have the influence to access those, but also understand the client's organizational culture, processes, and people. Without this knowledge, the complex relationship processes necessary for knowledge transfer are unlikely to succeed.

Knowledge Specialist

Knowledge specialists are the source of the knowledge and expertise on which the provision of services is based, so they are the heart of professional service firms. In many ways they are the key resource of the organization, and are usually treated as such. Depth and richness of knowledge is critical in order to add significant value to the client; however knowledge specialists are not always skilled at communication. A significant implication of the growing importance of knowledge transfer is that knowledge specialists can often no longer work only in their field of specialization with peers, but increasingly must communicate with a broader audience.

Knowledge specialists often work with their peers internally in order to perform black-box services for clients. In addition, they increasingly communicate with their peers at client organizations in knowledge sharing and transfer. Clearly, some knowledge specialists have the skills necessary to communicate their knowledge effectively to nonspecialist clients, and in any case professional service firms should specifically focus on developing the knowledge communication skills of their knowledge specialists. However, where knowledge transfer is required in a broader context, specialists may need to work with others to help communicate their knowledge effectively.

Knowledge Customizer

The fourth major role in knowledge relationships is that of knowledge customizer. This role comprises two related functions: customizing information and knowledge for the specific requirements of the client, and communicating that knowledge effectively. As we noted in Chapter 3, the customization of information is one of the most highly valued activities. It includes filtering, synthesizing, and presenting information so that it is directly relevant to the client. Professional service firms generate an enormous amount of high-value information and knowledge; however, the final step of customizing that base of knowledge to meet the client's specific situation arguably adds the greatest value.

Effectively performing the role of knowledge customization requires in-depth knowledge of the client, including what information and knowledge adds the greatest value, the client's decision-making processes and capabilities, and the cognitive preferences of key individuals in the client group. The role is often nominally a "sales" function, which is largely consumed by customizing and packaging specialist knowledge to make it most useful to clients.

With its large global auditing and consulting clients, Ernst & Young suggests to the client having a role of "knowledge steward" on the consulting team. This person is based at the client, and his or her sole function is to understand the state of the client's industry and its competitors, tap Ernst & Young's resources in the field, compile this input in a usable format, and provide it to the appropriate people in the client group. The role is commonly taken by a senior team member, and is rotated every few months, though usually supported by dedicated resources at Ernst & Young. This is largely a role of knowledge customization, combining adding value to information mainly by customizing it to a single client, and tailoring communication to give the greatest value for the specific audience.

Swiss financial institution UBS is one of the five largest banks in the world by market capitalization. Its private banking division is the largest operation of its kind worldwide, holding over $400 billion of the assets of high-net-worth individuals. Another of its divisions is Warburg Dillon Read (WDR), one of the largest investment banks worldwide. WDR generates an enormous base of knowledge and recommendations on investments in international financial markets for its corporate and institutional client base. These are customized for each institutional client by the WDR sales team, which knows their clients' interests and investment parameters. The WDR research is designed for institutions, however, and is often not appropriate or directly useful for its private banking clients. The UBS private banking group has instituted an Active Advisory Team (AAT), which adapts the WDR research to make it relevant for its own client base of high-net-worth individuals. In turn each private banking relationship manager again tailors the research further to provide directly applicable knowledge and advice for their individual clients. The AAT function is a pure example of the role of knowledge customizer, taking existing knowledge and customizing it for a specific market segment.

Senior and Junior Roles

There is an important distinction in knowledge relationship management between senior and junior staff. The most commonly heard criticism of professional service firms is that the senior "rainmakers" who secure and close the business are never seen again, and junior staff are allocated to execute the project. In a knowledge transfer context, clients note that the juniors—frequently fresh out of business school or other postgraduate studies—may have a lot of process knowledge, but scarce little industry-specific or other content knowledge that they can transfer.

This does not mean that junior staff should not be involved in these projects. Indeed, as David Maister points out, profitability and staff development in professional service firms depends to a significant degree on not having senior staff perform work that junior staff can do.[5] It does mean that the roles of junior and senior staff in knowledge transfer projects must be well thought-out. In most cases senior professionals should perform the lead for each knowledge role, with junior members playing a supporting role.

Client Knowledge Roles

Just as different knowledge relationship roles exist within professional service firms, there is a range of distinct roles in client organizations which relate to assimilating knowledge and value from suppliers. Understanding these roles and how they are structured in your clients is fundamental to designing an optimal approach to relationship management. To a large degree the client roles mirror the roles at the professional service firm.

The senior representative role on the client side is critical. Often clients nominate certain senior executives to be responsible for particular groups of professional service providers; they act as access points to the organization, but are usually not involved in the details of projects. They will play a key role in determining the style of the engagement.

An important group of roles is that of decision makers at the client organization. Adding value at the strategic decision-making level usually provides the greatest value in knowledge transfer, so that having the richest possible interaction with this group is very important. The senior representative—while often also a decision maker—can act as a filter to the decision-making group, which can either impede or facilitate effective knowledge transfer at this level. Line decision makers are often accessed in groups, or through information channels including electronic media. Service providers usually have ongoing access to portfolio decision makers, and can focus on them as individuals, as well as considering them as participants in portfolio management committees.

In project-based engagements, there will often be a project manager on the client side, who is the counterpart of the project manager or relationship coordinator at the service provider. In a similar way, client knowledge specialists often play important roles, mirroring those at the professional service firm. In knowledge transfer the knowledge specialists commonly prefer to deal with other specialists, and can have little patience for nonspecialists. Another important role is that of knowledge gatekeeper, as discussed earlier. This role can be played by the same people in any of the roles mentioned above, notably the senior representative and project manager, though there can also be other more junior gatekeeper roles which are relevant in ongoing interactions.

MODELS OF RELATIONSHIP MANAGEMENT

A diverse array of different models exist for relationship management. The best way to understand the differences between these models in the context of knowledge transfer is to examine how the four primary knowledge relationship roles combine and relate in each model. The knowledge roles can be woven together in many different ways, and ideally professional service firms will display flexibility in how they use their resources with different clients in order to add value and develop closer relationships.

Diamond or Mirror Model

The *diamond model* for client relationships, as illustrated in Figure 7–1, was developed and refined by 3M (Minnesota Mining and Manufacturing).[6] The core principle is that people communicate directly with their peers, as opposed to communication being channeled through a rela-

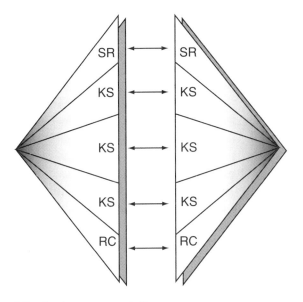

SR - Senior representative
RC - Relationship coordinator
KS - Knowledge specialist

FIGURE 7–1   The diamond or mirror model of relationship management.

tionship manager. Since the roles on the service provider side reflect those on the client side, this style of relationship structure can also be called the mirror model. Empirical research on interorganizational learning by Lane and Lubatkin suggests that the ability of a firm to learn from another firm is determined by the similarity of their knowledge bases, organizational structures, and ways of thinking, which supports the strength of this model of relationship management.[7]

In the diamond model, fairly evidently the senior representative liases with client senior management, knowledge specialists communicate with their peers at the client group, and the relationship coordinator or project manager works with the client project manager as well as organizing the rich array of client contact, as illustrated in Figure 7–1.[8] In this case, knowledge customizers or communicators will come into play when there is contact across groups between the service provider and client; for example, when specialists need to work with or communicate to client staff in other areas. A hallmark of this type of relationship is that there is often so much ongoing contact between different people that it cannot be managed in detail. Relationship coordinators can never know everything that is happening with a large client organization, and can only orchestrate resources on a broad basis, and when requested by specialists. This strategy usually results in far more dynamic relationships.

Guru Model

In the *guru model*, most high-value client contact is concentrated on an individual or small number of individuals, as shown in Figure 7–2.[9] They play the roles of senior representative, knowledge specialist, and large parts of the relationship coordinator and knowledge customizer roles. In reality, as much as possible of the supporting work behind each of these roles is performed by more junior staff. However, client contact is largely channeled through the "guru," who can command premium prices for his or her time, and justify the very high support levels required. The ratio of support staff to partners is often substantially higher in the guru model than in a typical professional service firm. Examples of the guru model include the professional service firms run by well-known consultants, such as Tom Peters' Tom Peters Group, Stephen Covey's Covey Leadership Center, or David Norton's Renaissance Solutions.

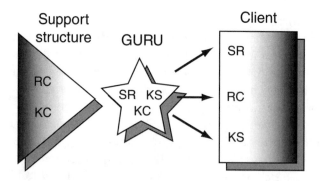

SR - Senior representative
RC - Relationship coordinator
KS - Knowledge specialist
KC - Knowledge customizer

Figure 7–2   The guru model of relationship management.

Giant Step

Chicago-based interactive marketing specialist Giant Step, a subsidiary of advertising agency Leo Burnett, uses a mirror relationship structure for its major projects. Developing Internet-based advertising and marketing programs requires the participation of a diverse array of client functions, ranging from information technology to marketing to media buying, and working with new media often falls outside of the existing experience and skills of the client organization. To address these issues, Giant Step forms joint project teams with the client. The overall project managers on the agency and client side work together in guiding the project, while every specialist group at Giant Step is allocated a counterpart at the client, to establish what is effectively two project teams linked together in a mirror image. Giant Step has established teams that specialize in each of the areas that would be represented on the client side in projects, specifically in order to be able to mirror those roles. It has also found that hiring people who have experience in their clients' functions means they can communicate effectively with their peers, and explain online marketing issues by relating them to the client team's existing expertise. This structure can also be valuable if there is insufficient communication within the client group, say between IT and marketing, as team members can help to bridge those communication gaps, and if necessary provide cross-training so each of the client teams can be familiar with the other teams' issues.

Giant Step sees training as an important part of the process, given that implementing online advertising is likely to be a new venture for many client executives. Projects begin with a one-day workshop, and other training programs are run as necessary. Executives at Giant Step think of the overall process as one of "co-mentoring," in which team members provide highly interactive guidance to the client on developing interactive marketing, and are simultaneously mentored by their client on its industry. Part of the quarterly assessment for project managers relates to how successful they have been at "client mentoring."

Since much new terminology has arisen in online advertising, and particularly website activity reporting, Giant Step has published a glossary of terms to ensure both sides have a common understanding. They encourage their staff and clients to keep this glossary in front of them when they are discussing these issues together. As an interactive marketing specialist, Giant Step naturally also provides extranets so clients can freely monitor work-in-progress, and access site performance analysis.

Portfolio Sales Model

Sales to portfolio managers, as typified by the financial market sales and research groups of investment banks, characterize another relationship model which can be seen in and adapted to other industries: the *portfolio sales model*, illustrated in Figure 7–3. Here the knowledge specialist role is represented by the research function, while different aspects of the sales function can be equated to the roles of relationship coordinator and knowledge customizer.

The relationship coordinator, who is effectively the relationship manager for the overall account, coordinates the array of specialists available within the firm, ranging from bond analysts to equity underwriters. The large investment banks are prototypical virtual organizations, with fluid movement of resources that must be brought together to be applied to specific client issues.[10]

Within each product area, a salesperson will have responsibility for servicing the client. Often the most important function of the salespeople is that of knowledge customization; they take the more general research generated by the analysts, and adapt it so that it adds value to their clients, for example, by being formulated as specific recommendations relevant to their current portfolios. In addition, they will monitor available sources of information in order to filter and customize it to provide value to their client base.

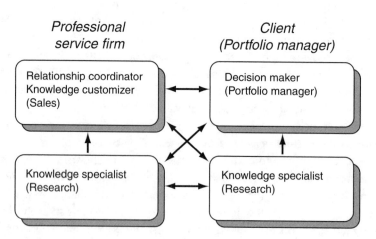

FIGURE 7–3   The portfolio sales model of relationship management.

Designing Relationship Management Models

Ultimately any model is a caricature that cannot express the detailed shape of client interaction, and the range and variety of client organizations. Service providers must design approaches to their client relationships that stem from their understanding of how they add value to clients, and are flexible enough to be readily adapted for different clients.

Particularly when knowledge transfer is an explicit or implicit objective, considering knowledge roles of the service provider and the client can be very helpful in the design process. This provides a ready tool to map the allocation of responsibilities and who should be interacting with whom at the client group in order to maximize knowledge transfer, added value, and deeper relationships.

INDIVIDUAL INTERACTION

In addition to designing the overall structure of client contact, issues relating to interaction between individuals must be considered and addressed. These include considerations in matching individual professionals with client staff, and organizing how they work together.

Personal Chemistry

As valuable knowledge transfer is usually part of a rich, dynamic interaction between people, how well individuals interact and understand each other plays an important role in the success of that knowledge transfer. People who get along well together will tend to have richer knowledge transfer than if they do not. The personal chemistry between people can make a significant difference to the business results achieved; this certainly applies in a sales context, but also in knowledge transfer. Many professional service firms allocate clients to relationship managers specifically on the basis of how good their chemistry is with the key contact at the client. In Chapter 8 we will look at how contrasting rather than matching personality styles can be valuable in knowledge creation; however, in designing relationship management the ability to communicate easily is the more important factor.

Client Postings and Staff Exchanges

Since interaction and dialogue are the heart of knowledge transfer, what better way to develop rich knowledge transfer than either posting staff at the client's offices, or having client staff work in your offices? It is fairly common practice among law firms to post staff at their major clients, sometimes only charging the client the salary of the lawyer rather than the usual hourly rate. This is an excellent example of the conjunction of rich two-way knowledge transfer and relationship development. The client learns both content and process knowledge through ongoing interaction over a period of months, while it builds a deep personal and business relationship, and becomes far more inclined to choose that law firm over others it knows less well.

While in any large project it is common for professional service firms to post staff at clients, at computer services giant EDS, effectively all professionals assigned to client projects are based at the client site. Some clients specifically ask their service providers for exchanges to promote knowledge transfer. Nicholas Applegate, an investment manager based in San Diego, California, which manages over $30 billion worldwide, has a formal analyst exchange program that brings analysts from the major stockbrokers that service it into its offices for a month at a time.[11]

CLIENT FEEDBACK

Rich client feedback is extremely valuable for professional service firms, as it enables them to improve their processes, both in adapting what they do to more closely suit the specific dynamics of each client, and in learning lessons which can be generalized to build overall better service. While this is of course fundamental to any business, it can be viewed specifically from the perspective of knowledge transfer. One of the great benefits of deliberately focusing on knowledge transfer with clients is that building a rich flow of knowledge to clients automatically starts to build knowledge flow in the other direction. This gives a strong advantage to the firms that have built this two-way knowledge flow, are able to understand their clients better, and get valuable feedback on which to base ongoing improvement of their services.

Building in Feedback

Professional firms should of course do all the usual things to gather feedback, including running client debriefings at the end of engagements, using well thought-out feedback forms, and so on. The key issue is designing ongoing rich feedback into the very structure of the relationship, which can be developed in a number of ways.

One useful initiative is staff training and development—developing skills in transferring knowledge to clients should always include approaches to make that knowledge flow two-way. Much of this process occurs simply through effective questioning and listening, which are core professional skills. However, while these are usually applied at the beginning of the process to define the engagement, they are less commonly used throughout the process and at the conclusion.

Another key issue is capturing the knowledge gained from the client. Good internal knowledge management practices, including providing the ability and motivation to capture and store valuable information, are necessary for this process to occur; however, there is rarely a specific focus on capturing knowledge from the client. This issue should be an essential element of a customer relationship management system, as covered later in this chapter. Better firms have some kind of "lessons learned" system for each engagement, but it is often not structured to identify feedback for specific purposes.

TECHNOLOGY IN RELATIONSHIP MANAGEMENT

The rapid increase in dependence on technology in all client communication is resulting in a dramatic change in the dynamics of relationships, as we began to explore in Chapter 6. There are certainly clear advantages to digital communication with clients, and undoubtedly an increasing proportion of contact (up to a point) will be digitally-based. On the other hand, digital communication is resulting in major changes in the nature of client relationships, and important issues and risks must be addressed by professional service firms in shifting their client communication to a largely technology-based platform.

Disintermediating Personal Client Contact

The most fundamental issue in relationship management with the advent of digital communication is that of making technology complement rather than replace direct client contact. There are significant advantages to digital forms of communication and interaction, which enable clients to access information directly and often use interactive applications.

In the broader context of business, a key advantage of technology is that it allows expensive people to be replaced by technology. An example is hardware and software support, as in the example of Cisco Systems given in Chapter 6. In the case of professional service firms, there can be substantial danger in providing lower-level services digitally, in that the personal contact on which relationships are predicated is disintermediated by technology, and starts to atrophy.

The critical issue here is that once client contact takes place mainly through technology, the interaction has implicitly become replicable and commoditizable. In order to maintain differentiation, and the premium pricing which goes with that, rich personal client contact—in other words people interacting with people—is essential. In addition, the disintermediation of personal contact means that the virtuous circle of continually understanding the client better and thus being better able to add value is broken, as shown in Figure 7–4.

One of the dilemmas of professional service firms is maintaining a balance between on one hand providing digital services which add value, are easier to use for the client, and cheaper to provide; and on the other hand running the risks of disintermediating personal contact. This is a vital aspect of the role of knowledge customization in relationships—it is specifically about adapting and interpreting generic information for clients in ways which technology is not capable of doing, maximizing the value of the information and systems provided, and communicating knowledge in a highly interactive fashion. There is a substantially higher cost to clients if they work with professionals rather than systems, although if it is a high-value situation then the extra value of personal customization and communication will certainly provide more-than-adequate compensation. Of course, this is also a sales issue—salespeople cannot sell if clients don't talk to them. But it is only by

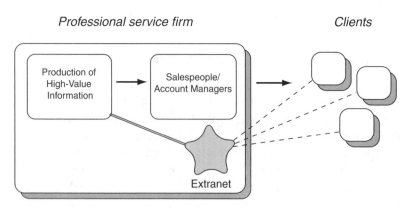

FIGURE 7–4   Technology can disintermediate personal contact with clients.

adding sufficient value—almost always through knowledge—that clients are motivated to speak to sales staff.

Ernst & Young has positioned its online consulting service Ernie, introduced in Chapter 6, as primarily targeted at mid-sized companies to which it cannot effectively provide a broad spectrum of fully personalized services at the right price. While there were initially uncertainties internally about whether to implement a service that was a potential competitor to more profitable services, Ernie has proved to be a successful complement to existing offerings. It leverages existing knowledge, maintains share-of-mind with clients, and at the same time as streamlining how it assists clients with a broad range of issues, establishes a solid base to win the larger projects that arise in this market. While clients can use Ernie to identify and begin to work on the issues they confront, they are very likely to go to Ernst & Young for the actual implementation of projects, which results in an efficient allocation of resources for both sides.

Access and Permissioning

Access to client-oriented online systems such as extranets is usually protected by passwords or other security. This built-in protection enables each user when logging-on to be given access to the level of information or services that it has paid for, or is justified by the profitability of its business. What you provide to your top few clients is likely to be different than what you provide your smaller clients.

This requires information on the site to be categorized either in terms of levels of value, service area, or field of interest. That in itself can create value by filtering out information that is not relevant to the client.

Controlling Information Flow

One of the issues with digital information is that once it leaves your organization, you effectively lose control over it. Clients can copy it, communicate it internally and externally, and modify it. There are some safeguards available, such as digital watermarks or client agreements, though these usually fail to address the issues.

Beyond intellectual property and revenue issues, there are also important implications for relationship management. When information is a large proportion of the value provided, and its flow cannot be controlled, to a large degree you lose control of the relationship, and the opportunity for leverage. An instance is when you have a relationship

Manpower

Manpower, Inc. is the largest staffing service in the world, providing temporary employees through 2,800 offices in almost 50 countries. While the core service provided by Manpower to its clients is providing temporary staff, it has recognized that it can increase the value added to clients and enhance its relationships by providing its clients with more knowledge about those relationships.[12]

The growth in use of browsers and intranets at its clients has enabled Manpower to develop extranet-based systems to provide this knowledge. It has developed a system it calls Virtual Account Management (VAM), which presents real-life stories about how Manpower has successfully worked with the client, as well as information on internal procedures for dealing with Manpower. In identifying and writing these stories for the client, Manpower wanted to make them relevant, useful, and interesting, without appearing to be obvious advertising. The VAM systems are designed specifically for each client, drawing on stories from that account. In addition, the "look and feel" of the site is tailored to fit into the client's intranet, and suit its corporate culture.

These customized extranets require substantial resources from Manpower, so they are provided only to large national or global accounts, although the relationship benefits are sufficient to allow them to be currently free of charge to clients. Manpower is considering also providing similar generic sites, or ones customized for specific client industries.

Manpower is a very decentralized organization, with no attempt to centrally control contact with the client. One intention of the extranet sites

with one division or group within a large organization, but not with others, or the nature of your relationship is different. Once you provide information to one group, it is very hard to control its flow to other departments or locations at the client.

Thundercloud Networks, based in Cambridge, Massachusetts, has specifically sought to address this issue. It provides a proprietary high-speed reliable network that links clients and service providers. The service provider maintains full control over information flow, being able to specify which individuals at which organizations have access to what information. This means the representatives in the knowledge customization role can both add substantial value by customizing information in a readily usable format, and ensuring that clients only receive is to make them as easy as possible for clients to identify and contact the appropriate manager or specialist at Manpower, so internal directories are provided on site. As the site is done in collaboration with the client, internal approval processes for hiring staff through Manpower are also posted.

One key aspect of the service is that it is based on stories, which is one of the most powerful ways of communicating knowledge. The stories represent real case studies from within the client organization, so are perceived as directly relevant to users of the system. Account directors gather these stories by tapping the experiences of all of its representatives. Manpower's intention behind VAM was not only to add greater value to its clients, but also to build partnership relationships and weave itself deeper into its clients' operations, which is reflected in the way the stories are gathered.

Other knowledge initiatives at Manpower include a "Global Learning Center," which is a virtual university providing over 600 interactive courses on the Internet to develop the skills of its temporary staff and the employees of its clients. This draws on its experience of over 20 years in delivering training to employees via classroom, CD-ROM, and other means. Providing this training in an easy-to-access format means it not only adds greater value to its corporate clients by providing more skilled staff, but also directly develops the skills and knowledge of its other customer base, which is its temporary staff. These courses are available free of charge to anyone who submits a resume and an application form.

information that is in line with the revenue they generate, as a tool for negotiating a higher level of business.

In another example, Fidelity Investments has given Merrill Lynch permission to install its own server at Fidelity's site. This allows Merrill Lynch to control the dissemination of its research and other high-value information within Fidelity, and implement customized relationship management and value-adding strategies for the different divisions within its client.

Mass-Customizing Information

One major advantage of digital communication with clients is the ability to mass-customize interaction at low cost. This is the basis of the rise of "one-to-one marketing," and other customer-focused approaches. Tapping technology to automate and customize client interaction is important in both adding value and containing costs. By its very nature, however, this type of interaction is quickly commoditized, and is unlikely to provide sustainable differentiation in its own right.

The role of mass-customized information and knowledge transfer is primarily focused in servicing lower-value clients, and as one element of overall interaction with highly profitable clients. The differentiation that allows ongoing premium pricing from major clients depends on the direct contact and interactivity associated with rich knowledge transfer.

Client Relationship Management Systems

The value of digital technology in helping to manage information about clients and client relationships was recognized early on, and the market for these systems is growing rapidly. Essentially these allow all people within a service provider who have client contact to input information on their client interactions into a database which can be accessed by everyone who works on that account.

These databases are primarily internal information management systems for service providers, and do not directly involve client knowledge transfer, so we will not choose to examine them in detail. What is most relevant about these systems in terms of adding value with knowledge is capturing information about the client that will facilitate greater knowledge transfer. Client relationship management systems should include information about client decision-making processes, cognitive styles, culture, and other factors that will assist effectively adding value with knowledge. Even at many prestigious professional service firms, it is surprising how often the relationship manager does not know their clients' investment approval processes or other basic and extremely valuable information. Staff should be explicitly guided in developing on an ongoing basis richer information on their clients' individual and organizational propensities in assimilating knowledge, which will assist more effective knowledge transfer. In most cases this same information can be used not only in ongoing relationship development, but also in specific sales processes, such as tendering for major projects.

SUMMARY: FIRM-WIDE RELATIONSHIP MANAGEMENT

Relationship management is at the heart of professional services; however, as these industries shift to be increasingly based on effective knowledge transfer, new dynamics and issues are coming to bear. Real value to clients comes with the institutionalization of knowledge transfer; some of the key skills required to achieve this include managing the knowledge gatekeepers and implementing practical approaches to project handover.

Effective structuring of relationship management is based on defining the key knowledge roles at the professional service firm and client organization, and structuring the relations between these in ways that allow interaction, knowledge transfer, and intimacy to flourish. Useful approaches include the diamond or mirror model, the guru model, and the portfolio sales model; however, these are just examples, and each organization must develop its own structures to suit its range of business situations. While technology plays a critical role in client communication, this raises important issues for relationship management, including the risk of disintermediating the sales force's personal contact with the client, and the necessity for controlling the flow of information.

If we follow the concepts of adding value with knowledge and developing closer relationships to their logical conclusion, we arrive at the idea of co-creating knowledge with clients. In Chapter 8, we explore the issues and dynamics of what is effectively a true partnership relationship with the client.

NOTES

1. O'Hara-Devereaux and Johansen offer valuable frameworks and suggestions for bridging cultural gaps. See Mary O'Hara-Devereaux and Robert Johansen, *GlobalWork: Bridging Distance, Culture, and Time* (San Francisco: Jossey-Bass, 1994).

2. Gary Hamel, "Competition for Competence and Interpartner Learning within International Strategic Alliances," *Strategic Management Journal* 12 (1991): 83–103.

3. Cohen and Levinthal discuss the role of gatekeepers in assimilating external knowledge. See Wesley M. Cohen and Daniel A. Levinthal, "Absorptive Capacity: A New Perspective on Learning and Innovation," *Administrative Science Quarterly* 35 (1990): 128–152.

4. See for example Cohen and Levinthal, 133, or Leonard, 159.

5. Maister, Chapter 4.

6. From Stewart (1997).

7. Peter J. Lane and Michael Lubatkin, "Relative Absorptive Capacity and Interorganizational Learning," *Strategic Management Journal* 19 (1998): 461–477.

8. Savage proposes peer-to-peer knowledge networking as one of the principles of the knowledge era. See Charles M. Savage, *5th Generation Management: Co-creating through Virtual Enterprising, Dynamic Teaming, and Knowledge Networking* (Boston: Butterworth–Heinemann, 1996): 199–204.

9. The guru model was suggested by Göran Roos of Intellectual Capital Services, London, UK.

10. Eccles and Crane offer an excellent description and study of investment banks as fluid and evolving organizations. See Eccles and Crane, op. cit.

11. "Nicholas Applegate: Where It's Research with a Sense of Urgency," *Investor Weekly* (December 14, 1998): 7.

12. Part of the information on Manpower can be found in Susan Elliott, "Manpower Creates Customer Loyalty through Shared 'Stories,' Information," *Knowledge Management in Practice* no. 3 (Houston, TX: American Productivity & Quality Center, 3rd Quarter, 1998).

Chapter 8

Co-Creation of Knowledge
Creating Value and Building Relationships

As I have emphasized throughout this book, relationship development and adding value to clients with knowledge are inextricably entwined. In order to transfer knowledge effectively, a deep and highly interactive relationship is required. As the channels for knowledge transfer deepen and widen, they add greater value to the client, providing increased momentum and breadth to the development of the relationship. Seen from another perspective, the direct and meaningful contact on which relationships depend is also the foundation for effective knowledge transfer.

If we continue to further develop the twin themes of knowledge sharing and relationship development, we logically arrive at the concept of co-creating knowledge with clients. The idea of co-creation epitomizes a true partnership, and represents one of the richest possible forms of relationships. Strong value is created for both parties, which usually could not be achieved by working in isolation.

Co-creation of knowledge is appropriate when neither party has an "answer" to the problem or issues at stake, but by working together they are more likely to create the knowledge relevant to those issues. In addition, involving the client in the actual process of knowledge creation means that it not only has the deepest possible understanding of the knowledge being created, but also develops its own abilities to create knowledge, as a very high level capability. Another benefit, of course, is that not just the client but both parties gain value from the knowledge created. In some circumstances, a firm can be paid handsomely to create knowledge that has very high value in itself.

Clearly, co-creating knowledge with a service provider depends on a high degree of trust, which is likely to have been generated through previous interaction. The intimacy created by project work for co-creating knowledge in turn engenders greater trust, which is a platform for more rewarding relationships. Co-creation should be regarded as a powerful relationship tool, beyond its intrinsic value.

BUSINESS MODELS FOR THE CO-CREATION OF KNOWLEDGE

Creating knowledge jointly with clients does not fit most traditional business models of professional service firms. The direction of the flow of value between clients and suppliers has already blurred substantially over the last decade, and the explicit co-creation of knowledge makes it even less clear as to who is creating and receiving value in the relationship.[1] This evolution means changes are often required in ways of thinking about relationships, and the business models on which they are founded. Knowledge co-creation can be seen as a simple extension of adding greater value to clients in a professional services environment, or it can start moving toward fundamentally different conceptions of the nature of business and the creation of value.

Adding Value with the Co-Creation of Knowledge

The nature of the co-creation of knowledge means that both parties allocate resources to a project, and expect to generate valuable knowledge. This makes the relationship far closer to a collaboration or alliance than a traditional client-provider relationship, and the client could ask why it should pay for this nature of collaboration.

There are a number of possible answers. Commonly the primary value added by the service provider stems from its expertise in structuring the collaboration and co-creation of knowledge so that it produces valuable results for the client. This is essentially an organization-wide form of knowledge elicitation. In the case of knowledge co-creation, however, the service provider is usually bringing to the party not only process knowledge of how to facilitate effective collaboration, but also content knowledge, which also provides major input to the project. It is true, however, that the dynamics of co-creation result in more of a peer-level relationship than maintaining the service firm as the knowledge "superior."

In many cases the nature of the knowledge on the client and provider side is substantially different in nature, which results in the value of the collaboration. Some industries well suited to the co-creation of knowledge bring together process knowledge from the professional firm regarding how best to create valuable outputs, company and industry-specific knowledge on the client side, and creativity from both sides. Examples of disciplines where these kinds of structures are common include advertising, engineering, design, and consulting. These approaches can equally well be applied in other industries, however. The outputs from this style of collaboration include not only knowledge-rich "products," but also many knowledge by-products including insights and understanding which are valuable in often-unforeseen ways.

Clearly, the exercise must add value to the client over and above what it could achieve on its own. The ability of the professional firm to achieve added value gives it the right to collect fees (or payment in other forms) for what could be seen as a collaboration. If the service provider obviously also receives substantial value from the project in its own right, then the client may be justified in trying to renegotiate the relationship to more of an alliance-based approach.

Client Relationships in the Co-Creation of Knowledge

The co-creation of knowledge suggests a substantially different basis of client relationships from traditional business models; however, the nature of these can vary substantially. Because these kinds of relationships must be founded on trust, they most commonly evolve from existing professional service relationships. In these cases, the structure is usually similar to that of other engagements in that client outcomes are specified, the professional service firm coordinates and draws on both its own and its client's resources in order to create the necessary knowledge for achieving these outcomes, and a time or project-based fee is charged.

When the co-creation of knowledge is more explicitly the intention, or even the starting point for the relationships, other structures for interaction are appropriate. These include multi-client projects, or going as far as establishing joint ventures as a vehicle for collaboration. Some other ideas for business models for collaborative relationships are given in Chapter 9, from the perspective of pricing knowledge.

Multi-Client Projects

It is becoming increasingly common for professional firms to work with a group of clients on a single knowledge-based project. The genesis of this structure was found in independent think tanks, which sought

---

St. Lukes

London-based advertising agency St. Luke's was created in 1995 from a split with Chiat/Day, which at the time was in the process of being acquired by Omnicom. It won *Campaign* magazine's 1997 Agency of the Year award; clients include Coca-Cola, IKEA, Eurostar, and Midland Bank. St. Luke's explicitly tells its clients that it doesn't have the answers to their issues, but that they have to create them together. Clients pay a scalable monthly retainer; St. Luke's chairman Andy Law says that knowledge multiplies in value when combined with the knowledge of others, so St. Luke's can only price sweat equity—the effort which it contributes to the co-creation of knowledge with its clients.

For the price of the retainer, the client receives an array of services. The service begins with an introductory workshop on creative thinking and the advertising process; the client's suppliers and its own clients are also invited to attend. The client gets a permanent office on the premises of the agency, which it can use for working on ideas, as its base in London, and to access the agency's library and other resources. This is called a brand room, and is decorated to reflect the feeling and mood of the client and its customers; the Eurostar room is complete with genuine train seats, while a cosmetic brand is decked out as a girl's bedroom. Strategy and advertising ideas are created in joint workshops with St. Luke's and the client, with constructive argument and contention emphasized in the process. The agency produces the advertising product on the basis of these workshops, but the entire process is performed interactively with clients rather than simply presenting them with a finished product.

St. Luke's says that it in its engagements it undertakes to provide an understanding of advertising, a high level of creativity, and knowledge of the processes which are likely to result in good advertising; while the client provides a deep understanding of its industry, its own clients, and its culture. Its entire business model is based around the co-creation of knowledge—Law states that St. Luke's will not accept any clients that want it to go away and produce advertising as a product.

---

funding for research projects from a range of organizations that would benefit from the likely outcomes of the research. The most common format for multi-client projects remains very similar, with a fixed contribution allowing entry into the syndicate; the members participating throughout the process of knowledge creation; and customized briefings and reports of the findings distributed to each client member. There are a multitude of examples in the field of knowledge management—Arthur Andersen and Ernst & Young's Center for Business Innovation, as well as other firms, have run multi-client projects on the business lessons from knowledge management.

In the multi-client project model, commonly much of the knowledge generation is expected to come from the professional firm or research institute; however, there is also usually substantial input from the participants, especially in group interaction. The value of a group of complementary organizations working together on an issue of common relevance can be immense. Again, part of the value the supplier provides lies in its skills in structuring and guiding knowledge flow and development, as well as its relationships, which allow a diverse group of organizations to be brought together in a mutually beneficial format.

One important issue is whether the clients involved in the project are competitors. Often multi-client projects are designed to have only one client from any given industry, although with careful design, projects can provide opportunities for competitors to be involved. Global Business Network has many clients in industries such as energy and chemicals, and finds that much of the value perceived by clients is specifically in providing a forum in which they can engage in constructive interaction with real or potential competitors.

Establishing Joint Ventures

The ultimate implementation of knowledge co-creation is establishing a joint venture or alliance to develop and exploit knowledge. This puts both partners on a more obviously equal footing, and addresses the issue of remuneration in line with the value of knowledge contribution, as discussed in Chapter 9.

Universities tend to prefer licensing the technology that they develop rather than entering into partnerships, although Stanford University has taken innovative approaches for developments which merit the effort. When an inventor at Stanford developed a new music synthesis technology, it created a trademark, Sondius, which would have a life and revenue potential beyond the patent expiration for the technology. Stanford then established a partnership with Yamaha, combining the music company's intellectual property with its own to form a portfolio of more than 400 patents. The first products developed using the joint intellectual property hit the market in 1998.[2]

DESIGNING THE CO-CREATION OF KNOWLEDGE

As we have seen, the expertise in the *process* of co-creating knowledge usually comes from the professional service provider, and having responsibility for this justifies the fees charged by the service provider. Effective management of the process of knowledge co-creation depends on understanding the issues in designing processes for working with knowledge collaboratively, and then managing the ongoing dynamics of the process. We will look first at some of the structures of knowledge creation that will help us design successful processes, and then at the dynamics of co-creation.

Knowledge Development Loops

The development of knowledge is an iterative process, in which experience and lessons provide the basis for deeper understandings in ongoing feedback loops. A loop-based framework for understanding learning and knowledge development was developed by David Kolb; this still provides a foundation for much of our understanding of adult learning.

Kolb suggested that there are four phases in the learning cycle. The first is experiencing, which stems from doing and activity. The second phase is engaging in reflection on the experience, which is followed by conceptualization, through interpreting the events and the relationships between them. The fourth stage is the planning of further action based on the learning, which brings it full circle back to engage in further experience.[3] The entire process is illustrated in Figure 8–1.

The feedback loop as a foundation for knowledge development has also been applied to organizations. Nonaka and Takeuchi have suggested a knowledge spiral in organizational knowledge development, which proceeds successively through the phases of socialization, externalization, combination, and internalization, as shown in Chapter 2, building from the level of the individual to that of the organization and beyond.[4]

Knowledge feedback loops are at the heart of knowledge creation within organizations. While knowledge creation is by its nature iterative, how the loop functions will be different between organizations. Which part of the cycle is emphasized and the linkages between each phase will vary substantially. Understanding the nature and detail of this feedback loop provides insights into how to structure all knowledge transfer with clients.

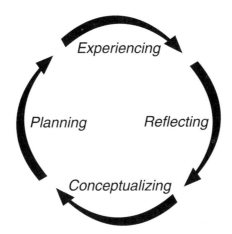

FIGURE 8–1   The learning cycle.

Since the co-creation of knowledge involves at least two organizations, it is very valuable to understand the dynamics of the knowledge creation loop, not only within the client, but also within your own organization. Figure 8–2 shows how the knowledge development loop within two individual organizations can be combined to become a shared process of creation and development between two organizations. This framework can be a valuable tool to help design effective collaboration processes. Once the differences and relative strengths of each phase of the knowledge development loops in each company are understood, they can then be combined into an interorganizational knowledge development loop which best encompasses and uses the loops and strengths within each organization. This larger loop focuses attention on and helps define which elements of the knowledge creation cycle should be performed by each organization, and specifically what communication channels and content will maximize the richness of feedback and development.

DYNAMICS OF THE CO-CREATION OF KNOWLEDGE

Knowledge is almost always created in some form of collaboration rather than by individuals working alone. Fostering the kinds of motivation and interaction that result in valuable knowledge creation within a company is a complex challenge, and some organizations are clearly more successful at this than others. Taking this collaboration to a multi-

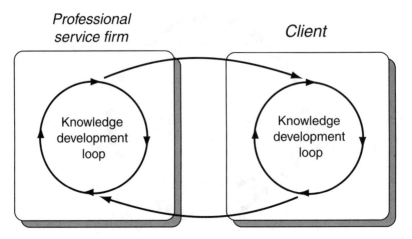

FIGURE 8–2   The knowledge development loop within and between organizations.

organization situation makes it far more complex and difficult again, with the boundaries between organizations creating major challenges in facilitating collaborative knowledge creation. On the other hand, one advantage of having organizations jointly engage in knowledge creation is that it forces a more explicit model for collaboration, and clarity in the constituent processes, which in itself can create substantial value.

Process Management

In collaborative knowledge creation, it is usually preferable for one organization to hold primary responsibility for managing the creative process. The professional service firm will usually take this role, and in any case should position itself to take this responsibility, as this is arguably the major source of value and typically the primary success factor in the project.

Part of this role is essentially project management—ensuring that the resources are brought together to make happen whatever is necessary. This is still subsidiary to managing the process of knowledge creation, which includes consideration of all of the dynamics of this volatile undertaking. Managing the creation of knowledge is certainly far more of an art than a science, a key part of which is finding the delicate balance between directing the process and letting it happen.

Facilitation

The primary process in knowledge creation is facilitation. It is not only critical in co-creation, but in all knowledge-rich situations; this skill should be deeply embedded in every professional service firm, both for its own internal knowledge creation, as well as in adding value to clients. Facilitation could be described as the process of bringing together disparate knowledge in a complementary and useful way. It is intrinsically unstructured, to best allow the most useful interaction between participants in ways which will achieve a valuable combination of knowledge.

Facilitation is a very high-level skill which to be accomplished successfully must draw on a rich understanding of people, groups, knowledge, paradigms, and business. It is often applied within the frame of knowledge elicitation, in getting clients to make the most of the latent knowledge within their organization. However, it is even more fundamental to the co-creation of knowledge, in bringing together knowledge and ideas that have probably been developed from substantially different perspectives.

Brainstorming

Brainstorming has become a core tool in business facilitation since the process was developed by Alex Osborn.[5] The original principles of putting forward all ideas, not criticizing, looking for quantity, and combining and improving the initial suggestions, are still used by organizations worldwide. While generating a large number of ideas is the avowed intention and basis of the brainstorming methodology, the greater value is in the subsequent combination of those ideas, and the dynamics created by the situation. It is typically just one element in the overall process of knowledge creation, but can play an important role, particularly in setting a frame for the desired dynamics of knowledge interaction.

IDEO of Palo Alto, California, the largest product design consulting firm in the United States, bases a significant part of its reputation on its brainstorming ability. It has found that in addition to generating valuable ideas and knowledge internally, and assisting in the sharing and development of knowledge, it also produces useful ideas and knowledge for clients, and helps generate business for the firm.[6]

Projects at IDEO routinely start with the client explaining the problem or situation to a brainstorming group of designers. Clients are taught the basic principles of brainstorming, and are reminded of the rules if they break them when participating in workshops. One of the perceived benefits of running a brainstorming session is simply that it is an efficient way for clients to get ideas compared to individual meetings or reports. While brainstorming is used in essentially all projects as part of IDEO's core methodology, some clients choose to hire IDEO just to run brainstorming sessions.

Creative Abrasion and Matching People

One central issue in running successful projects involving the co-creation of knowledge is the effective interaction of staff from both organizations. Dorothy Leonard suggests that "creative abrasion" is one of the most important elements for the generation of knowledge.[7] If people with similar ways of thinking are brought together, there is far more likely to be groupthink than the generation of the sparks that results in volatile knowledge creation. Knowledge often emerges from the collaboration of people with very different ways of looking at their field. Indeed Nissan Design International, for example, deliberately puts together teams by hiring people with contrasting cognitive styles.[8]

This suggests that joint knowledge creation teams should be designed to provide this level of creative abrasion. Building in this abrasion does require very strong facilitation and supervision skills, however, as interpersonal abrasion can clearly also result in less pleasant outcomes. Deliberately matching professionals with client staff having different cognitive styles is certainly risky, but also can result in far richer knowledge creation for the client, both on individual and organizational levels. One way of reducing risk is discussing with the client beforehand the deliberate introduction of this creative abrasion, and the potential wrinkles on the way. This purposeful use of creative abrasion in knowledge creation projects should be contrasted with knowledge communication-based engagements and sales relationships, which are more likely to succeed if cognitive styles are matched, as discussed in Chapter 7.

Developing External Communities of Practice

Since the idea of "communities of practice" was first introduced—probably by John Seely Brown, the chief scientist at research and development institution Xerox PARC—it has emerged as one of the key concepts in knowledge management. A community of practice brings together practitioners within a field of specialization in order to share high-level knowledge and experience.[9] These communities have always existed and are an intrinsic part of all knowledge development, as knowledge specialists will always seek out their peers in order to develop their own knowledge.

The issue is how to assist these communities to develop in ways that are useful for all participants. Since knowledge specialists are usually eager to establish interactions with their peers, it can come down to making it easy for people to share knowledge and ideas, which is often a technology issue of connecting people in easy and useful ways.

Communities of practice commonly exist within a single organization, or across highly specialized fields of science or engineering. In many cases knowledge specialists have greater loyalty to their field of knowledge than their organizations. It is possible for professional service firms specifically to create communities of practice either with single clients, or groups of clients.

Linking a professional service firm's knowledge specialists with their peers in clients in a community of practice will certainly add substantial value to clients through the useful sharing of knowledge, as will assisting clients to create and develop their own communities of practice. Many professional service firms have developed expertise in building these communities in the process of leveraging their internal knowledge, and can pass on this expertise to their clients. Another perspective is considering the knowledge roles introduced in Chapter 7, and seeing the building of communities of practice as taking the richness of interaction between knowledge specialists at the service provider and their peers at the client as far as it will go.

Taking the concept a step further, professional service firms can add significant value by building communities of practice among groups of its clients. This adds value by providing the technology infrastructure for them to share knowledge, bringing together a group with common interests, and sometimes facilitating the interaction.

Arthur Andersen's KnowledgeSpace is an online consulting resource which provides access to databases, interactive modules, and consultants; it is very similar in concept to Ernst & Young's Ernie, which we discussed in Chapter 7. In addition to these resources, it provides moderated online forums and discussions that allow Arthur Andersen clients who face similar issues to exchange ideas and access tailored information. The KnowledgeSpace virtual communities include CFOs, internal auditors, oil and gas companies, and digital communications. Linking clients together in this way not only provides intrinsic value, but can also build loyalty and share of mind.

Conferences and Roundtables

While bringing communities together online provides a valuable forum for exchange, it does not have the same power in terms of exchanging and creating knowledge as bringing people together in the same place. Conferences are a wonderful, time-tested way of bringing people together; many attendees find greater value in the informal exchanges and discussions with other delegates than in the formal presentations. While it is "old technology," bringing together people in this way will always be immensely valuable. Many organizations host conferences that bring their clients together, with many benefits such as knowledge exchange and formation of communities of practice among their users.

Roundtables are more focused, and provide a forum for exchange of views, information, and knowledge among participants. Fannie Mae operates in the secondary market to provide home financing targeted to low, moderate, and middle-income people; it is the largest source of funds for home mortgages in the United States. While its end-customers are primarily families, it deals directly with lending institutions, and has other stakeholders including local government and business. Fannie Mae regularly hosts regional roundtables and forums, bringing together lenders, business leaders, local politicians, research organizations such as universities and think tanks, and other parties. The participants' objectives in making home ownership more accessible are highly aligned, so the forums provide them with the opportunity to create solutions together, drawing on their complementary knowledge, as well as helping Fannie Mae to develop new products and services appropriate for evolving markets.

Sharing Technology

The same factors which enable communication channels to be useful for knowledge communication, also make them effective in the collaboration required for knowledge creation. Of these factors, interactivity is clearly the most important. Anything that improves the bandwidth and scope of interactivity will contribute positively to the results of knowledge creation. The true advantage of digital communication is not only effectively linking people who are geographically distributed, but also providing rich means of interaction.

Electronic bulletin boards well preceded broad use of the Internet as the first tool for knowledge sharing through digital technology; these allowed people to post comments for others to view. These have progressed to threaded discussions, which allow discussions to follow different strands and themes in a conversational style, with chat room software now bringing in many more features and allowing more dynamic interaction.

Videoconferencing is gradually replacing telephone conferencing for situations in which rich interaction is required, including knowledge co-creation. Electronic whiteboarding is another very valuable tool, which enables people in different locations to use web-based technology so each can write and draw simultaneously on the same "whiteboard." There is currently massive development of and strong growth in demand for Internet-based collaborative technologies; some of these are likely to become broadly used. While there is no substitute for face-to-face meetings, when they are not possible the most interactive technologies possible should be used.

Knowledge Capture

As discussed in Chapter 5, a substantial proportion of the value gained by clients can be found in the capture of knowledge in a usable form. In addition to the knowledge capture which would be part of the engagement anyway, in the context of knowledge co-creation it is very valuable to document the actual process by which the knowledge is generated. This documentation can allow the client to gain not only the knowledge content, but greater facility in the creation process.

Since the process of knowledge creation usually generates a broad array of ideas that are then refined to produce specific outcomes, a great deal of latent value often remains in the ideas left behind on the way. These can be revisited later to solve other issues or simply to mine for gems. The spinoffs from NASA space research have been as diverse as better pillows and detecting cherry pits in cherry pie filling; however, commercializing the research behind these advances required both capturing the lessons from the steps in the process, and choosing to follow-up on them. Wherever possible, recording the process of knowledge co-creation and providing it to the client in a usable format, and possibly making that a specified outcome of the project, can greatly increase the value proposition for the client.[10]

ISSUES IN THE CO-CREATION OF KNOWLEDGE

There are significant issues and potential problems in the co-creation of knowledge, not least of which is the ownership of any intellectual property created. The complexity of these issues can prove to be a strong disincentive for organizations to engage in knowledge co-creation, and illustrates why trust is critical even in the initiation of knowledge co-creation projects.

Mutual Trust

The most fundamental rule in co-creating knowledge is working from mutual trust; if it is not present to a sufficient degree at the beginning of an engagement, the project is not likely to be viable. The trust must be reciprocal—it is equally important for the service provider to trust its client as the other way around.

Researchers who have studied joint ventures have concluded that however much participating firms try to cover all potential issues in contracts, success ultimately depends on trust.[11] This is not to suggest that legal agreements should not be used, but that there is no way for agreements to cover all contingencies, and no substitute for trust.[12] The bottom line is that the benefits of the co-creation of knowledge are severely limited without significant mutual trust. These kinds of projects, therefore, are more likely to stem from an existing strong relationship than to be a starting point for collaboration.

Even given reasonable levels of mutual trust, it is still critical to discuss and agree from the outset how the most important issues, such as ownership of intellectual property, will be handled. While it is impossible to foresee all eventualities, the more possibilities that are discussed, the more likely that situations can be handled in a way that benefits all parties and builds rather than destroys relationships.

Confidentiality is already a bedrock of professional service engagements, and thus should need no further emphasis. The depth of client information and knowledge obtained in the process of knowledge co-creation can be a significant step beyond that shared in other styles of working, and therefore requires a greater degree of confidentiality, and again, strong mutual trust.

Ownership of Intellectual Property

Knowledge is a valuable asset, and if two or more parties create knowledge together, the issue of the ownership of that knowledge will inevitably arise. Intellectual property is essentially knowledge or intellectual capital that can be legally protected. This definition includes, for example, documents that can be copyrighted, inventions that can be patented, and process names that can be trademarked. Most ideas or processes themselves cannot be patented, however, and while formal documentation of this knowledge can be legally protected, the knowledge itself cannot. As such, much of the actual valuable knowledge generated in a project will be extremely difficult to protect, and thus is not intellectual property in the legal sense.

When intellectual property in the form of patents and copyrights is generated from a project, it can be relatively straightforward to allocate ownership and benefits, as long as this eventuality has been discussed and agreed upon beforehand. The way in which this is approached will depend on the nature of the collaboration, and vary from vesting all intellectual property with the client, to sharing ownership or licensing rights, or occasionally vesting ownership with the professional service firm. Professional service firms often seek to specify that they and the client both have the right to use processes and methodologies developed during a project, as most of these innovations are generated in the course of client engagements. The ability to use this knowledge can be restricted in ways that make sense to both parties; for example consulting firms can be permitted to apply any methodologies developed in all industries other than those of the client. Clearly, whatever is agreed upon regarding the allocation of eventual intellectual property should be established contractually.

Trade secrets or confidential information law protects ideas that have not entered the public domain or that cannot be protected by copyright or patents. This is often more relevant than intellectual property law in the co-creation of knowledge, and agreements should usually contain confidentiality clauses. Of course, whenever there are potential legal or contractual issues, please seek specialist legal advice.

SUMMARY: CO-CREATING KNOWLEDGE WITH CLIENTS

The closest and richest type of knowledge-based relationship is one in which the professional service firm and client create knowledge together.

This implies different business models from the usual experts-for-hire approach, including the possibilities of establishing joint ventures and running multi-client projects.

In order to add value in the co-creation of knowledge, service firms must have expertise not only in their specialist fields, but also in the dynamics of knowledge collaboration, including effective process management, facilitation, and brainstorming. Developing external communities of practice creates real value in allowing clients to share knowledge on an ongoing basis. Mutual trust is a prerequisite of effective knowledge co-creation projects, partially in order to be able to negotiate and work with issues such as the ownership of any intellectual property created.

Building far closer relationships with clients—including implementing the co-creation of knowledge—means that the boundaries between organizations blur, and traditional approaches to pricing services begin to become ineffective. In Chapter 9 we review some of the more common approaches to pricing knowledge-based services, and examine a range of ways to implement pricing models reflecting the value created for the client.

NOTES

1. Davis and Meyer explore in detail the theme of blurring in the direction of flow of value. See Davis and Meyer, op cit.
2. See Lawrence M. Fisher, "Technology Transfer at Stanford University," *Strategy & Business* (4th Quarter, 1998).
3. David A. Kolb, *Experiential Learning: Experience as the Source of Learning and Development* (Englewood Cliffs, NJ: Prentice Hall, 1984).
4. Nonaka and Takeuchi, op. cit., 71–73.
5. Alex F. Osborn, *Applied Imagination.* 3rd rev. ed. (New York: Charles Scribner's Sons, 1963): 151.
6. Information on IDEO is drawn from Robert I. Sutton and Andrew Hargadon, "Brainstorming Groups in Context: Effectiveness in a Product Design Firm," *Administrative Science Quarterly* 41 (1996): 685–718.
7. Leonard, op. cit., 63–65.
8. See Leonard, op. cit., 79–81; and Katharine Mieszkowski, "Opposites Attract," *Fast Company*, no. 12 (December 1997): 42.
9. John Seely Brown and Estee Solomon Gray, "The People Are the Company," *Fast Company*, no. 1 (November 1995): 78.

10. See Gary Abramson, "Their Pain, Your Gain," *CIO Enterprise* (October 15, 1998).

11. See Kathryn R. Harrigan, *Strategies for Joints Ventures* (Lexington, MA: Lexington Books, 1986), as quoted in Gary Hamel, "Competition for Competence and Interpartner Learning within International Strategic Alliances," *Strategic Management Journal* 12 (1991): 83–103; and Leonard, op. cit., 174.

12. Ring and Van de Ven suggest that in high-commitment relationships informal agreements will increasingly replace legal contracts, as their experience with each builds trust. See Peter S. Ring and Andrew H. Van de Ven, "Developmental Processes of Cooperative Interorganizational Relationships," *Academy of Management Review* 19, no. 1 (1994): 90–118.

Chapter 9

Pricing Knowledge
Implementing New Revenue Models

Information and knowledge behave in very different ways to most products or simple services. For example, if you transfer knowledge to a client—or even many clients—you still have that knowledge, and in fact probably more than you started with. Very importantly, there is often little relationship between the cost of inputs and the value of knowledge outputs. And much attention has been paid to how knowledge is often subject to increasing returns rather than diminishing returns: it can increase in value the more it is shared.[1]

All of these characteristics suggest that the pricing of knowledge and knowledge-based services should be very different from that of more traditional products and services. Yet still many of the same approaches to pricing are used. One important reason is simply the immense difficulty of valuing and pricing knowledge. As we have seen, the value of knowledge depends on its context and the client.

The organic, fluid nature of knowledge means there is no easy way to price it, and no neat, glib answer as to how professional service firms should charge for their services. Certainly, however, professional service firms need to reexamine the basis on which they charge, and at least experiment with different approaches to pricing. This chapter aims to cover many of the most common approaches to pricing knowledge, as well as some more novel methodologies. As with much of this book, the intention is to provide practitioners across the professional industries with lessons from their counterparts in related fields. The focus of this book is knowledge transfer to clients; however, here we will deal with the dynamics of pricing knowledge-based services more generally.[2]

188

BEYOND TRADITIONAL PRICING MODELS

Over the past decade new pricing models have started to emerge, often as a result of deregulation and the competitive forces of un-bundling covered in Chapter 2. Legal and consulting firms historically have tended to charge according to the time they spend working on a job, irrespective of the quality of the knowledge going into the engagement and the value to clients. Stockbrokers and advertising agencies have traditionally charged a percentage of the transactions in which they are involved, in the same way as a rug on consignment in a flea market.

While these approaches are still common, and will continue to be used in many situations, new models and approaches are emerging. Innovators will experiment with new forms and find what works and what doesn't, leading the way for professional service industries to move on from the traditional approaches. In the coming years, clients will be confronted with a far broader choice of pricing models as well as services, and ultimately will choose the offerings which give them the greatest value for the price they pay.

Of course, an easy way of making prices relate to client-perceived value is to charge high fees, and the clients you get are the ones that perceive higher value than they are charged. Textbook pricing theory can be used to find a profit-maximizing pricing level; however, in reality a more flexible system will result in greater revenue, as the nature of knowledge-based services is far more fluid than the products on which most pricing theories are based.

In an environment in which services have been unbundled, one of the key issues is distinguishing between the commoditized and differentiated elements of the offering. There will always be an element of the range of services offered which are commoditized, and competitive pricing strategies must be applied in these cases. However, the differentiated elements of the offering should be priced as much as possible based on the value to the client. When an offering is differentiated, then it is throwing money away and devaluing the offering to price it in the same way as a commoditized offering. Another key issue in developing pricing models is that of client relationships—certainly you wish to maximize revenue for work performed, however, if the quality of the client relationships suffers, then long-term profitability could be affected.

TRADITIONAL PRICING MODELS

Here we will look at the more traditional approaches to pricing knowledge and knowledge-based services, which include time-based pricing, fees, bundled pricing, and commissions. In the following section we will examine approaches to pricing which attempt to link price more directly to value. The fact that the approaches covered here are more traditional does not mean that they are not necessarily useful or appropriate in many situations, however, they have distinct limitations that mean the use of alternative pricing models often proves valuable.

Time and Cost Pricing

The most common method for professionals to charge is based on their time. In most organizations this is fairly closely related to their cost in terms of salary, overheads, and proportion of billed time. Professional practice management is largely focused on managing these factors.

Most professional firms pay as salary in the order of 20–40 percent of the overall service revenue generated directly by their nonpartner staff. When there are substantial costs involved other than salaries and basic overheads, such as major infrastructure or capital requirements, as in the case of investment banking, this proportion can be substantially less. Because the major cost of most professional service firms is their staff, time-based pricing is essentially a type of "cost plus" pricing, which takes the costs of providing a service, and adds a margin.

While billing by time spent is easy, convenient, and relatively transparent to clients, it may have very little relation to the value to the client. Should a brilliant innovation generated in a minute's inspiration be charged out for a fraction of the cost of drafting a standard letter? And while expertise and usable new ideas in a particular field may take months or years of unbilled time to develop, should these then be available for the price of an hour's time, or less if some of the core lessons have been distilled and made explicit in a document which can be copied or faxed? Some professional service firms are experiencing significant problems with these issues.

Time-based charging will always have a role, however, because of its simplicity, and in the end the hourly or daily rate can be adjusted to meet market demand. One key factor is that clients are used to paying by time in many industries. This means it can initially be difficult to wean clients off these approaches. Perhaps the most important problem with time-based charging is that there is not necessarily a direct relation to value generation for the client.

Fixed Fees and Retainers

Many professional service firms charge a fixed fee to carry out a specified project, without the client seeing how the fee is made up of the time and cost of staff required. There has been a strong shift to fees from time or commission measures over the last years, notably in consulting and advertising. In reality the fee is almost always calculated on a time and cost basis, with possibly an additional premium if the client is likely to bear it. Even so, project-based pricing increasingly provides the opportunity for professional service firms to price their work and knowledge transfer based on the value they believe the client is likely to accrue, and to convince their client that the value they will receive from the project is greater than the price they will pay.

Cambridge Technology Partners, a software implementation firm based in Cambridge, Massachusetts, built annual revenues of over $600 million in the seven years since its founding in 1991. This impressive growth is partially based on its novel approach of setting a fixed time and fixed price for large projects, as well as its substantial undercutting of competitors' fees.

Hybrid models, which involve combinations of fees and time-based pricing, are becoming more common. These include charging a fixed fee for prespecified services and charging on a time basis for any additional work, or time-based charging up to a pre-specified limit.[3] These essentially represent types of risk sharing arrangements, which are discussed later in this chapter.

Bundled Pricing: Knowledge Transfer as Differentiation

Since knowledge is so hard to value, it is often easier to bundle it together with a product or service which itself can more easily be priced. As we saw in Chapter 1, all client offerings can be viewed as a combination of products, black-box services, and knowledge transfer. When these are bundled together as a single offering, any part of that offering can be used to price the package. In this case knowledge can act to differentiate the offering from its competition.

Michael Porter stated that differentiation allows firms to command a premium price; however, he defined premium price as either gaining a higher price for products, selling more products at the same price, or gaining equivalent benefits such as customer loyalty.[4] Knowledge transfer in particular is a key source of differentiation, although its presence does not necessarily translate into higher pricing, but may simply result in clients choosing your offering over those of your competitors at the same price.

This means that clients will use the knowledge transfer component to distinguish between and select the better value proposition between similar products and services. For example, industrial chemicals may be priced by the pound or kilogram, but the business can be won by adding value to the manufacturing processes in which they are used.

Commissions

A related approach to pricing knowledge is charging a commission or percentage on the value of transactions. This has traditionally been the case in a range of professional service industries, although deregulation and the associated competitive forces have resulted in major strains on the system, and substantial changes in commission-based charging. For example, a fixed percentage commission on share transactions is increasingly rare, and in the advertising industry the traditional model of charging a percentage of the cost of media billing is rapidly being overtaken by new pricing trends.

A fixed commission system still holds in some fields, such as equity underwriting. In all industries, however, this approach is under continued pressure from new entrants who offer more attractive pricing structures. While measuring value added by a professional service firm as a proportion of the dollar amount of the transaction involved is a rather crude approach, it does provide a yardstick, and allows competitive advantage to be determined by the quality of services and other value added by the service firm.

Retainers and Membership Fees

Retainers in their most basic form provide access to a firm's services. Commonly they include the provision of a pre-agreed (often time-based) amount of services, beyond which further fees are charged. This is, of course, essentially another variation on time-based pricing. META

Group's services model, as described in Chapter 6, gives an example of the range of services that can be covered with a retainer.

Since knowledge transfer is most effectively based on ongoing conversations and interaction, it can be appropriate to charge clients a membership fee to join these dialogues. This approach can either provide access to professionals at the service provider in informal ways such as telephone conversations, or participation in broader communities including other clients. Global Business Network's core services, including conferences, subscriptions, and access, are all covered with an annual membership fee. Generally, membership fees can be used to provide access to high-level dialogue in a range of ways, notably conferences, or online forums such as those in Arthur Andersen's KnowledgeSpace.

Tenders

Knowledge-based services are often subject to tendering, where the client specifies its requirements and asks for the lowest price and best performance within its specifications. The use of tendering implies that the services are commoditized, and that they are driven purely or primarily by price. Unless service providers can differentiate themselves within the tender process, which is difficult, there is little or no opportunity for premium pricing. As much as possible, firms need to establish their differentiation with the client before tenders are called, and build relationships that avoid direct price-competitive situations.

PRINCIPLES OF VALUE-BASED PRICING

The Holy Grail of professional services is to find a way of charging which is based on the value received or perceived by the client. Of course, in order to get business in the first place the client must perceive substantially greater value than the price charged. Some firms have a policy of only taking on assignments that give a demonstrable value-to-price ratio. Global management consulting firm Proudfoot PLC, based in Surrey, UK, states that the firm will only take on work which it can demonstrate will add value equal to at least three times the cost of the project. McKinsey & Co. and many other major consulting firms have a similar tacit policy, sometimes specifying far higher multiples.

One of the most important aspects of implementing value-based pricing is that it helps to align the objectives of clients and service providers. If both sides benefit when projects are successful and suffer when they don't go well, then they have clearly made a strong move to a true partnership-style relationship. This means that, while service providers are eager to establish value-based pricing in order to earn larger fees than they could otherwise, there is also a strong incentive for organizations to reward their service providers in ways which mean they will be highly motivated to ensure successful outcomes.

Implementing value-based pricing is deeply tied to developing knowledge-based client relationships. The types of agreements and disclosure of information required by many models and approaches requires strong mutual trust—they are far more likely to happen once there is already a deep level of familiarity. And that disclosure, along with the alignment of objectives that is intrinsic to many of these approaches to pricing, helps to develop intimacy and far closer relationships.

Measuring Value

Ideally in establishing knowledge-based pricing models we would be able to measure value created for clients as a result of engagements or relationships, and many new pricing models attempt to do this. The problems are legion, however, which means that except in cases such as contingency fees for litigation, few firms have implemented these broadly.

The greatest difficulty is in isolating the contribution of the professional service firm from the many other factors that impact performance. If a consultant assists a client in refining its strategic positioning, and sales go up 30 percent, is that a result of the consulting engagement, or because of an upturn in the economy, or production problems at a competitor?

The key issue in determining whether value-based measures are likely to be usable in any given circumstances is the scope of the project or relationship relative to the scope of what is being measured. There is no way of completely isolating the value impact of external professional services; however, if this factor is sufficiently large, then both sides can agree to share in changes in performance.

If what is being measured is narrower in scope, it is easier to believe that the engagement is responsible for enhanced results. Work with smaller companies or divisions, or at the product level, is more likely to impact revenue and profitability. It is possible for an engagement with a large multinational corporation to significantly impact group profitability, but it would have to be on a massive scale.

These issues also mean that cost, revenue, profitability, shareholder value, and share price represent increasing orders of difficulty for use as measures of value. The variables which impact costs are usually far more under control than those for revenue, and these can often be identified, so that the impact of the engagement can more easily be measured. In addition, costs can usually be fairly readily measured or allocated down to a departmental basis, which is not possible for revenues. Profitability includes both cost and revenue variables, while shareholder value and share price are affected by a wide variety of macro issues. These can be used for executive compensation, but there would usually have to be a very close relationship with an external service provider—or for it to be a smaller organization—to link these to its fees.

Mutual trust is a critical issue in these kinds of measures of client value. Cost figures and other accounting measures are easy to fudge, so unless the service provider trusts the client's assessment of the figures, cost-impact charging will not be implemented.

Risk Sharing

The concept of risk sharing is central to all value-based pricing. Sharing the rewards of a project between a service provider and its client—essentially getting participation in the value created—means there must also be more sharing of risk. Clients have little reason to give away bonuses to their service providers, without also sharing some of the potential downside. With clients that have a low tolerance for risk or cost, it represents an opportunity for the service provider to take on some of that risk in exchange for a larger proportion of the benefits. Since organizations' tolerance for risk varies substantially, risk-sharing arrangements must be negotiated on a case-by-case basis.

As suggested above, implementing risk-sharing pricing arrangements—whether or not they are formally articulated as such—means that the service provider and client share in both the upside and downside of the success of projects. This alignment of objectives can be contrasted to the win/lose stance in which each is trying to get the most out while putting the least in. The way in which risk sharing is most commonly implemented is by charging clients a base fee that represents the service firm's labor and overhead costs, plus perhaps a nominal margin, and sharing in the value created by the engagement.

Agreed Objectives

When final value creation in terms of profitability or related measures is difficult to relate directly to the work performed, other yardsticks can be applied which represent indirect value to the client, but over which the service provider has more control. Among many others, these can include results of surveys of client or product awareness or image for advertising agencies and public relations firms, changes in quality or failure rates in production for consultants, or time for project completion for construction firms or software developers.

In a knowledge transfer-based engagement, the agreed objectives can be knowledge outcomes specified at the outset, as discussed in Chapter 7. These can include skill levels of client staff and the effectiveness of capabilities; the issue is making it demonstrable that greater knowledge or capabilities exist after the end of the engagement.

Client Perceived Value

In cases in which it is impossible or impractical to measure the impact of services performed, assessing client perception of value can sometimes be used. This is perhaps particularly relevant in adding value to others' decision making, where it is impossible to separate the various inputs to the final decision, and only the decision makers can judge what was valuable to them in their decision.

There are clearly many difficulties in using client perception of value—in many situations it becomes simply a subjective bonus, which is rarely satisfactory to both parties. One of the most important conditions for client perceived value to be used effectively as a basis for or component of pricing is that the client indeed believes it receives substantial ongoing value from its suppliers, and is highly motivated to reward excellent performance. It is very hard to work in an isolated engagement that is not part of an ongoing relationship. It also tends to be more effective if the client uses a limited panel of service providers with which it has ongoing relationships. This means that the client can determine an approximate fee pool to be shared among its panel of service providers, possibly linking this to its own performance by various measures, and then allocating this pool between the panel on the basis of perceived value added by each over a period. This kind of approach has been most fully implemented in the institutional stock broking industry, and is described later in the chapter.

DDB Worldwide Communications Group

Advertising network DDB Worldwide Communications Group, based in New York, was nominated by *Advertising Age* as Global Agency Network of 1997, and in 1998 achieved global billings of $11.6 billion. Chairman and CEO Keith Reinhard has been an active proponent of pay-for-results approaches to fees.

In 1991, DDB Worldwide Communications Group began by offering to guarantee results on its advertising campaigns under certain conditions. This first initiative did not work as well as had been hoped, partially because while the CEOs of client organizations were enthusiastic about the concept, the brand managers preferred to have control over the relationship, and were sometimes reluctant to share information.

Since then the agency has shifted from offering a guarantee to making part of its compensation based on results. This involves a basic fee structure that allows the agency to cover its costs plus a basic margin, with bonuses paid based on the results achieved by the client.

The key issue in establishing the bonuses is agreeing on measures for results that are aligned with the clients' marketing objectives, and are as directly as possible attributable to the agencies' efforts. Some measures used include sales and profit of the client as a whole or for the relevant division, media or production savings, and survey measures of brand or advertising awareness and intention to purchase. If the objective of the client were to increase distribution, this would represent a different type of assignment that could be measured, for example, by number and diversity of distribution channels. In 1998, the agency made $6 million in incremental revenue from these schemes, which went straight to its bottom line.

Since a core element of DDB Worldwide Communications Group's business is developing brands, it is actively seeking to create its own brands, and license these to clients, thus keeping the intellectual property in-house. In one example, it created the brand H_2OPE, which it has licensed for an annual fee to the Stockholm Water Foundation, which on-licenses it to companies. Reinhard says that he wants his business to become more like the music industry, in which the creators do not sell their ideas for a fixed price, but instead license them to generate ongoing revenue.

IMPLEMENTING VALUE-BASED PRICING MODELS

Since in professional services every engagement is customized to whatever degree, it presents a marvelous opportunity for creativity and experimentation in developing and implementing value-based pricing models. There is no one solution, and within professional services each industry and even each client may merit a different approach. While for smaller clients or engagements the effort of negotiating a tailored arrangement may not be worthwhile, any significant project or relationship offers the potential for client and service provider to align their interests in the way they agree on pricing. Consenting adults can choose to engage in whatever form of pricing structure they believe meets their respective objectives. The survey of approaches given here is by no means exhaustive, but covers a range of useful and innovative structures, with examples of firms that have successfully implemented these.

Cost, Revenue, and Profitability Impact

Developing pricing models that are based on measuring the impact on cost, revenue, and profitability can only be done effectively in certain conditions, as discussed above. Implementing these is essentially an issue of nominating an appropriate measure, and determining how this will be linked to the service provider's remuneration. Both sides have to agree that whatever measure is used—be it cost, revenue, or profitability in a given domain—is substantially linked to the contribution of the professional service firm. The link to fees can be structured in many ways, including taking a percentage of value created and bonuses for achieving specified targets.

In one recent example of cost impact pricing, Booz•Allen & Hamilton negotiated an agreement with its client to allocate a proportion of the fees for a cost-reduction reengineering project to the success in achieving the targeted savings. Together they established a scorecard of measures, including the number of people, costs associated with functions, new processes established, and so on across several divisions in the organization. The initial project and implementation lasted several months, with regular meetings over the following six months to review progress, to take remedial action where necessary, and at specified milestones to establish the achievement of agreed indicators on which further payments were based. The regular follow-up meetings also served to establish a deeper and richer dialogue and relationship with the client.

The most common situations in which revenue-related measures can be used are individual products, particularly new products, where the service provider creates or co-creates the entire marketing strategy or campaign, or even the product itself.

Contingency and Success Fees

Contingency fees—which are fees payable depending on success—are effectively a variation on revenue-based fees. They are most commonly used in litigation, where an agreed proportion of the possible winnings goes to the law firm; this is clearly also a form of risk sharing, since often no other fees are payable and thus the law firm risks getting no return on its efforts. Contingency fees in law have always been standard practice in the United States; however, they were only made legal in the United Kingdom, Australia, and New Zealand through the late 1990s, and are not accepted practice in most other jurisdictions. Success fees are also routine in investment banking, where fees can be payable depending on the success of a range of outcomes, including acquisitions, protection from takeover, or share price increase.

Licensing

Licensing is an important vehicle used in charging for knowledge, and especially knowledge transfer. In its basic form, it provides an ongoing payment for the use of specified knowledge. This is most often applied to intellectual property such as patents, trademarks, or copyrighted material, where organizations pay a fee for use of the intellectual property. These licensing fees often include a basic annual payment, with an additional payment per use or as a proportion of revenue.

Consulting firm Intellectual Capital Services (ICS), based in London, uses a licensing approach in charging for its services. ICS applies proprietary research and models within its clients to develop company-specific performance and intellectual capital models, or to value intangible assets. A fixed fee is charged for this initial process, and any subsequent processes in developing the systems and models. Clients then pay 18 percent annually of the cumulative fees paid through the relationship for the right to continue to use the systems and models. This fee is invested in further research and development. For their fee, the client receives an annual quality review of the systems or models in use as well as an option on the use of further research results.

Training courses are a good example of a knowledge "product" that can be licensed to clients to generate ongoing revenue as they derive ongoing benefit from knowledge development in their organizations. These can be sold for a single fee that depends on the size of the organization, or an up-front fee supplemented by a licensing fee for each trainee or time the course is run.

Idea Fees and Licensing

A large proportion of value creation comes from good ideas, yet in general ideas cannot be protected by law as intellectual property. Any way of charging for ideas—which are often flashes of inspiration based on years of experience or remarkable creativity—is a big step toward more effective knowledge-based pricing. Rainey Kelly Campbell Roalfe/Y&R, a young advertising agency in London that has recently been acquired by global communications group Young & Rubicam, has since its inception based all of its charging on idea fees.

The agency charges a monthly fee based on the resources needed to manage the client account; this is intended simply to cover costs and break even. In addition, it agrees up front with the client a value—and therefore price—for the idea that will achieve the client's objectives. This pricing is established before the idea is created; however, it is only payable if and when the agency generates an idea that the client believes meets its needs. All terms are agreed upon and established contractually at the outset, so that the ideas are protected by contract law rather than intellectual property law, which would be of little use in these circumstances.

The value given to the idea is different for each client, and is intended to reflect the likely impact on client revenue rather than be related to costs such as spending on media. If it is difficult to identify a relationship between advertising and sales revenue, the agency may take a percentage of the budget of the marketing initiative the idea will drive. No commissions are charged on any production or research, so there are no vested interests in increasing costs to the client.

In most cases the ideas are intended to be used over the long term to build brands; if so, there is usually an ongoing annual payment—resembling a licensing fee—as long as the idea is used. If the client changes advertising agencies but wants to continue to use the idea, there is a buy-out charge specified in the contract. Joint chief executive M.T. Rainey acknowledges that it is easier to implement these principles from the outset of client relationships, but emphasizes that the agency's intention is to be in the business of ideas, and as such, it wants to charge for the ideas that it generates.

Equity and Stock Options

Equity can be a powerful reward for knowledge, particularly as knowledge-based services can have a major impact on the client's success. This is only likely to happen when the client is cash-poor, and prefers to pay its suppliers in equity or stock options. However, these are also the kinds of situations in which service provider input is most likely to have a significant impact on the company's value.

Industrial design firm Palo Alto Design Group (PADG) specifically seeks clients that are prepared to offer stock options, warrants, or royalties in return for its services. PADG helped design the enclosure for Palm Computing's Palm Pilot at the concept stage in return for a small fee and warrants in Palm stock, which paid off handsomely when Palm Computing was subsequently bought by U.S. Robotics.[5]

Venture capital can be regarded as knowledge transfer in exchange for equity. The venture capital firm provides capital as well as knowledge of the process of developing a firm through its initial stages, and applies and transfers that knowledge to the firm in which it is investing. In return it takes equity in the firm.

Joint Ventures

Joint ventures can be an ideal vehicle for the commercialization of knowledge which has been co-created by two companies. They can also be established explicitly for the joint development and subsequent exploitation of knowledge. As suggested in Chapter 8, these approaches truly establish the two firms as partners, and represent very powerful means of aligning their goals and objectives.

In 1997, EDS won the largest financial services IT outsourcing contract in the world from the Commonwealth Bank of Australia (CBA), essentially taking over its information technology operations for a minimum of 10 years, with an expected contract amount of $A5 billion. At the same time CBA took a 35 percent stake in EDS Australia for $A240 million. This has resulted in an immense alignment of interests and objectives of the two parties—both risks and rewards are shared in a true partnership relationship. As part of the ongoing relationship EDS and its management consulting subsidiary A.T. Kearney establish "Value Discovery" teams to identify ways in which they can create value together with CBA. The fee structure for each initiative is discussed and negotiated on a case-by-case basis, wherever possible being based on measurement of the value created. The closeness of the relationship allows the ready implementation of innovative pricing structures.

Institutional Stockbroking Pricing Model

The institutional stockbroking industry provides an excellent model of pricing based on client perceived value. This has arisen due to industry dynamics, in which institutional investors are highly motivated to reward adequately the stockbrokers who provide timely information, insights, and ideas that improve their investment performance. Since portfolio decisions are ultimately made by the fund managers, however, only they can judge how much value the brokers added to their decision making. Previously this was handled in an ad-hoc way by awarding transactions to the broker who had contributed the most to the investment idea or had been helpful recently, but this informal system was not clear enough in rewarding the brokers for what was most valuable to the fund managers.

It is now becoming the norm for institutional investment managers worldwide to use a formal quantitative value-based voting system for allocating commissions to their stockbrokers. In Europe, for example, about half of all major fund managers use this kind of system, with many more using a similar informal system. Typically, investment managers calculate how much brokerage commission they would generate in a year, and then allocate that among their panel of stockbrokers on the basis of the value they perceive has been added to their decision making. This is calculated by quarterly or semi-annual voting by every individual fund manager and analyst who has contact with the brokers.[6]

Merrill Lynch Mercury Asset Management, a subsidiary of Merrill Lynch headquartered in London, manages over $180 billion in assets worldwide. Every six months it formally reviews the performance of its panel of stockbrokers in adding value. The three primary functions of their stockbrokers that are reviewed are research, sales, and execution. Mercury's fund managers rank the top five analysts in their field of specialization, looking for the broader perspectives they offer rather than more generic number-crunching ability; these ratings are then weighted according to the importance of the sector. Fund managers also allocate votes on sales service by the brokers, focusing on the originality of their ideas, and speed of reaction to market developments. The dealers at Mercury whose responsibility is to get orders executed also vote on the brokers' quality of execution of trades. These votes are then combined to yield an overall ranking of brokers and a rating on a scale of 1 to 50. The results are discussed with the brokers, focusing on the areas in which they can improve their added value and rankings. While actual commission allocation is not necessarily exactly aligned with the ratings, Mercury ensures that over time the business executed with each broker is in line with its established ratings of perceived added value.

It is possible that similar arrangements will arise in other industries in which comparable dynamics are evolving. While these are more likely to be initiated on the client side, they can also be proposed by service firms; as long as sufficient value is created by the service providers, this style of system can benefit all parties.

Auctioning

Where the demand for a service provider exceeds its ability to perform services (which is most often the case for a solo practitioner or small specialized firm), it can auction its time. Its time is a limited resource, and if there is an effective auctioning system the price paid for its work will reflect the value placed on it by their clients, and where its application will add the greatest value. Some professional speakers auction their availability on any given date for speaking engagements, accepting the highest offer for their time.

Start-up company Advoco.com has established an online market for services, including business and technology consulting, which enables potential clients to bid for the services of specialist service providers. The growth of use of the Internet has helped auctioning develop rapidly as a means of achieving efficient pricing in a wide variety of markets; it has the potential to become commonly used for pricing services that are highly specialized or in limited supply.

Free!

While giving away knowledge for free could hardly be called value-based, no survey of approaches to knowledge-based pricing would be complete without including this strategy. Kevin Kelly, Executive Editor of *Wired* magazine, is one of the new apostles of giving away products and services.[7] Kelly notes that in situations where products and services become more valuable as they are more plentiful, it can make sense to give them away for free or at low prices.

If goods, services, or knowledge are given away, revenue can be generated in a number of ways. Some of these include charging for them once value has been established by ubiquity, charging more for related products or services, and exploiting the valuable attention of the user audience through advertising. More directly relevant in professional services, giving knowledge away establishes expertise and credibility, and can help justify premium pricing for other services.

The genesis of The RiskMetrics Group (RMG), introduced in Chapter 5, was J.P. Morgan's creation of a methodology for financial market risk management that was made freely available to all financial institutions, including both clients and competitors. Not only did it provide detailed instructions on implementing the methodology, but it also supplied free daily data updates to allow others to use the methodology. The methodologies and data are still available for free.[8]

J.P. Morgan benefited in a number of ways, including establishing itself as the de facto leader in financial risk management, and providing a base for the sale of software to implement the methodologies. Probably more importantly, it contributed to better risk management practices in the financial sector, which benefits all participants. Since then RMG has introduced new products which are priced in more conventional ways, such as its CorporateMetrics® methodology, data, and software for corporate financial risk management.

SUMMARY: IMPLEMENTING NEW PRICING MODELS

Knowledge behaves very differently from products and simple services, and requires different approaches to pricing. Traditional pricing models, such as time and cost pricing, fixed fees, and commissions have both advantages and disadvantages, but fail to address many of the important issues surrounding knowledge-based services.

A key objective of professional service firms is to implement ways of pricing which are based on the value added to clients. Some of the principles of value-based pricing include attempting to measure the value created, sharing both upside and downside risk with clients, agreeing on measurable objectives for engagements, and assessing client perceived value. Some specific approaches being implemented include measuring cost and revenue impact, licensing, idea fees, equity and stock options, and the institutional stockbroking model.

Having covered some of the key issues of implementing knowledge-based client relationships—managing communication channels, structuring firm-wide relationship management, co-creating knowledge, and applying new pricing models—we now need to pull these strands together to establish an overall implementation strategy. Chapter 10 examines the issues that professional service firms need to address in implementing these principles. Ultimately knowledge and relationships are connected by people and effective communication between them, so we propose practical approaches to these critical enablers of knowledge-based relationships.

NOTES

1. See for example Brian W. Arthur, "Competing Technologies, Increasing Returns, and Lock-In by Historical Events," *The Economic Journal,* no. 99 (March 1989): 116–131; Kevin Kelly, *New Rules for the New Economy: 10 Radical Strategies for a Connected World* (New York: Viking, 1998); and the treatment of positive feedback and lock-in in Carl Shapiro and Hal Varian, *Information Rules: A Strategic Guide to the Network Economy* (Boston: Harvard Business School Press, 1998).

2. For further ideas on knowledge-based pricing, see Karl-Erik Sveiby's article "Fourteen Ways to Charge for Knowledge," at www.sveiby.com.au/Twelve Ways.html.

3. Geoffrey James, "Methods of Payment," *CIO Enterprise* (October 15, 1998).

4. Porter, 120.

5. Eric Ransdell, "Redesigning the Design Business," *Fast Company*, no. 16 (August 1998): 36–38.

6. Benjamin Ensor, "European Brokers Survey: Pulling Away from the Pack," *Euromoney* (November 1997).

7. Kelly.

8. See The RiskMetrics Group website, at www.riskmetrics.com.

Chapter 10

Creating Value in the Knowledge Economy

People, Strategy, Relationships, and Communication

In our exploration of the nature of knowledge-based client relationships, it has become apparent that knowledge is ultimately about people and relationships, which is why knowledge *must* be thought about beyond the boundaries of an organization. Knowledge is created, developed, and applied by individuals and people working together. As such, effective communication between people is the foundation of the knowledge economy and professional services, both in creating and applying knowledge in useful ways, and in adding the greatest value to clients. In this chapter, we will draw together some of the threads we have developed throughout the course of the book, and present an overview of practical implementation issues for professional service firms to apply in improving their capabilities in developing knowledge-based client relationships. We will focus in particular on enhancing capabilities in client communication.

EVOLVING STRATEGY AND ORGANIZATIONAL STRUCTURES

The challenges and rapid pace of change of the knowledge economy mean that professional service firms must reexamine the basis of their strategy and organizational structures, particularly in managing their interaction with key clients. While the implementation of change in large organizations usually cannot help but be evolutionary, the conception of change must be revolutionary. Rather than thinking about how to gradually evolve existing organizational beliefs and structures, professional service firms need first to draw a clean slate on the underlying structures and strategy that are required by the dynamics of a world in which knowledge transfer is central to building and maintaining profitable relationships. Once the likely future shape of the firm has been conceived, a transition strategy can be developed to take it from where it is to its desired form.

New Business and Revenue Models

The existing business and revenue models in place in many professional service firms may not provide sound foundations for building closer and more rewarding knowledge-based client relationships. As the dynamics of business change and evolve with the growing importance of knowledge in the economy, it will become critical to implement new ways of conceiving of the way value is created, and appropriating that value between the client and service provider.

Professional service firms must go through an active process of examining their implicit business models, and the assumptions underlying them. This provides a foundation for being able to reexamine the core competencies and capabilities of the firm in the context of the knowledge economy, and how these can be developed and reinforced within evolving business models. One of the most important issues to address is that value is increasingly created together with the client, and business and pricing models need to take that into account.

Within established firms, new approaches to pricing often can be implemented gradually, by being applied to clients in situations in which they are well suited. Traditional pricing methodologies have many strengths, and in many cases they are the easiest and most appropriate ones to use. When value-based pricing models are suitable, they can initially be implemented on a project-by-project basis. Some clients are reluctant to move from more familiar pricing models, but they can become enthusiastic partners when they see the real advantages in a greater alignment of objectives with their service providers.

Positioning

On one level, positioning is about the strategic selection of the company's range of offerings in relation to a targeted client base. Taking it to a higher level, strategic positioning for professional service firms must encompass decisions about how they create knowledge relative to their clients, and how they use that knowledge to create value for clients. Many professional service firms' stance on these issues is based on deeply embedded assumptions about the nature of the industry in which they work, however these assumptions need to be brought to light and fully considered.

The most fundamental choice that every business must make is whether it will follow the path of commoditization—in which it competes on cost and price—or differentiation—in which it competes on greater value to the client, with the potential to achieve premium pricing. Those who choose the path of differentiation must accept that it will always be eroding, and they will have to continually keep running just to stay in the same spot, let alone move ahead. And while it is easy for professionals to say they are taking a path of differentiation, they must clearly identify what the source of that differentiation is, and how it will be reinforced rather than eroded over time.

Another basic choice to be made lies in the distinction presented throughout this book—where the firm falls on the spectrum between providing black-box services and knowledge transfer (see Figure 10–1). This choice is implicit in the way all professional service firms do business, however, should also be explicitly discussed and agreed. Some of the other broad issues and choices that professional service firms need to address in their positioning include their commitment to creating their own knowledge, how they create that knowledge, how much they draw on external knowledge in their work, and how much they involve clients in the creation of knowledge.

In a global marketplace there is room for any number of different positioning strategies, and aiming at providing differentiated services at

**Black-
box**

**Knowledge
transfer**

FIGURE 10–1   Where do you stand on the spectrum from black-box services to knowledge transfer?

premium pricing is by no means the only viable strategy. However, I believe that in the future sustained differentiation in professional services will depend on sharing knowledge as a foundation for developing closer client relationships. Continually creating knowledge is a prerequisite for sustained value creation, and this applies not only to professional service firms, but also to their clients. As such, the greatest value is increasingly in helping clients to create, develop, and apply knowledge for themselves. Clients' perception of the highest value creation will gradually shift towards knowledge elicitation—helping them to develop their own knowledge—as a source of far higher value than black-box services or even communicating existing knowledge.

Communication Channel and Relationship Management

Since communication is at the heart of professional relationships, developing and structuring communication channels and client contact are perhaps the most vital tasks in building business in professional service firms; the fundamentals of communication and relationship management were developed in Chapters 6 and 7. The firm's business and revenue models form the foundation for business development, within which relationship and communication strategies can be established. These too require an active and ongoing process of examination and management, both in terms of providing approaches and structures that can be used as a template across the organization, and in adapting those approaches to meet the needs and idiosyncrasies of each client.

STRATEGIC IMPLEMENTATION OF TECHNOLOGY

The implementation of technology cannot be allowed to happen in an ad-hoc fashion, simply in response to new developments. Technology strategy in professional services is fundamental to the firm's positioning, and must be developed within the context of the overall business strategy in developing knowledge-based client relationships. There is no doubt that technology will have a dramatic impact on the shape of professional services, both in building richer communication and in developing interactive services. However, implementing technology without due consideration of its fit within the strategy and directions of the business has the potential to take the firm in unanticipated directions.

Part of this is the issue of commoditization; having too great an emphasis on technology can result in the danger of entering a realm of competition that can too easily be commoditized. Another critical issue is the potential disintermediation of direct contact with the client, as discussed in Chapter 7. Unconsidered implementation of technology-based services can take away the richness of contact that results in intimate and profitable relationships.

Richer Communication and Interactivity

A good frame for implementing technology in client relationships is in terms of communication channel management, the focus of Chapter 6. This puts digital communication channels into the context of the entire spectrum of client communication, and how the portfolio of channels interacts and complements each other as a whole. Using technology as a basis for proactively building broader and richer communication and contact as a complement to face-to-face interaction is a great source of value and an important part of developing intimate and valued relationships.

Another vital and increasingly important aspect of technology is its role in providing interactive systems and services. Computer-based training and other interactive applications start to frame technology as an enabler for people in internalizing and developing their knowledge, rather than simply a means of providing access to information. These applications will never provide a complete substitute for personal interaction, although they mean that technology can play a significant role within a broad strategy for developing knowledge-based client relationships.

Ernst & Young's Ernie and Arthur Andersen's KnowledgeSpace, as described in Chapters 6 and 8, are good examples of well-thought-out implementations of technology in professional services, and address both issues of facilitating communication between people, and providing interactive services. While the intentions of each were somewhat different, both very deliberately focus on complementing existing and forthcoming services, addressing a broader range of clients, and supplementing rather than replacing contact with core clients.

PROFESSIONAL SKILL DEVELOPMENT

Since knowledge is all about people and interaction between people, one of the most promising fields for enhancing capabilities lies in developing the skills of professionals who use and create knowledge, and work with clients. Much of the current range of training and development courses intended for professionals can be useful. Establishing a strategic-level framework for understanding the intrinsic nature of professional services, however, enables skill development to be positioned to result in the greatest benefits.

One implication of the importance of interpersonal interaction in professional services relates to the types of people who will perform effectively. Knowledge specialists who are happiest when deeply involved in the minutiae of their fields and are decidedly less happy when they have to speak with clients will always have a role to play, but they will be increasingly edged out by those who can interact with others in ways that create and transfer knowledge. Much of the training available in business communication is not aimed at professional knowledge transfer and is too generic to be very valuable in high-level professional services. Development specifically aimed at the challenges of making clients more knowledgeable is essential.

Information and Knowledge Skills

Professionals are quintessential knowledge workers—every aspect of their work involves dealing with information and knowledge. As such, their skills in effectively working with information and knowledge are at the heart of their capabilities. Certainly they need continual development of the specialist knowledge which enables them to add value; however, their most basic skills, on which their effectiveness and success is founded, are information and knowledge skills.

These skills include assessing relevance and filtering information overload, reading and note taking, analysis, synthesizing information, pattern recognition, and decision making. These are all components of the basic skill set of professionals, and essential to their tasks, so most are already good or excellent at these functions. This level of proficiency does not mean that those skills cannot or should not be developed further; in fact, developing these skills is one of the prime ways of achieving differentiation in professional services, and usually provides an excellent return on investment.

All these skills can be developed in classroom training. However, one of the most useful approaches to developing knowledge skills lies in facilitating knowledge workers in developing their own information strategies—taking them through all aspects of the processes, from accessing and filtering information, to decision making and communication. Each professional, with unique job characteristics and his or her own preferences and style for dealing with information, will benefit from a different approach to dealing with information and knowledge. Taking professionals through this process gives them the basic tools they require. It allows them the opportunity to stand back from their work, and enhance their personal skills from the perspective of adding value to information and knowledge, especially in the context of how that creates value for clients.

Knowledge Communication Skills

Knowledge communication skills may be a subset of communication skills, but to be developed effectively they require substantially different approaches to most types of communication training. Most communication training is related to sales functions, gaining a fairly basic understanding of personality types, or writing business letters. While these are important skills, these should be considered foundation skills. Knowledge communication is based on far more than clarity and persuasion; it is about being able to effect in others a changed understanding of sophisticated concepts.

The primary skills and knowledge underlying knowledge communication are an understanding of cognitive styles and the structure of mental models, especially the psychology of decision making. These basic skills can be applied to adapting interaction to individual clients, developing presentations, facilitating meetings, and designing effective written and visual communication.

Knowledge communication skills can be developed in a classroom environment, but must be practiced. For example, training in cognitive styles should include exercises that force professionals to adapt their communication of recommendations and concepts to clients with different styles. Many training courses implement similar approaches for application in a sales environment; however, few do so in a knowledge communication context.

Facilitation and Knowledge Development

Developing knowledge is a cooperative process largely based on the interaction of people with contrasting mental models. Facilitation is *the* foundation skill for knowledge elicitation and creation. Good facilitation is essentially about achieving the best from a group of people. This involves resolving apparent conflicts resulting from divergence in group members' mental models, and together building a frame or result which respects and builds on the diversity and difference of perspective and experience in the group. Facilitation is a fundamental skill, which draws on a specific range of interpersonal capabilities, but can be developed over time. Many training and development programs are available which focus on facilitation; it is helpful if these are framed specifically in a knowledge development context. Some related skills also central to knowledge creation and development were covered in Chapter 8; these include brainstorming, process management, and the development of organizational and interorganizational knowledge creation loops.

Flexibility in Communication

The law of requisite variety, introduced in Chapter 4, suggests that the more flexible your behavior, the more likely you are to achieve your desired outcomes. This is very clearly the case in communication. People who have a narrow repertoire of communication styles experience limited success in communicating with others, whereas those with extensive flexibility in their approaches to communication are far more effective. They are able to keep on trying new and different approaches to communicating until they achieve the results they are looking for, rather than simply continuing to try the same approach even if it gives inconsistent results. This is one of the most critical skills in facilitation. A good facilitator has access to a very broad repertoire of behaviors, and is constantly willing to experiment with new approaches in order to allow groups to achieve what they want.

Developing flexibility should be an overriding objective of all training and development in communication. It is an ongoing process, and only over time are people able to broaden their access to different approaches to communicating with others.

COMMUNICATION DESIGN

One of the most important areas in enhancing the value added to clients is designing the presentation of information so that it can be readily assimilated and internalized as knowledge. The effective presentation of information has always been a major focus in professional services; however, focusing on effective knowledge transfer rather than simple provision of information brings out the value of using more innovative approaches.

Structuring Communication

Information presented as written documents must be organized effectively in order to be readily used by clients. This is traditionally accomplished in a hierarchical structure, which enumerates points and sub-points. This is perhaps best encapsulated in the well-known "pyramid principle," which Barbara Minto developed when she was responsible for communications at McKinsey & Co., and which is still the de facto standard for writing at the firm.[1]

This principle proposes that communication should be structured in a pyramid, with the apex representing the purpose or conclusions of the message, and supporting information and ideas providing more detail as you move further down the pyramid, based on grouping ideas logically. The most efficient way to provide concepts to readers is from the top down, which means that they get the essence of the communication at the outset, and can choose how much detail they access in supporting the primary message.

Digital communication allows far greater flexibility than paper documents in the structure of information and communication. One advancement that has profoundly changed the design of documents is hypertext, which allows references to other electronic documents to be followed up with the click of a mouse. The great advantage of this is that it intrinsically allows a tiered structure; people can read the top-level overview, and immediately access greater detail or references whenever they wish. It is also possible to implement toolbars on the computer screen that indicate exactly where in the hierarchy and network of documents or concepts one is currently located, giving an inherent sense of overall structure.

Stories and Metaphors

People learn best through stories, metaphors, and analogies. Supporting evidence for this is presented in the Appendix. Most people will acknowledge that they learn most easily when they are presented with stories having personal relevance, metaphors enabling them to relate their experience to new areas, and analogies between concepts. The richness and open-ended nature of these forms of communication facilitates people in integrating new ideas into their ways of thinking, and developing their own enabling knowledge structures. The process of knowledge acquisition is essentially one of forming relationships between new and existing experience and concepts; using approaches to communication that intrinsically relate to the relationships and structure of experience allows for the easiest and richest learning. Clearly, these approaches are not only very effective for communicating knowledge, but also assist people in creating their own knowledge by introducing different perspectives on their existing knowledge.

3M has applied these principles to reform its business planning process around the use of stories, which it calls strategic narratives. These have replaced the traditional "bullet-point" or list-based approach to planning, which 3M found did not evoke the richness of thinking necessary for effective strategic planning.[2] Manpower, as discussed in Chapter 7, has designed its client extranet around stories, giving people concrete examples of how their peers have achieved successful results. This approach not only allows them to integrate that knowledge easily, but also makes it entertaining and accessible, while attracting scarce attention.

VISUAL REPRESENTATIONS FOR KNOWLEDGE COMMUNICATION

Visual representations are one of the areas with the greatest scope for enhancement of knowledge communication. The Appendix reviews the evidence that visual representations greatly increase the comprehension and retention of conceptual information, when used as a complement to text. In addition, good visuals attract the eye and help to cut through the flood of documents received by busy executives.

Information and Concept Visualization

Data and information visualization are well-developed fields that use graphics to represent and convey large quantities of complex data. Yale University's Edward Tufte has helped take information visualization to an art form with his books *Envisioning Information* and *The Visual Display of Quantitative Information*.[3] The ready availability of advanced software to transform data to graphs and other visual representations has meant these approaches are becoming far more widely used. This is making it considerably easier for people to assimilate large quantities of information, and sometimes the relationships within it, although in general visual representations could still be used far more widely and effectively.

Concept visualization is distinct from information visualization; it seeks to convey conceptual understanding rather than simply information. The precept is to design visual representations—usually as a complement to text—which maximize the effective internalization of knowledge. This can be framed both as knowledge communication in conveying specific conceptual frameworks, or as knowledge elicitation in the sense of providing clients with an opportunity to frame and structure their knowledge in a useful way.[4]

Concept Structure and Representation

The heart of effective visual concept representation is in presenting the concepts in a structure that is aligned with or similar to the structure of the mental models of the person seeing the diagram. In the Appendix we discover that mental models are generally associative, hierarchical, and systemic in nature. Concept representations should be based on these structural features, and can also draw on other aspects of the way people think and act, such as causality, alternative scenarios, and others. There are many useful approaches to visual concept representation; the core of the idea is that the intention is to impact the way people understand or think about certain issues, rather than simply to impart information. A simple example of a concept representation is given in Figure 10–2.

Three-dimensional representations can be very valuable in showing the relationships between concepts, as people's mental representations are often spatial rather than simply flat images. Virtual Reality Markup Language (VRML) is a convention that allows the presentation of three-dimensional images on Internet browsers, including "fly-through" representations of actual or conceptual spaces; this can be applied to show complex relationships between concepts.

Mind-Mapping

One approach to visual representations which is beginning to be used fairly broadly in the business community is mind-mapping, a tool originated by Tony Buzan.[5] It makes use of a visual format to show the relationships between ideas, which for many people is a far easier way to represent their thinking, and allows all the key concepts of a given subject to be visible in one diagram. A simple mind-map of some of the concepts illustrated in this book is shown in Figure 10–3; wherever possible it is valuable to incorporate color into mind-maps, as it attracts attention better and can facilitate the assimilation of ideas.

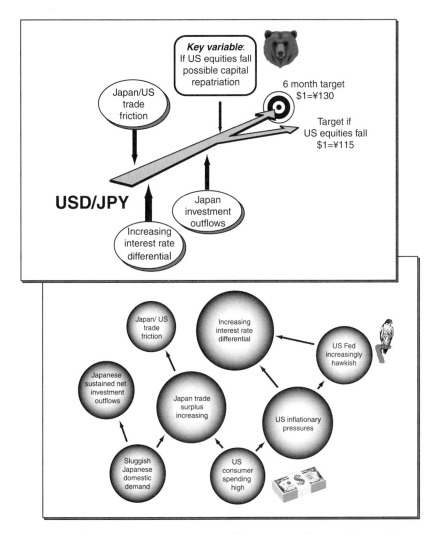

FIGURE 10–2   Concept representation of the primary forces affecting the level of the Japanese yen. Source: AHT Financial Research, a division of Advanced Human Technologies. Used with permission.

New York-based Inferential Focus synthesizes information about emerging trends in society and business for its client base of major corporations and institutional investors. In order to communicate these trends and ideas to its clients the firm uses mind-maps, which help bring together disparate information in a way that clearly shows the relationships and relevance to the user.[6]

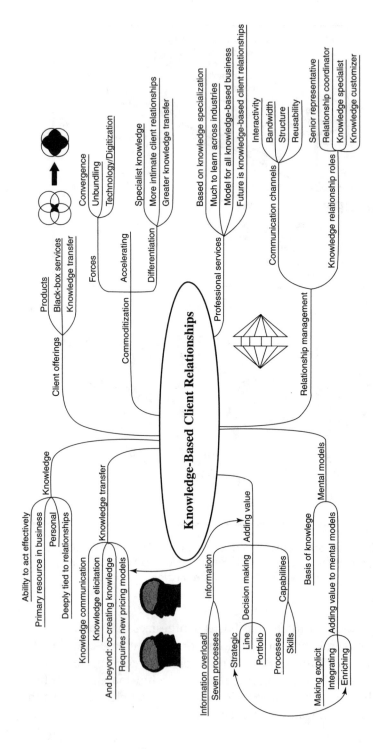

FIGURE 10–3 Mind-map of key concepts in this book.

Visual Metaphors

The use of visual metaphors can allow very powerful communication of concepts and ideas. People can directly relate to the concepts presented in visual metaphors, which are broadly accessible, and easy to internalize. Root Learning of Perrysburg, Ohio produces learning maps for its clients based on visual metaphors. Much of its work is in strategic planning and change management programs, in which the issues facing the organization and its strategic directions are presented in a number of detailed four-by-six foot graphics. The intention is for staff and executives to quite literally see the big picture.[7] Inter Action Corporate Communications of Sydney, Australia does similar work, using powerful visual metaphors as the basis for internal communication programs in large government and corporate clients.

THE FUTURE OF PROFESSIONAL SERVICES: CREATING VALUE IN THE KNOWLEDGE ECONOMY

The future of business is all about knowledge and relationships. Relationships will become increasingly critical in every industry, as customers and clients gain more choices and knowledge, and increasingly go to the cheapest source to meet their needs, barring the existence of prior ties or affinity with any supplier. Knowledge is and will be the overriding source of value created in the economy. Much of that will be in the form of "embedded knowledge," in which products and services are superior to their competitors because of the knowledge that has gone into their creation. However, in professional services knowledge transfer and sharing will be the primary means for adding value to clients with knowledge and the key source of sustainable differentiation.

Knowledge is about people. It is people who have the "capacity to act effectively" in the enormously complex and dynamic arena which is the business world of today. And relationships are also clearly about people. Knowledge-based relationships are ultimately based on the richness of interaction between people, and their ability to communicate effectively and bring together their varied experience and mental models to create value far exceeding that which they could as individuals.

Perhaps in the future there will be nonhuman "intelligent systems"; at the moment there are certainly systems which embed knowledge in a capacity to act, however, the scope in which they can act is very narrow, and they remain tools to which people delegate specialist tasks. For the foreseeable future, by far the most valuable knowledge will be that of people. Certainly the nexus between knowledge and relationships is formed by people, and the focus in business will be on this critical dimension.

Knowing that the future of professional services is about people, knowledge, relationships, and effective communication, we must work to better understand the process by which people acquire, create, and develop knowledge. Applying this understanding effectively is perhaps the heart of creating greater value in a knowledge-based economy. The science of cognitive psychology has much to teach us in terms of understanding how people think and work with their knowledge; however, much work remains to be done in applying these insights in practical ways in a business context. The Appendix offers a framework for some of the research that has been done in the field, in a way that lends itself to adaptation to business processes.

This kind of understanding of the nature of knowledge and mental models can assist us greatly in eliciting people's knowledge, and in drawing out greater possibilities in the way they think and make decisions. Enriching people's mental models and enabling greater flexibility of behavior are some of the highest and most lasting forms of value creation, and must be based on intimate interactions and relationships, as well as the facilitation skills which embody professionals' deep understanding of people and organizations.

While parts of business and society will become increasingly mechanized, the opportunity also exists for a far deeper appreciation of people's abilities to create and apply knowledge individually and collectively. Bringing people together in order to jointly enrich their knowledge, perhaps especially across organizational boundaries, will become a finer art and science, and increasingly central to the creation of value in the knowledge economy. I am deeply optimistic about the future of business, because I see people all around the world who believe in their own and others' potential, and want to work more closely with others to create knowledge and build deeper, closer relationships between people. I believe that this is the only way to achieve lasting commercial success, as well as being the pathway to gain the greatest joy and satisfaction from your work. I hope to meet you on the journey.

NOTES

1. Barbara Minto, *The Minto Pyramid Principle: Logic in Writing, Thinking, and Problem Solving* (London: Minto International, 1996).

2. Gordon Shaw, Robert Brown, and Philip Bromiley, "Strategic Stories: How 3M Is Rewriting Business Planning," *Harvard Business Review* (May-June 1998).

3. Edward Tufte, *Envisioning Information* (Chesire, CT: Graphics Press, 1990) and *The Visual Display of Quantitative Information* (Chesire, CT: Graphics Press, 1992). A less spectacular, but useful and exhaustive review of approaches to conveying information visually is given by Robert Harris in *Information Graphics* (Atlanta: Management Graphics, 1996).

4. Richard Saul Wurman has done much to develop the scope of visual communication. He has presented the work of some of the leading practitioners in the field in a beautiful book; see Richard Saul Wurman, *Information Architects* (New York: Graphis, 1997).

5. Tony Buzan with Barry Buzan, *The Mind Map Book*, rev. ed. (London: BBC Books, 1993).

6. Mark Fischetti, "Masters of the (Information) Universe," *Fast Company* (August/September 1997): 181–187.

7. See Sherman Stratford, "Bringing Sears into the New World," *Fortune* (October 13, 1997).

Appendix

The Nature of Mental Models
How People Acquire Knowledge

The effective transfer of knowledge is predicated on understanding how people acquire knowledge and understanding. Cognitive science is based upon the study of how people learn, think, and communicate, and thus can provide us with valuable lessons in this domain. Here we will review some of the findings from the field of cognitive science— which is comprised of a broad array of disciplines including cognitive psychology, linguistics, neuroscience, and philosophy—to identify lessons we can apply directly in business. These disciplines are rich and diverse, and our objective in drawing on them is very specifically to learn how to be more effective at implementing knowledge transfer.

Cognitive science is divided by many arguments over fundamental issues in the field. Ray Jackendoff, a leading researcher in the field, delicately refers to the "unfortunate sociological problems in cognitive science."[1] Without attempting to resolve any of these arguments, I will draw on the most relevant research and thinking in the field to provide useful lessons for business professionals. Despite the diversity of approaches of scientists working in the field, major progress has been made over the last decades in understanding many of the fundamental issues of human cognition. Delving into the theoretical and empirical background to the foundations of knowledge acquisition will be very valuable in building an understanding of how to design effective client communication and interaction. Unfortunately, this Appendix offers only a brief overview of the field, but I hope it stimulates interest and further study in what I believe is an increasingly critical aspect of leading business practice.

223

COGNITIVE STRUCTURE AND COGNITIVE STYLE

The two major topics we will cover are cognitive structure and cognitive style. Cognitive structure deals with the *structure* of the conceptual models on which people base their understanding of their environment. Understanding the common structure of people's mental models is extremely valuable in a variety of ways. Structuring ideas and information in ways that are aligned with the structural forms of mental models means they can be more easily assimilated and internalized. Familiarity with the structure of the mental models of individuals and groups enables far more effective approaches in enriching those models, and adding value to the decision-making processes on which they are based.

While cognitive structure examines common ground in human cognition, cognitive style looks at the *differences* between people as to how they take in information from their environment, make sense of it, and act on it. As such, understanding cognitive styles is very valuable in customizing presentations to and interactions with individuals and groups in order to result in the greatest knowledge transfer and perceived value.

MENTAL REPRESENTATIONS

We can never experience reality directly; we must rely on the information provided by our senses. Sensory experience is all we have on which to base how we think about the world. We must form internal representations of the world from our experiences in order to be able to think about it.

The terms *mental representation* and *mental model* are defined and used in a wide variety of ways by different scholars. To avoid confusion with others' definitions, I will use "mental representation" to mean how people represent their experiences, memories, imaginings, and concepts of the world; these constitute the basic elements used in their thinking. The term "mental model" refers to models of the world that people use to understand their environment and guide how they think and act in order to achieve their objectives; these are constructed from the building blocks of mental representations.

The idea that how people think is based on mental representations is widely (though not universally) accepted by cognitive scientists. Much of the debate focuses on the nature of the representations that people hold in their minds, and how they are used for thinking and knowledge acquisition.

It is worth pointing out that it is very difficult to gain awareness of our own mental processes, and while many will recognize some of the elements of mental representations in themselves, they are not likely to perceive them with any degree of accuracy. Still, most of the aspects we will discuss have been demonstrated empirically, and have proven to be useful in the effective communication of knowledge.

The Nature of Mental Representations

While the concept of mental representation has formed a basis for much of the study of cognitive psychology, there has been heated debate on the nature of those mental representations. The two major types of mental representations that have been proposed are analogical and propositional.

Analogical representations are internal sensory-based representations of external experience, which are effectively analogies of that experience. They are usually taken to mean visual imagery, though they can just as well refer to internally generated or perceived sounds, feelings, or other experiences. Essentially they are sensory constructs, meaning representations based on our five senses.

Propositional representations are abstract in that they are based on symbols and the relationships between them. As such, they are similar to language or mathematical formulae, though they function on a more fundamental level, representing the underlying concepts and relationships that people translate into and from language.

Other researchers have suggested other types of representation, however, analogical and propositional representations—with some variations on these—together cover most of the proposed formulations of the nature of mental representation. Much of the debate in cognitive science has centered on which of these two types of representation is correct, and the specifics of how they are manipulated in knowledge acquisition and reasoning.

Dual-Coding Theory

Dual-coding theory, proposed by Allan Paivio, has been perhaps the most influential approach to understanding mental representations.[2] This suggests that people in fact use both analogical and propositional representations in independent but interconnected systems. There has been strong experimental evidence to support the dual-coding theory.[3]

Each of the two representational systems specializes in representing and processing distinct types of information. The propositional system is mainly oriented to language and other tasks requiring sequential processing. The analogical system is usually considered to represent images, and as such deals with visual representations and other tasks requiring spatial or concurrent processing. Each system is proposed to use different units or symbols for representation, but related symbols are linked between the two systems. For example, the mental image of a cat would be linked to the concept and word "cat." The dual-coding theory is represented diagrammatically in Figure A–1.

This separation of representational systems into propositional and analogical components, or more crudely, words and pictures, reflects the popular distinction between left brain and right brain processing. Indeed evidence suggests some correlation between propositional and analogical processing and the hemispheres of the brain, though it would be a mistake to take these for the same idea.[4]

Sensory-Based Representations

People use analogical representations based on their senses. In other words, people primarily form internal representations that are visual

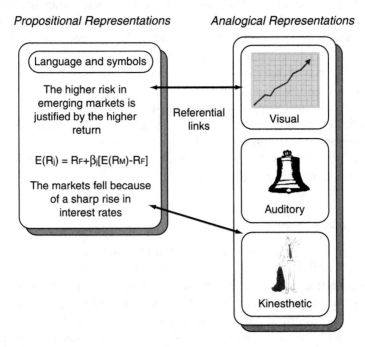

FIGURE A–1   A diagrammatic representation of dual-coding theory.

(images or pictures), auditory (sounds), or kinesthetic (physical sensations or feelings); though they can also be olfactory (referring to the sense of smell) and gustatory (referring to the sense of taste—for example, when we read a menu and form representations of what we would most enjoy eating).

Visual representations are in many situations the most efficient system for information and high-level concept manipulation. An immense amount of information can be contained in a visual representation, often more than in any single propositional representation, and in a way that can be manipulated and processed with speed and flexibility. Anecdotally, business people tend to show a preference for visual internal representations.

What are usually referred to as visual representations are better thought of as visuospatial—that is, combining visual representations with the apprehension of spatial relationships. This faculty can be particularly important in conceptual thinking and skills, and has been linked to mathematical ability. Forming internal visuospatial representations does not come easily to everyone, although these kinds of images can be extremely effective for communicating complex concepts to the right audience.[5]

One of the many useful distinctions from the field of neurolinguistic programming (NLP), originally developed by John Grinder and Richard Bandler in the early 1970s, is the idea of *submodalities,* which takes our understanding of analogical representations to a further level of richness.[6] These introduce further distinctions within each of the major modalities of the representational systems. For example, submodalities or distinctions within internal visual representations could include how bright or dim the representation is, how clear or blurred, how near or far and so on. The concept was actually first introduced by the American psychologist William James in 1890;[7] however, the field of NLP has found that varying the submodalities of representations can have a significant impact on understanding, emotion, and belief. Later in the Appendix we will examine preferences in the use of representational systems as a key element of cognitive style.

Language

Language is the primary structure used for propositional representations, and the basis of many aspects of thought. The topic of language as a basis for knowledge is clearly too vast to address here; however, a few distinctions will help us to understand language within the context of mental representations and models.

The great linguist Noam Chomsky in his early work on transformational grammar made the distinction between the *surface structure* and *deep structure* of language.[8] The surface structure consists of the actual words and syntax used in communication, while the deep structure is the structure of the underlying meaning beneath the communication and the relationships between the component concepts. In a simple illustration, the sentences, "He gave her the report," and "She was given the report by him," have different surface structures, but an identical meaning, and thus the same deep structure. Mental representations of language are formed at the level of deep structure or meaning rather than surface structure or the actual words used.[9] The act of interpreting the meaning of a sentence is the same as that of forming a mental representation of it.

Chomsky's work is largely based on the principle that all humans are born with a "language faculty," which means that we naturally learn whatever language we are exposed to when we are young, although that language faculty only allows certain rules in the structure and syntax of language. As such, while there are many thousands of languages in the world, every one of them has in common the same underlying "universal grammar," which is in fact determined by our biological nature. As such, the mental representations to which people have access in understanding language are based on this universal grammar.[10]

MENTAL MODELS

To review our definition from Chapter 4, a mental model is the model or representation we hold in our mind of the way we believe the world or some part of it works. Mental models are based on mental representations which are either or both analogical or propositional. They provide a framework that helps to give meaning to our perceptions in relation to our previous experiences.

Mental Models as the Foundation of Knowledge and Understanding

Our working definition of knowledge as "the capacity to act effectively" gives us insight into what it means to understand something. To be able to act effectively within a system requires us to have a model not only of how that system has worked in the past, but also of how it will act in the future, and our relationship with that system. That is what will allow us to act in a way that will (if our model is useful) achieve the results we desire.

Kenneth Craik, the first modern exponent of these ideas, wrote in 1943 that "If the organism carries a 'small-scale model' of external reality and its own possible actions within its head, it is able to try out various alternatives, conclude which is the best of them, react to future situations before they arise, utilize the knowledge of past events in dealing with the present and future, and in every way to react in a much fuller, safer, and more competent manner to the emergencies which face it."[11]

In a similar vein, Philip Johnson-Laird, author of the seminal book *Mental Models*, explains that: "If you know what causes a phenomenon, what results from it, how to influence, control, initiate or prevent it, how it relates to others' states of affairs or how it resembles them, how to predict its onset and course, what its internal or underlying 'structure' is, then to some extent you understand it. The psychological core of understanding, I shall assume, consists in your having a 'working model' of the phenomenon in your mind. If you understand inflation, a mathematical proof, the way a computer works, DNA, or a divorce, then you have a mental representation that serves as a model..."[12]

People's mental models can also be understood as their belief systems. People act on the basis of their mental models, meaning that they implicitly behave as if the foundations and assumptions on which their models are based are true. One way to get insight into people's mental models is to observe the implicit beliefs that guide their attitudes and behaviors.

Internalization and Integration

Internalization is the process of converting information and experiences into personal knowledge; this is a critical stage in knowledge transfer and all knowledge management. In order for experience and information to become knowledge, it must be integrated into our existing knowledge and understanding in some form. If there is no integration or connection to what we know already, then these are simply remembered facts, and do not contribute to our understanding of the world. New experience or information is integrated into our existing understanding by forming connections and associations to existing knowledge and experience, which ultimately means integrating it into our mental models. Since our mental models form the basis of our understanding and chosen action, new information must be integrated in some way into them in order to become knowledge.

The way these connections and associations are formed is based on the intrinsic structure of mental models, which is discussed below. Understanding these principles gives us real insight not only into mental models, but how information and experience is internalized into these mental models.

Bower and Hilgard noted that the more objects, patterns, and concepts are stored in memory, the more easily new knowledge about these is acquired and used in new contexts. Since learning is associative in terms of making linkages with existing concepts, the ease of acquiring new knowledge depends on the breadth of the categories into which knowledge is organized, the differentiation of those categories, and the richness of linkages across them.[13] This is a critical issue in knowledge acquisition; it means that diversity of knowledge and experience is one of the most fundamental factors in the ability to develop new knowledge, and that people who are overly focused in their experience and knowledge base can be handicapped in further knowledge acquisition.

More generally, the richer the connections and associations we make with our existing experience, the more powerful and useful the knowledge gained. If we hear or read some information, and we can relate it only weakly to our existing mental models, it will have limited impact. If we perceive many different associations and perspectives on the new information, it will have a significant impact on the content and possibly the structure of our mental models, and result in changed understanding.

This is a key reason why dialogue is one of the most powerful sources of changed understanding and richer mental models. Rich interaction between two or more different mental models and perspectives in the process of an ongoing conversation uncovers many potential associations, connections, and perspectives. In presenting information, giving multiple perspectives that relate as broadly as possible to the experience and knowledge base of the client will result in the most valuable knowledge acquisition.

THE STRUCTURE OF MENTAL MODELS

The basic structures of mental models are common to all people. As noted cognitive philosopher Jerry Fodor states, some of the most fundamental aspects of thought and belief are "grounded in the 'architecture' of mental representation."[14] We can never know the actual representations of the world that people hold in their minds, but we can discover some of the structures of their mental models, and how ideas and concepts are related within them. Understanding these structures provides us with a very powerful tool for instructing how we design the communication or elicitation of knowledge, and all interaction with our clients. As Alfred Korzybski pointed out, while a map or model is *not* the territory that it represents, its usefulness is based on it having a similar structure to its subject.[15]

Research in the field of cognitive science has allowed us to identify some of the underlying structures and forms of mental models that people have in common. Johnson-Laird suggests that the structures of mental models are identical to the perceived structures of the situations they represent.[16] What this in fact tells us is that the structures we perceive in our environment are aligned with the structures available to us in building our mental models.

The structure of mental models has three central attributes:

- Associative
- Hierarchical
- Systemic

We will go on to apply these principles in examining how stories, scenarios, and metaphors are used in the acquisition of knowledge.

Associative

Aristotle first proposed that all knowledge is based on associations between ideas; the idea of associations as a basis of knowledge and understanding has played an important role throughout the history of philosophy. Clearly people form associations between concepts and ideas. This has been modeled in cognitive psychology in the form of *semantic networks*, which describe the concepts that are associated mentally; and sometimes the degree of association or similarity between them, which determines the likelihood that one concept will "trigger" another. Semantic networks have been shown to be good models for predicting some experimental findings in memory and recognition, and they provide a basic framework for understanding the nature of the way associations are formed and used in cognition. A simple example representing part of one person's semantic network is illustrated in Figure A–2.

The primary ways in which associations between concepts are formed are:

- Similarity and Analogy
- Causality
- Contiguity
- Contrast

Similarity and Analogy

The most fundamental and important means of association is through perceived similarity. It can be argued that the foundation of thought is how people identify similarity between different things. This issue has been at the heart of much research in cognitive psychology, in an attempt to gain an understanding of how people categorize perceptions and concepts, and thus form associations between them.

Two things are perceived to be similar if they have one or more *attributes* in common. In Tversky's influential model, the degree of similarity between two concepts is based on the attributes they have in common, lessened by the attributes which are different or distinct.[17] Each person will perceive differently what the relevant attributes are, and

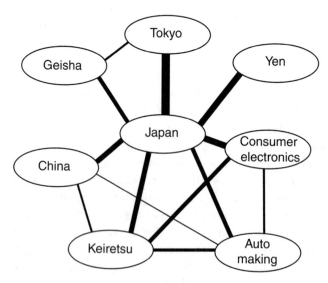

FIGURE A–2   Part of a person's semantic network.

their degree of similarity, although there is a common structure in how this is done. For example, some of the common attributes of Spain and Italy include being Mediterranean countries, predominantly Catholic, and having related Romantic languages, while some of the different attributes include the types of food they eat and their political systems. Based on their perception of the importance, and similarity or difference of these and other attributes, most people see greater similarity between Spain and Italy than, say, Spain and Germany.

While similarity refers to the commonality of attributes between concepts, analogy refers to the commonality of the relational structure of attributes between concepts. As such, in analogy the attributes of two concepts may not be common, and in fact usually are not, however, the structure of the relationships between the two concepts is similar. A couple of examples will help to distinguish between similarity and analogy. A mouse is like a rat, because they have a number of attributes in common: they look alike, they have whiskers, they both eat cheese, and so forth; that is, they are similar. However, an atom is like a solar system, not because electrons are like planets, but because the relationship of electrons to the nucleus is similar to the relationship of planets to the sun: the solar system is an analogy for an atom.

Dedre Gentner notes that our understanding of analogies "conveys a system of connected knowledge, not a mere assortment of independent facts," and proposes that when people use an analogy the relations that are mapped across domains are dominated by the higher-order relations.[18] Since understanding is largely based on the relationships between concepts, this mapping across domains of the high-level structure of relationships shows why analogies are one of the richest tools for knowledge communication.

Causality

Causality is a very important element underlying our mental models, and in indicating how different concepts are associated or linked. Our judgments of causality that are implicit in our mental models are critical in determining how we act in seeking the outcomes we desire.

On one level, the basic rules that people use to judge causality hold no major surprises, and experimental evidence generally supports what the philosopher David Hume proposed more than 200 years ago. For example, whether one event causes another is often judged according to the time interval and regularity between the perceived cause and effect, and how physically close the two events are. The covariation—the degree to which two events occur or do not occur together—is an important cue to judging causality.[19]

On the other hand, the way people judge causality and probability has been shown to be subject to many errors and distortions, and a whole field of study on "cognitive bias" has arisen to research how people misjudge expectations of events and the relationships between them. Just one example is the so-called "conjunction fallacy," in which people often judge the probability of two events happening together as higher than that of one of them happening in isolation.[20]

Contiguity

Association between two ideas is often engendered because they have been experienced as contiguous, that is occurring close together in time or in space. For example, if you heard a particular song on your first date with your partner, hearing that song again will often evoke those associations and memories.

Contrast

In addition to similarity, association can be formed by contrast, in linking ideas because they are perceived to be opposites. In this way black can be associated with white, and fat with thin. This is usually less important than other means of forming associations, but is still common.

Chunking and Hierarchies

George Miller proposed in his landmark paper "The Magical Number Seven, Plus or Minus Two" that people can only think about approximately seven "chunks" of information simultaneously.[21] This is still generally accepted as valid. The term "chunk" is used to mean an integrated unit of information, such as a number, word, or concept. Herbert Simon discovered that the number of chunks people could hold depended on the complexity of the chunks; he later stated that in many situations people only hold four to five chunks simultaneously.[22] One of the critical lessons from these ideas is that we cannot expect people to take in simultaneously more than five to seven concepts or ideas, so that in communication and presentation we must limit ourselves to this number of concepts.

If you group a number of concepts together on the basis of similarity or any other association, you can then label this group and think of it as a single unit—it has become a single chunk. This frees up our limited thinking capacity to take in additional concepts. For example, if China, India, Thailand, Indonesia, Brazil, Ukraine, and Hungary are determined to be emerging markets for your services, these can then be grouped together and thought about as a single concept of "emerging markets."

If the chunks formed by grouping similar concepts are in turn grouped with others, similar chunks—in the instance above "emerging markets" may be grouped with, say, "developed markets" and "minor markets"—then a hierarchy of concepts is formed. In this way, the limitations of human thought—specifically on the number of ideas it can hold in mind simultaneously—automatically lead to a hierarchical structure of thinking.[23] This is shown in Figure A–3.

This process of chunking concepts to form hierarchies is in fact the basis of the development of expertise. Once people have sufficient familiarity with a topic to perceive the underlying similarities between concepts, they can form chunks that are more meaningful in their relationships, and build a hierarchical structure of knowledge that is relevant and useful in classifying concepts and instances. It is only in building this hierarchy over time that experts can acquire a "big picture" view of their field of expertise, which reflects the structure and relationships of the key relevant concepts.

This model has been supported by a range of experiments. One asked novice and expert physicists to classify problems into related groups. It emerged that the novices grouped problems in terms of the surface features that were evident in their initial appearance, while the experts grouped them based on the underlying principles relating the problems.[24]

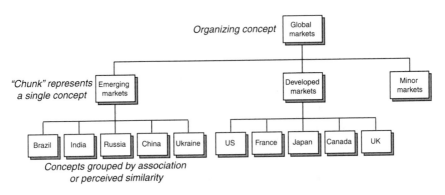

FIGURE A–3   Chunking builds a hierarchical structure of concepts.

Systemic

In addition to being associative and hierarchical, mental models are also systemic, in the sense of incorporating nonlinear and recursive structures. Systemic thinking is about perceiving and understanding the complex network of relationships that defines a system as opposed to an isolated element. A consequence of these multiple relationships is that the effects of one element of the system can flow through the system to end up influencing and impacting that same element, meaning that thinking about systems must incorporate feedback and self-reference, and cannot rely solely on linear thought processes. Douglas Hofstadter in his Pulitzer Prize winning classic *Gödel, Escher, Bach* developed the theme that consciousness, as well as other phenomena such as imagery and analogies, is based on recursivity, or what he called "Strange Loops,"[25] while cognitive scientists Maturana and Varela have argued that cognition is a biological phenomenon stemming from the intrinsic circularity of the organization of living systems.[26] Pursuing another angle, M.I.T.'s John Morecroft found that the broadly accepted view that human decision making is based on bounded rationality, as originally proposed by Herbert Simon and his colleagues, results directly in the feedback structures on which system dynamics are based.[27] Today cognitive mapping techniques consistently incorporate these recursive and self-referential aspects of mental models.[28]

Systems diagrams have been explicitly designed to represent systemic models and situations, notably in their implicit portrayal of causality, and are a very effective means of communicating complex relationships and principles. A simple example of a systems diagram is shown in Figure 1–2 in Chapter 1 of this book; basic guidelines for developing systems diagrams are can be found in Senge, and O'Connor and McDermott.[29]

Scenarios and Stories

People think about and understand the world in terms of scenarios and stories. Neurobiologist Ingvar, by examining the role of the prefrontal cortex in how people organize their cognition of time, proposed that it is through our "memories of the future"—which are imagined scenarios of what may happen—that we perceive meaning in the world.[30] This implies that it is intrinsically human to form scenarios of the future as a basis for reasoning and action.

Research by Tversky and Kahnemann suggests that people will judge the probability of a given scenario to be higher if it is more detailed, contains representative events, and is causally linked.[31] Stimulating people's imagination through the presentation of scenarios will cause them to add further detail, thus building richer mental representations of those scenarios, and the attribution of a higher likelihood to them. This has implications in many domains of human behavior, however, emphasizes the importance of rich and detailed descriptions of possible scenarios or events in knowledge communication.

Many practitioners have emphasized the importance of stories in knowledge acquisition. Part of the reason for this is the way people organize their understanding of causality temporally, as studied by Ingvar. We experience the world as a sequence of events, so it is far easier for us to find similarities and internalize knowledge based on other sequences of events, which we call stories. In addition, stories are rich in the potential for analogies; people will find their own useful analogies and lessons that they can map against their mental models in order to find more effective ways of thinking.

Metaphors

Metaphors are tools. Metaphors are poetry. Metaphors are bridges to connect our knowledge. Many people think of metaphors as linguistic flourishes, but they are in fact at the very heart of the way we think, and very powerful tools for communicating knowledge effectively. People acquire knowledge by relating it to their existing experience and understanding. Presenting ideas and information with the aid of metaphors inherently provides people with a means and structure for integrating these into their mental models, in a way that draws out the key salient points, and enables rich connections to form.

Leading linguists and cognitive scientists George Lakoff and Mark Johnson, in their delightful and influential book, *Metaphors We Live By*, explore in detail the nature of the metaphors that guide our everyday perceptions and communication.[32] They find that most of our conceptual system is metaphorical in nature, and in fact argue that "human thought processes are largely metaphorical." Metaphors are a very valuable resource in evoking conceptual understanding, of course as a complement to more prosaic approaches.

Applications of the Structure of Mental Models

Understanding the underlying structure of people's mental models is the best possible foundation for designing the communication of conceptual knowledge. The associative, hierarchical, and systemic nature of the structure of mental models suggests that these structures should also be implicit in the information and ideas we present.

Hierarchy has traditionally been a fairly strong feature of much business communication, though it could be used in far more diverse means, particularly in presenting systems of knowledge, and in positioning specific communications within a broader context and framework. The lateral associations and relationships between concepts are less commonly explicit in communication, partially as this is very hard to represent effectively and succinctly in text. The failure to address the systemic nature of concepts has been a major weakness in most business communication, however, this is rapidly changing as these ideas become more widely accepted. Systems diagrams and other illustrations that indicate the recursive nature of causality are valuable tools. Generally, the adequate representation of these key structural attributes in communication requires the complementary use of text and images.

There is strong empirical evidence that scenarios and stories are among the most powerful means of conveying structured information and ideas. Not only should story-based approaches be used extensively in high-value communication, but these should involve as broad a range of styles and media as possible, including print, voice, movies, and enactment. Metaphors are one of the most useful tools for conveying conceptual information, and can be presented either in words and images or both. In order to be effective, however, they must be well thought-out, as the complex relationships between two ideas may not always fully support the intended communication.

COGNITIVE STYLE

The idea of cognitive style recognizes that we all have different approaches and styles to thinking and acting. Cognitive style can be considered a subset of the broader field of personality style, which encompasses all aspects of how a person thinks and behaves. The fields can be difficult to distinguish, and both are useful to us. However, our primary intention and focus here is to understand better the differences in how people perform knowledge-based functions such as taking in information, analyzing it, and making decisions. The idea of personality styles has been applied, for example, to teaching salespeople to adapt their approaches to match the personality and preferences of their clients, more commonly as a sales tool than as a way of adding greater value. Much of the value of understanding clients' cognitive styles is enabling you to match their preferences for dealing with information with the way in which you present information and communicate with them, thus building a foundation for rich client relationships.

Myers-Briggs Type Indicator

The most widely used personality profiling test in business is the Myers-Briggs Type Indicator (MBTI), which was developed in the early 1940s and is now administered to more than three million people annually. It is based on the original personality distinctions of psychologist Carl Jung, though it has been developed into a more rigorous and testable framework. While it is more a measure of personality style than cognitive style per se, it is useful in many ways, such as in engineering the creative abrasion described in Chapter 8, and has significant cognitive aspects.[33]

The MBTI categorizes people along four dimensions, each defined by two polar opposites of their primary orientation or preference. These dimensions are Extrovert/Introvert; Sensor/Intuitor; Thinker/Feeler; and Judger/Perceiver.

The dimension of Extrovert/Introvert examines attitudes toward the external world which are reflected in behaviors. Sensor/Intuitor is an important cognitive dimension. Sensors are oriented to concrete information, evidence, and facts—what they can sense directly— whereas Intuitors tend to perceive abstract relationships and meaning, and rely more on their intuition than descriptive facts in understanding the world. Thinkers tend to think rationally, and attempt to be objective in assessing their actions, while Feelers choose a subjective approach, and are inclined to base decisions on their values rather than analysis. Judgers prefer order, structure, and predictability in their environment, whereas Perceivers tend to be spontaneous and to assess and respond to situations as they develop, rather than plan in detail.

Understanding the preferences of our clients along these dimensions is clearly very valuable in a broad range of contexts, including many aspects of relationship development and management. Many companies provide salespeople as well as other staff with training in the MBTI to increase their awareness and ability to communicate effectively with people who have contrasting personality styles. Of the four dimensions in the MBTI, an understanding of Sensor/Intuitor is the most directly relevant in designing knowledge communication, although the others are all valuable in developing richer communication and client relationships.

Learning Style Inventory

The Learning Style Inventory (LSI) was developed on the basis of work by David Kolb on learning cycles, described in Chapter 8. It identifies how people prefer to learn; as such it is directly relevant to our concerns of maximizing the utility of knowledge transfer. Understanding the diversity of different learning styles can be very valuable in adapting and tailoring our communication.

The LSI combines the four phases in the learning cycle—abstract conceptualization, active experimentation, concrete experience, and reflective observation—into pairs of preferences. This results in four learning style types: converger, diverger, assimilator, and accomodator. In brief, convergers are best at identifying practical uses for ideas, divergers prefer to observe situations from many perspectives, assimilators are best at taking in diverse information and synthesizing it into a structured form, and accomodators learn mainly from direct experience and experimentation. Each style demonstrates different preferences in taking in information and developing personal knowledge.[34]

This framework is probably more useful than the MBTI in constructing teams for, say, knowledge co-creation. The LSI is certainly a useful tool for people to develop greater awareness and thus flexibility in their own learning styles, but also very much for gaining insight into clients' preferences in dealing with information and learning in the course of professional service relationships, and using that to refine their approaches and interactions.

Representational System Preference

We have seen that people use visual, auditory, and kinesthetic representations in their mental representations. Everyone uses each of these representational systems to some degree, however, most individuals will demonstrate a preference for one of these systems in any given situation. This concept, originally introduced by the field of NLP, has been taken and applied broadly in many contexts. In the context of knowledge transfer, it is most useful in designing interaction and the presentation of information.

It is also useful to contrast analogical and propositional representations, and to note that not only do people demonstrate preferences among sensory representational systems, but also between these and propositional representations. Some people are heavily oriented to propositional representations, and almost only think in "language," whereas others favor visual or other sensory-based "thinking."

Metaprograms

Metaprograms in general describe the perceptual or behavioral preferences or orientation of a person along a given dimension. For example, the four dimensions of the Myers-Briggs test can be considered to be metaprograms. The value of the concept is that it allows us to focus on and develop the metaprograms or dimensions that particularly interest us, in this case effective knowledge communication and elicitation.

One basic metaprogram that we have found to be of value in professional communication is that of Complexity/Simplicity. In communicating rich conceptual information, for example, research on international financial markets or emergent industries, people tend to show preferences for complexity or simplicity of the causal structures implicit in the presentation. Some people tend to accept only explanations or analyses that exceed a certain level of complexity, whereas others prefer frameworks that contain a limited number of elements and interrelationships. Considerably greater refinement is possible in understanding the diversity of people's preferences in taking in highly conceptual information, however, applying even this simple filter of cognitive preference can greatly enhance communication.

Scenario Formation

As we have seen, people often think and make decisions on the basis of possible future scenarios which they have generated. Gaining insight into the structure of how clients form and work with mental scenarios in their analysis and decision making can be very valuable in tailoring communication. This process is clearly challenging, as clients very rarely have any perception of this themselves. Still, it is possible to gain some understanding of these processes within an ongoing relationship.

Scenario formation is an aspect of cognitive style, as people display different preferences for how they form scenarios in their analysis and decision making. Some of the key dimensions include the degree to which thinking is focused on a single central scenario, as opposed to several scenarios that are all considered reasonably plausible; in how much detail the central scenario is developed; to what degree secondary scenarios can be contradictory to the central scenario; and how flexible the central scenario is in changing given new information. Another important preference is whether people form scenarios in analogical or propositional forms (or both). This parameter will vary depending on the context—situations involving personal experience such as social interaction are more likely to be represented by images or conversations, while conceptual issues such as the state of the economy will tend to be more propositional in nature. Nevertheless, individuals will show markedly different individual preferences. Having even some idea of these aspects of how a client forms mental scenarios in making decisions can be very valuable in being able to present information and ideas more effectively, and add greater value.

Applications of Cognitive Style

As we have seen, there are a wide variety of frames and perspectives on the diversity of cognitive styles. The broader study of personality styles assists us in the full scope of our interactions with others, while understanding cognitive styles is primarily valuable in enhancing the communication and development of knowledge with others.

The greatest value of understanding cognitive styles is in direct contact with clients, so front-line professionals need training and development in an appropriate model or models of cognitive style, selected for relevance to the ways in which they usually interact with their clients. This should be specifically framed to provide a starting point for professionals to develop their understanding on an ongoing basis as they apply what they learn in their client interactions.

The most obvious application of cognitive styles is in tailoring interaction with individuals and small groups to result in the most effective flow of knowledge. These are basic skills in the tool-kit of the facilitator, especially in knowledge creation projects.

On a broader level, understanding the diversity of cognitive styles means that all communication and interaction should be designed to be useful and accessible to all people, rather than a narrow group of people. The design of everything from documents to conferences should specifically consider these issues. Most people (and professionals are perhaps more guilty than most!) tend to communicate and interact in ways that suit their own cognitive style, on the implicit assumption that others think like they do. Educating professionals to communicate more effectively to a broader audience can result in substantial benefits.

ELICITING MENTAL MODELS

Immense value can be derived from helping to make an individual's or group's mental models explicit, as we saw in Chapter 4. Some of the benefits of this process are that it allows clients:

- To understand better the basis on which they are making decisions, and their underlying assumptions
- To enrich and enhance the usefulness of their mental models for the situation
- To integrate individual mental models within a group
- To create a framework for constructive discussion
- To establish whether the actions they are taking are in fact consistent with their mental models

Over the last couple of decades, a number of researchers have been developing and experimenting with approaches to making mental models explicit. As Eden points out, however, "the process of articulation is a significant influence on present and future cognition."[35] In other words, the process of making mental models explicit changes the mental models. For academic purposes, this is a significant problem in understanding the nature of people's mental models, and how they relate to their behavior. In professional services and consulting, this is not a significant issue, as virtually invariably the changes that happen in making mental models explicit result in richer and more useful mental models.

Gaining insight into how you think requires and provokes reflection and consideration, which can only result in enhancements. As such, simply engaging in the process of making clients' mental models explicit can add very significant value in itself, by the knowledge development it evokes. Cossette and Audet write of the "emancipatory" properties of cognitive maps, and distinguish research in the field into the use of cognitive maps as decision-making tools, and their application to "personal development," in which self-examination facilitates the modification of attitudes and behavior.[36]

Individual and Group Mental Models

The basic concept of mental models clearly refers to individuals. It is individuals who build mental models based on their experience, and use these to understand the world and decide how best to act effectively. While some scholars suggest that it is inappropriate to treat a group or organization as though it has a mental model in the same way as that of an individual, it clearly can be done; and in a business context the issue is whether it is *useful* to do so, and if so how best to adapt approaches to suit groups.[37]

Certainly groups have at least some shared experiences and commonality in terms of understanding their environment, and use this to make decisions that reflect what is in effect an implicit group mental model. In order for a group to come to an effective decision, there must be some element of shared meaning.[38] As a group works together, there will be further shared experience; and in the ongoing discussion of the meaning and relevance of that experience, the group's mental models will be reinforced, in terms of greater integration of the individuals' mental models, and ability to make effective group decisions.[39] This process of integrating individual mental models within a group and developing a useful and flexible group framework for making decisions is greatly facilitating by thinking in terms of the group's mental models, and working with the group at that level. The fundamental approaches of much strategy consulting work, for example, are based on an implicit assumption that the client's senior executives have collective mental models.

Cognitive Mapping

Cognitive mapping covers a broad range of techniques for developing visual and sometimes data-based representations of a person or group's cognition of some part of their environment. Other terms such as "concept mapping" and "causal mapping" are sometimes used for related ideas. Here our focus is on cognitive maps that help to make explicit people's mental models, in the sense of their understanding of behavior and causality on which they base their decisions and actions in a particular domain.

A wide variety of approaches has been developed and used for building cognitive maps.[40] These techniques can be used for capturing expertise and knowledge, studying organizational decision making, and a variety of other processes; however, we are primarily interested in using them as practical tools for working with individuals and groups to enrich and integrate their mental models. This goal is most easily achieved in a facilitated process, which draws out people's perceptions of key concepts, the relationships between them, and maps these visually so people can iteratively refine their collective understanding through consideration and discussion. These can be mapped on whiteboards or paper, or alternatively software can be used to represent the cognitive maps and analyze the resulting framework.[41] One of the valuable focal points for discussion is getting agreement on the meanings of the core concepts or units on which the map is based—this facilitates building a shared vocabulary for the group.

More structured approaches can sometimes be valuable. In these, individuals are commonly interviewed using consistent methodologies to uncover the key elements and causal relationships implicit in their mental models, and shown the resultant maps for feedback. The cognitive maps of the individuals can then be used as a basis for work as a group, or combined into composite maps.

A simple example of a basic style of cognitive map, depicting part of one professional's thinking, is shown in Figure A–4; a "plus" symbol on an arrow indicates that this relationship supports the target concept, while a "minus" symbol indicates erosion of the concept. A preliminary glance at this simple map suggests an awareness of key business issues but a lack of strategic clarity on the part of the subject. Building a more complex map of existing thinking would usually be just the first step in developing an enhanced conception of the strategic direction of the organization in the context of a systemic understanding of its business environment.

VISUAL KNOWLEDGE ACQUISITION

Because people to whatever degree think visually, it makes sense that showing people visual representations will help their understanding and acquisition of knowledge. Acquiring knowledge is largely about forming associations and relationships within and between concepts and domains. Visual representations implicitly allow the depiction of relationships in two and even three dimensions, with variables such as size, direction, type and strength of relationship, and many more easily represented.

The empirical evidence strongly supports the value of visual representations in knowledge acquisition. One researcher has stated that "probably no other instructional device leads to more consistently bene-

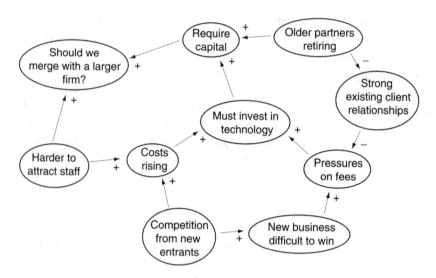

FIGURE A–4   An example of a basic cognitive map.

ficial results than does adding pictures to text," noting that those benefits have been shown to extend across a wide variety of tests, subjects,
and types and functions of pictures.[42] In studies of the use of visual representations in the development of mental models in science education,
researchers found evidence that visuals resulted in superior mental
models, including better and more accurately organized concepts.[43]
Interestingly, these and other studies have also shown that the addition
of graphics can improve the performance of high-IQ students more than
low-IQ students. Winn suggests that more able students are better able
to handle and use the greater information load given by pictures supplementing text, which can overburden less able students.[44]

The key issue is that if people perceive and think visuospatially as
well as propositionally, then we need to present information and ideas
to them both propositionally (in words and equations) and visually (in
diagrams and illustrations). As such, visual representations will almost
never stand alone, but are an incredibly valuable *complement* to text,
especially for concepts that are hard to verbalize. Text is still often used
alone, limiting its ability to be effectively internalized as knowledge.

Cognitive load theory, developed by John Sweller, suggests that
instruction will be more effective if it takes into account the limitations
of working memory.[45] One of the techniques this implies is avoiding
splitting the attention of learners. In situations in which text and visuals

provide complementary messages, integrating these into a single representation that incorporates the necessary text into the diagram will facilitate learning.

On a very practical level, well-designed visual representations help cut through information overload in a number of ways. Visuals attract the eye, drawing clients' valuable attention. Not only do people tend to look at the diagrams in documents before text, but the reduced time required to assimilate information using visuals means that people will consistently prefer those documents, and have their information burden eased.

Symbols and Conventions

A wide variety of symbols and conventions is used in visual representations. Some of these reflect how people without preconceptions tend to understand diagrams, others are learned through convention, and some differ across cultures. Without trying to cover these conventions exhaustively, it is worth pointing out a few that represent the sorts of issues that can be useful in the design of visual concept representations. They include:

- The size of the representation of a concept is perceived to be related to its importance.
- In a diagram that shows associated concepts, their physical proximity on the page or screen are considered to show how closely related the concepts are.
- A number of boxes placed in a line below a single box are assumed to represent a hierarchy.
- A left-to-right string of tasks or events is perceived to represent a sequence occurring over time.

Using these types of conventions allows the implicit communication of conceptual relationships in easily assimilated representations. Many of these types of conventions are taken for granted when designing visuals; it can be useful to use them more deliberately in order to structure the communication of complex ideas.

SUMMARY: MENTAL MODELS AND KNOWLEDGE ACQUISITION

To transfer knowledge effectively we must understand how people acquire knowledge and understanding. Cognitive science and related disciplines provide valuable lessons for business professionals. An understanding of these fields will become an increasingly important part of the core knowledge and expertise required by all professionals.

Our mental models are the foundation of how we understand our world and act in order to achieve the results we desire. Knowledge acquisition is about integrating new experiences and information into our existing mental models; the breadth and richness of our existing mental models determines how easily and usefully we can internalize new experience. If we understand the *structure* of how people build mental models, and the *differences* in how they take in information and act on it, we are able to communicate far more effectively in allowing others to integrate it as their own personal knowledge.

Much empirical evidence exists to help us to understand the fundamental nature of the structure of mental models, as well as a range of frameworks and tools we can use to gain an understanding of the cognitive styles of our clients. Cognitive mapping, which covers a broad range of approaches, is a powerful tool for eliciting, enriching, and integrating the mental models of individuals and groups, while the judicious use of visual representations can greatly assist effective knowledge acquisition.

These insights, tools, and techniques are potentially very useful and effective in the context of all knowledge-based client relationships, but are by no means simple to learn and apply. It is an ongoing journey to gain deeper insight into how the people you work with acquire knowledge, and to refine the ways you interact with them so as to facilitate their ability to acquire and develop knowledge. The rewards, however, are immense, as the strong positive feedback loop of knowledge-based client relationships means that gaining even a slight edge over your competitors in your ability to develop richer knowledge-based client interaction will result in ever-closer and more profitable relationships, with abundant value creation for both you and your clients.

NOTES

1. Ray Jackendoff, *Languages of the Mind: Essays on Mental Representation* (Cambridge, MA: MIT Press, 1995), 18.

2. See for example Allan Paivio, *Mental Representations: A Dual-Coding Approach* (Oxford, UK: Oxford University Press, 1986).

3. See for example Allan Paivio, "The Empirical Case for Dual Coding," in *Imagery, Memory, and Cognition: Essays in Honor of Allan Paivio*, J. C. Yuille, ed. (Hillsdale, NJ: Lawrence Erlbaum Associates Inc., 1983).

4. For a review of experimental evidence on the dual-coding theory, see for example Michael Eysenck and Mark Keane, *Cognitive Psychology: A Student's Handbook*, 3rd ed. (Hove, UK: Psychology Press, 1995).

5. For a detailed study of visuospatial cognition, see Manuel de Vega and Marc Marschark, eds. *Models of Visuospatial Cognition* (New York: Oxford University Press, 1996).

6. See for example Robert B. Dilts, Todd Epstein, and Robert W. Dilts, *Tools for Dreamers: Strategies for Creativity and the Structure of Innovation* (Capitola, CA: Meta Publications, 1991): 372.

7. William James, *The Principles of Psychology*, 1890, chap. 18. James also described the principles of mental representations in his groundbreaking book, which is available on the Web at www.yorku.ca/dept/psych/classics/James/Principles/index.htm.

8. See Noam Chomsky, *Aspects of the Theory of Syntax* (Cambridge, MA: MIT Press, 1965).

9. For an example of experimental confirmation of this see Philip N. Johnson-Laird and R. Stevenson, "Memory for Syntax," *Nature* 227 (1970): 412.

10. See for example Noam Chomsky, *Language and Problems of Knowledge: The Managua Lectures.* (Cambridge, MA: MIT Press, 1988).

11. From Kenneth Craik, *The Nature of Explanation* (Cambridge, UK: Cambridge University Press, 1943), as quoted in Philip N. Johnson-Laird, *Mental Models: Towards a Cognitive Science of Language, Inference and Consciousness* (Cambridge, UK: Cambridge University Press, 1983).

12. Johnson-Laird, op. cit., 2.

13. Gordon H. Bower and Ernest R. Hilgard, *Theories of Learning* (Englewood Cliffs, NJ: Prentice Hall, 1981).

14. Jerry A. Fodor, *Concepts: Where Cognitive Science Went Wrong* (Oxford, UK: Oxford University Press, 1998): 27.

15. Alfred Korzybski, *Science and Sanity: An Introduction to Non-Aristotelian Systems and General Semantics*, 2d ed. (Lancaster, PA: International Non-Aristotelian Library Publishing, 1941): 58.

16. Johnson-Laird, op. cit.

17. Amos Tversky, "Features of Similarity," *Psychological Review* 84 (1977): 327–352.

18. Dedre Gentner, "Structure-Mapping: A Theoretical Framework for Analogy," *Cognitive Science* 7 (1983): 155–170.

19. See Hillel J. Einhorn and Robin M. Hogarth, "Judging Probable Cause," *Psychological Review* 99, no. 1 (1986): 3–19.

20. Amos Tversky and Daniel Kahneman, "Extensional versus Intuitive Reasoning: The Conjunction Fallacy in Probability Judgment," *Psychological Review* 90 (1983): 293–315.

21. George A. Miller, "The Magical Number Seven, Plus or Minus Two," *Psychological Review* 63 (1956): 81–93.

22. Herbert A. Simon, "How Big Is a Chunk?" *Science* 183 (1974): 482–488.

23. Miller, Galanter, and Pribram suggest that all intentional behavior is guided by hierarchical plans, driven by the attempt to use our limited memory capabilities. See George A. Miller, Eugene Galanter, and Karl H. Pribram, *Plans and the Structure of Behavior* (New York: Holt, 1960): 130–132.

24. From M. T. H. Chi, P. J. Feltovich, and R. Glaser, "Categorization and Representation of Physics Problems by Experts and Novices," *Cognitive Science* 5 (1981): 121–152; and M. T. H. Chi, R. Glaser, and E. Rees, "Expertise in Problem Solving," in *Advances in the Psychology of Human Intelligence*, vol. 2, ed. R. J. Sternberg (Hillsdale, NJ: Lawrence Erlbaum Associates, Inc., 1983), as described in Eysenck and Keane.

25. Douglas Hofstadter, *Gödel, Escher, Bach: An Eternal Golden Braid* (New York: Basic Books, 1979).

26. H. Maturana and F. Varela, *Autopoiesis and Cognition: The Realization of the Living* (Dordrecht, Netherlands; Boston: D. Reidel, 1980).

27. John D. W. Morecroft, "System Dynamics: Portraying Bounded Rationality," *Omega* 11, no. 2 (1983): 131–142.

28. See for example Michel Bougon, Nancy Baird, John M. Komocar, and William Ross, "Identifying Strategic Loops: The Self-Q Interviews," in *Mapping Strategic Thought*, A. S. Huff, ed. (Chichester, UK: John Wiley & Sons, 1990); and Colin Eden and Fran Ackerman, "The Analysis of Cause Maps," *Journal of Management Studies* 29, no. 3 (May 1992): 309–323.

29. See Senge; Joseph O'Connor, and Ian McDermott, *The Art of System Thinking: Essential Skills for Creativity and Problem Solving* (London: Thorsons, 1997).

30. D. H. Ingvar, "'Memory of the Future: An Essay on the Temporal Organization of Conscious Awareness," *Human Neurobiology* 4 (1985): 127–136.

31. Tversky and Kahnemann, op. cit.

32. George Lakoff and Mark Johnson, *Metaphors We Live By* (Chicago: The University of Chicago Press, 1980).

33. Dorothy Leonard specifically suggests using the MBTI to design creative abrasion. See D. A. Leonard and S. Straus, "Putting Your Company's Whole Brain to Work," *Harvard Business Review* 75, no. 4 (July-August 1997).

34. Kolb.

35. Colin Eden, "On the Nature of Cognitive Maps," *Journal of Management Studies* 29, no. 3 (May 1992): 261–265.

36. Pierre Cossette and Michel Audet, "Mapping of an Idiosyncratic Schema," *Journal of Management Studies* 29, no. 3 (May 1992): 325–347.

37. See for example Eden, op. cit.

38. For a good review of the relevant literature on consensus and shared meaning, see Choo, 80–84.

39. See Kees van der Heijden and Colin Eden, "The Theory and Praxis of Reflective Learning in Strategy Making," in *Managerial and Organizational Cognition: Theory, Methods and Research*. Colin Eden and J. C. Spender, eds. (London: Sage, 1998): 58–75.

40. Very useful reviews of a range of approaches to cognitive mapping are provided in Anne S. Huff, ed. *Mapping Strategic Thought* (Chichester, UK: John Wiley & Sons, 1990); and Colin Eden and J. C. Spender, eds. *Managerial and Organizational Cognition: Theory, Methods, and Research* (London: Sage, 1998).

41. An example of cognitive mapping software is Decision Explorer (previously COPE), distributed by Banxia and Scolari.

42. B Weidermann, "When Good Pictures Fail," in *Knowledge Acquisition from Text and Pictures,* H. Mandl and J. R. Levin, eds. (Netherlands: Elsevier Science Publishers B.V., 1989).

43. W. D. Winn, "The Effect of Block-Word Diagrams on the Structuring of Science Concepts as a Function of General Ability," *Journal of Research in Science Teaching* 17 (1980): 201–211; and R. E. Mayer, J. L. Dyck, and L. K. Cook, "Techniques That Help Readers Build Mental Models from Scientific Text: Definitions, Pretraining, and Signaling," *Journal of Educational Psychology* 76 (1984): 1089–1105, as quoted in W. D. Winn, "Design and Use of Instructional Graphics," in *Knowledge Acquisition from Text and Pictures,* H. Mandl and J. R. Levin, eds. (Netherlands: Elsevier Science Publishers B.V., 1989): 135.

44. Winn (1989) again quotes Winn (1980), as well as P. E. Parkhurst and F. M. Dwyer. "An Experimental Assessment of Students' IQ Level and Their Ability to Profit from Visualized Instructions," *Journal of Instructional Psychology* 10 (1983): 9–20.

45. See for example P. Chandler and J. Sweller, "Cognitive Load Theory and the Format of Instruction," *Cognition and Instruction* #8 (1991): 293–332.

Bibliography

Abramson, Gary. "Their Pain, Your Gain." *CIO Enterprise* (October 15, 1998).

Allee, Verna. *The Knowledge Evolution: Expanding Organizational Intelligence.* Boston: Butterworth–Heinemann, 1997.

Argyris, Chris. "Single-Loop and Double-Loop Models in Research on Decision Making." *Administrative Science Quarterly* (21 September 1976): 363–375.

Arthur, Brian W. "Competing Technologies, Increasing Returns, and Lock-In by Historical Events." *The Economic Journal*, no. 99 (March 1989): 116–131.

Ashby, W. Ross. *An Introduction to Cybernetics.* London: Chapman & Hall, 1956.

Badarraco, Joseph L. *The Knowledge Link: How Firms Compete through Strategic Alliances.* Boston: Harvard Business School Press, 1991.

Bartlett, Christopher A., and Sumantra Ghoshal. "Managing across Borders: New Organizational Responses." *Sloan Management Review* (Fall 1987): 43–53.

Bateson, Gregory. *Steps to an Ecology of Mind.* London: Paladin, 1973.

Beach, Lee Roy. *The Psychology of Decision Making: People in Organizations.* Thousand Oaks, CA: Sage Publications, 1997.

Bolman, Lee, and Terrence Deal. *Reframing Organizations: Artistry, Choice, and Leadership.* 2d ed. San Francisco: Jossey-Bass, 1997.

Bougon, Michel, Nancy Baird, John M. Komocar, and William Ross. "Identifying Strategic Loops: The Self-Q Interviews." In *Mapping Strategic Thought*, edited by A. S. Huff. Chichester, UK: John Wiley & Sons, 1990.

Bower, Gordon H., and Ernest R. Hilgard. *Theories of Learning.* Englewood Cliffs, NJ: Prentice Hall, 1981.

Bresnahan, Jennifer. "The Latest in Suits." *CIO Enterprise* (October 15, 1998).

Brooking, Annie. *Intellectual Capital: Core Asset for the Third Millenium Enterprise.* London: International Thomson Business Press, 1996.

Brown, John Seely, and Estee Solomon Gray. "The People Are the Company." *Fast Company*, no. 1 (November 1995): 78.

Buzan, Tony, and Barry Buzan. *The Mind Map Book.* Rev. ed. London: BBC Books, 1993.

Capon, Andrew. "Setting Sail into the Digital Age." *Global Investor* (April 1999).

Chandler, P., and J. Sweller, "Cognitive Load Theory and the Format of Instruction." *Cognition and Instruction* 8 (1991): 293–332.

Chomsky, Noam. *Aspects of the Theory of Syntax.* Cambridge, MA: MIT Press, 1965.

———. *Language and Problems of Knowledge: The Managua Lectures.* Cambridge, MA: MIT Press, 1988.

Choo, Chun Wei. *The Knowing Organization: How Organizations Use Information to Construct Meaning, Create Knowledge, and Make Decisions.* New York: Oxford University Press, 1998.

Clarke, Thomas, and Stewart Clegg. *Changing Paradigms: The Transformation of Management Knowledge for the 21st Century.* London: HarperBusiness, 1998.

Cohen, Wesley M., and Daniel A. Levinthal. "Absorptive Capacity: A New Perspective on Learning and Innovation." *Administrative Science Quarterly* 35 (1990): 128–152.

Cossette, Pierre, and Michel Audet. "Mapping of an Idiosyncratic Schema." *Journal of Management Studies* 29, no. 3 (May 1992): 325–347.

Craik, Kenneth. *The Nature of Explanation*. Cambridge, UK: Cambridge University Press, 1943.

Daft, Richard L., and Robert H. Lengel. "Information Richness: A New Approach to Manager Information Processing and Organization Design." In *Research in Organizational Behavior*, Vol. 6, edited by B. Staw and L. L. Cummings. Greenwich, CT: JAI Press, 1984.

_____. "Organizational Information Requirements, Media Richness, and Structural Design." *Management Science* 32, no. 5 (May 1986): 554–571.

Davenport, Thomas H. "The Fad that Forgot People." *Fast Company*, no. 1 (November 1995): 70.

Davenport, Thomas H., and Laurence Prusak. *Working Knowledge*. Boston: Harvard Business School Press, 1998.

Davis, Stan, and Christopher Meyer. *Blur: The Speed of Change in the Connected Economy*. Reading, MA: Perseus, 1998.

Dawson, Ross. "Information Overload—Problem or Opportunity?" *Company Director* (October 1997): 44–45.

_____. "Performance Management Strategies for Knowledge Organisations." *Reward Management Bulletin* 2, no. 3 (February/March 1998): 183–186.

_____. "Managing Professional Knowledge." *Company Director* (March 1998): 22–23.

_____. "Did You Forecast Asia? Scenario Planning in Portfolio and Risk Management." *The Australian Corporate Treasurer* (August 1998).

_____. "Now, A Net for Clients Who Need That Extra Bit." *Australian Financial Review*, Special Report: Intranets and Networking (November 24, 1998): 6.

de Geus, Arie P. "Planning as Learning." *Harvard Business Review* 66, no. 2 (March-April 1988): 70–74.

Dembo, Ron S., and Andrew Freeman. *Seeing Tomorrow: Rewriting the Rules of Risk*. New York: John Wiley & Sons, 1998.

de Vega, Manuel, and Marc Marschark, eds. *Models of Visuospatial Cognition*. New York: Oxford University Press, 1996.

Dilts, Robert B., Todd Epstein, and Robert W. Dilts. *Tools for Dreamers: Strategies for Creativity and the Structure of Innovation.* Capitola, CA: Meta Publications, 1991.

Drucker, Peter. *Managing for the Future.* Oxford, UK: Butterworth–Heinemann, 1992.

_____. *Post-Capitalist Society.* New York: HarperCollins, 1993.

Eccles, Robert G., and Dwight B. Crane. *Doing Deals: Investment Banks at Work.* Cambridge, MA: Harvard Business School Press, 1988.

Eden, Colin. "On the Nature of Cognitive Maps." *Journal of Management Studies* 29, no. 3 (May 1992): 261–265.

Eden, Colin, and Fran Ackerman. "The Analysis of Cause Maps." *Journal of Management Studies* 29, no. 3 (May 1992): 309–323.

Eden, Colin, and J. C. Spender, eds. *Managerial and Organizational Cognition: Theory, Methods, and Research.* London, UK: Sage, 1998.

Edvinsson, Leif, and Michael S. Malone. *Intellectual Capital: Realizing Your Company's True Value by Finding Its Hidden Roots.* New York: HarperBusiness, 1997.

Einhorn, Hillel J., and Robin M. Hogarth. "Judging Probable Cause." *Psychological Review* 99, no. 1 (1986): 3–19.

Elliott, Susan. "Manpower Creates Customer Loyalty through Shared 'Stories,' Information." *Knowledge Management in Practice* no. 13 (3rd Quarter, 1998), American Productivity and Quality Center.

Ensor, Benjamin. "European Brokers Survey: Pulling Away from the Pack." *Euromoney,* (November 1997).

Evans, Philip B., and Thomas J. Wurster. "Strategy and the New Economics of Information." *Harvard Business Review* (September-October 1997).

Eysenck, Michael, and Mark Keane. *Cognitive Psychology: A Student's Handbook.* 3rd ed. Hove, UK: Psychology Press, 1995.

Fischetti, Mark. "Masters of the (Information) Universe." *Fast Company* (August/September 1997): 181–187.

Fisher, Lawrence M. "Technology Transfer at Stanford University." *Strategy & Business* (4th Quarter, 1998).

Fodor, Jerry A. *Concepts: Where Cognitive Science Went Wrong.* Oxford, UK: Oxford University Press, 1998.

Ford, G. W. "Technology Transfer, Technocultures, and Skill Formation: Learning from Australian Experience." *Asia Pacific Human Resource Management* (Summer 1991): 67–73.

Gentner, Dedre. "Structure-Mapping: A Theoretical Framework for Analogy." *Cognitive Science* 7 (1983): 155–170.

Goldhaber, Michael H. "Attention Shoppers!" *Wired* (December 1997).

Goldman, Steven L., Roger N. Nagel, and Kenneth Preiss. *Agile Competitors and Virtual Organizations: Strategies for Enriching the Customer.* New York: Van Nostrand Reinhold, 1995.

Hamel, Gary. "Competition for Competence and Interpartner Learning within International Strategic Alliances." *Strategic Management Journal* 12 (1991): 83–103.

Harris, Robert. *Information Graphics.* Atlanta: Management Graphics, 1996.

Hofstadter, Douglas. *Gödel, Escher, Bach: An Eternal Golden Braid.* New York: Basic Books, 1979.

Huff, Anne S., ed. *Mapping Strategic Thought.* Chichester, UK: John Wiley & Sons, 1990.

Ingvar, D. H. "'Memory of the Future': An Essay on the Temporal Organization of Conscious Awareness." *Human Neurobiology* 4 (1985): 127–136.

Inkpen, Andrew C. "Creating Knowledge through Collaboration." *California Management Review* 39, no. 1 (Fall 1996): 123–140.

Irvine, Stephen. "The Year of Retrenchment." *Euromoney* (September 1998).

Isenberg, Daniel J. "How Senior Managers Think." *Harvard Business Review* (November-December 1984).

Jackendoff, Ray. *Languages of the Mind: Essays on Mental Representation.* Cambridge, MA: The MIT Press, 1995.

James, Geoffrey. "Methods of Payment." *CIO Enterprise* (October 15, 1998).

Janis, Irving L. *Groupthink: Psychological Studies of Policy Decisions and Fiascoes*. Boston: Houghton-Mifflin, 1982.

Johnson-Laird, Philip N. *Mental Models: Towards a Cognitive Science of Language, Inference, and Consciousness*. Cambridge, UK: Cambridge University Press, 1983.

Johnson-Laird, Philip N., and R. Stevenson. "Memory for Syntax." *Nature* 227 (1970).

Kelly, Kevin. *New Rules for the New Economy: 10 Radical Strategies for a Connected World*. New York: Viking, 1998.

Kintsch, Walter. "The Role of Knowledge in Discourse Comprehension: A Construction-Integration Model." *Psychological Review* 95, no. 2 (1988): 163–182.

Koestler, Arthur. *The Act of Creation*. London: Hutchinson, 1964.

Kolb, David A. *Experiential Learning: Experience As the Source of Learning and Development*. Englewood Cliffs, NJ: Prentice Hall, 1984.

Korzybski, Alfred. *Science and Sanity: An Introduction to Non-Aristotelian Systems and General Semantics*. 2d ed. Lancaster, PA: International Non-Aristotelian Library Publishing, 1941.

Kuhn, Thomas S. *The Structure of Scientific Revolutions*. Chicago: University of Chicago Press, 1970.

Lakoff, George, and Mark Johnson. *Metaphors We Live By*. Chicago: The University of Chicago Press, 1980.

Lane, Peter J., and Michael Lubatkin. "Relative Absorptive Capacity and Interorganizational Learning." *Strategic Management Journal* 19 (1998): 461–477.

Leonard, Dorothy. *Wellsprings of Knowledge: Building and Sustaining the Sources of Innovation*. Boston: Harvard Business School Press, 1995.

Leonard, D. A., and S. Straus. "Putting Your Company's Whole Brain to Work," *Harvard Business Review* 75, no. 4 (July-August 1997).

Liedtka, Jeanne M., Mark E. Haskins, John W. Rosenblum, and Jack Weber. "The Generative Cycle: Linking Knowledge and Relationships." *Sloan Management Review* (Fall 1997): 47–58.

Liedtka, Jeanne M., and John W. Rosenblum. "Shaping Conversations: Making Strategy, Managing Change." *California Management Review* 39, no. 1 (Fall 1996): 141–157.

Maister, David H. *Managing the Professional Service Firm*. New York: The Free Press, 1997.

Mandl, H. and J. R. Levin, eds. *Knowledge Acquisition from Text and Pictures*. Amsterdam, Holland: Elsevier Science Publishers B.V., 1989.

March, James. *A Primer on Decision Making: How Decisions Happen*. New York: Harvard Business School Press, 1994.

Markides, Constantinos. "Strategic Innovation." *Sloan Management Review* (Spring 1997): 9–23.

Maturana H., and F. Varela. *Autopoiesis and Cognition: The Realization of the Living*. Dordrecht, The Netherlands; Boston: D. Reidel, 1980.

Mieszkowski, Katharine. "Opposites Attract." *Fast Company*, no. 12 (December 1997): 42.

Miller, George A. "The Magical Number Seven, Plus or Minus Two." *Psychological Review* 63 (1956): 81–93.

Miller, George A., Eugene Galanter, and Karl H. Pribram. *Plans and the Structure of Behavior*. New York: Holt, 1960.

Minto, Barbara. *The Minto Pyramid Principle: Logic in Writing, Thinking, and Problem Solving*. London: Minto International, 1996.

Mintzberg, Henry. *The Nature of Managerial Work*. New York: Harper & Row, 1973.

_____. *Mintzberg on Management: Inside Our Strange World of Organizations*. New York: Free Press, 1989.

Morecroft, John D. W. "System Dynamics: Portraying Bounded Rationality." *Omega* 11, no. 2 (1983): 131–142.

Negroponte, Nicholas. *Being Digital*. New York: Knopf, 1995.

Nicou, Monica, Christine Ribbing, and Eva Åding. *Sell Your Knowledge: The Professional's Guide to Winning More Business*. London: Kogan Page, 1994.

Nonaka, Ikujiro, and Hirotaka Takeuchi. *The Knowledge-Creating Company*. New York: Oxford University Press, 1995.

Normann, Richard, and Rafael Ramírez. "From Value Chain to Value Constellation: Designing Interactive Strategy." *Harvard Business Review* (July-August 1993): 65–77.

O'Connor, Joseph, and Ian McDermott. *The Art of System Thinking: Essential Skills for Creativity and Problem Solving.* London: Thorsons, 1997.

O'Hara-Devereaux, Mary, and Robert Johansen. *GlobalWork: Bridging Distance, Culture, and Time.* San Francisco: Jossey-Bass, 1994.

Paivio, Allan. "The Empirical Case for Dual Coding." In *Imagery, Memory, and Cognition: Essays in Honor of Allan Paivio,* edited by J. C. Yuille. Hillsdale, NJ: Lawrence Erlbaum Associates, Inc., 1983.

_____. *Mental Representations: A Dual-Coding Approach.* Oxford, UK: Oxford University Press, 1986.

Peppers, Don, and Martha Rogers. *The One to One Future: Building Relationships One Customer At a Time.* New York: Currency Doubleday, 1993.

_____. *Enterprise One to One: Tools for Competing in the Interactive Age.* New York: Currency Doubleday, 1997.

Peters, Tom. *Liberation Management: Necessary Disorganization for the Nanosecond Nineties.* New York: Fawcett Columbine, 1992.

Polanyi, Michael. *The Tacit Dimension.* London: Routledge & Kegan Paul, 1967.

Porter, Michael E. *Competitive Advantage: Creating and Sustaining Superior Performance.* New York: The Free Press, 1985.

Porter, Michael E., and Victor E. Millar. "How Information Gives You Competitive Advantage." *Harvard Business Review* (July-August 1985): 149–160.

Pralahad, C. K., and Gary Hamel. "The Core Competence of the Corporation." *Harvard Business Review* (May-June 1990).

Prokesh, Steven E. "Unleashing the Power of Learning: An Interview with British Petroleum's John Browne." *Harvard Business Review* (September-October 1997).

Quinn, James Brian. *Intelligent Enterprise: A Knowledge and Service Based Paradigm for Industry.* New York: The Free Press, 1992.

Quinn, James Brian, Philip Anderson, and Sydney Finkelstein. "Managing Professional Intellect: Making the Most of the Best." *Harvard Business Review* (March-April 1996): 71–80.

Ransdell, Eric. "Redesigning the Design Business." *Fast Company*, no. 16 (August 1998): 36–38.

Rempel, John K., John G. Holmes, and Mark P. Zanna. "Trust in Close Relationships." *Journal of Personality and Social Psychology* 49, no. 1 (1985): 95–112.

Reuters, *Dying for Information?* London: Reuters, 1996.

Ring, Peter S., and Andrew H. Van de Ven. "Structuring Cooperative Relationships between Organizations." *Strategic Management Journal* 13 (1992): 482–498.

_____. "Developmental Processes of Cooperative Interorganizational Relationships." *Academy of Management Review* 19, no. 1 (1994): 90–118.

Roos, Johan, Göran Roos, Leif Edvinsson, and Nicola Dragnetti. *Intellectual Capital*. Basingstoke, UK: Macmillan Press, 1997.

Savage, Charles M. *5th Generation Management: Co-Creating through Virtual Enterprising, Dynamic Teaming, and Knowledge Networking*. Boston: Butterworth–Heinemann, 1996.

Schön, Donald A. *The Reflective Practitioner: How Professionals Think in Action*. New York: Basic Books, 1983.

Schrage, Michael. "Provices and Serducts." *Fast Company*, no. 4 (August/September 1996).

Schwartz, Peter. *The Art of The Long View: Planning for the Future in an Uncertain World*. New York: Doubleday Currency, 1991.

Senge, Peter M. *The Fifth Discipline: The Art and Practice of the Learning Organization*. New York: Currency/Doubleday, 1994.

Shapiro, Carl, and Hal Varian. *Information Rules: A Strategic Guide to the Network Economy*. Boston: Harvard Business School Press, 1998.

Shaw, Gordon, Robert Brown, and Philip Bromiley. "Strategic Stories: How 3M Is Rewriting Business Planning." *Harvard Business Review* (May-June 1998).

Shelley, G. C. "Dealing with Smart Clients." *Ivey Business Quarterly* (Autumn 1997): 50–55.

Simon, Herbert A. "How Big Is a Chunk?" *Science* 183 (1974): 482–488.

_____. *Administrative Behavior: A Study of Decision-Making Processes in Administrative Organizations.* 4th ed. New York: The Free Press, 1997.

Stalk, George, Philip Evans, and Lawrence E. Shulman. "Competing on Capabilities: The New Rules of Corporate Strategy." *Harvard Business Review* (March-April 1992).

Stata, Ray. "Organizational Learning—The Key to Management Innovation." *Sloan Management Review* (Spring 1989): 63–74.

Stewart, Thomas A. "Your Company's Most Valuable Asset: Intellectual Capital." *Fortune* 130, no. 7 (October 3, 1994).

_____. "The Dance Steps Get Trickier All the Time." *Fortune* (May 26, 1997).

_____. *Intellectual Capital: The New Wealth of Organizations.* New York: Doubleday, 1997.

Sutton, Robert I., and Andrew Hargadon. "Brainstorming Groups in Context: Effectiveness in a Product Design Firm." *Administrative Science Quarterly* 41 (1996): 685–718.

Sveiby, Karl Erik. *The New Organizational Wealth: Managing and Measuring Knowledge-Based Assets.* San Francisco: Berrett-Koehler, 1997.

Treat, John E., George E. Thibault, and Amy Asin. "Dynamic Competitive Simulation: Wargaming as a Strategic Tool." *Strategy & Business* (2nd Quarter, 1996).

Tufte, Edward. *The Visual Display of Quantitative Information.* Cheshire, CT: Graphics Press, 1983.

_____. *Envisioning Information.* Cheshire, CT: Graphics Press, 1990.

Turner, Arthur N. "Consulting is More Than Giving Advice." *Harvard Business Review* (September-October 1982).

Tversky, Amos. "Features of Similarity." *Psychological Review* 84 (1977): 327–352.

Tversky, Amos, and Daniel Kahneman. "Extensional versus Intuitive Reasoning: The Conjunction Fallacy in Probability Judgment." *Psychological Review* 90 (1983): 293–315.

van der Heijden, Kees. *Scenarios: The Art of Strategic Conversation*. London: John Wiley & Sons, 1996.

van der Heijden, Kees, and Colin Eden. "The Theory and Praxis of Reflective Learning in Strategy Making." In *Managerial and Organizational Cognition: Theory, Methods, and Research*, edited by Colin Eden and J. C. Spender, 58–73. London: Sage, 1998.

Violino, Bob, and Bruce Caldwell. "Analyzing the Integrators." *Information Week* (November 16, 1998).

Wack, Pierre. "Scenarios: Uncharted Waters Ahead." *Harvard Business Review* 63, no. 5 (September-October 1985): 71–90.

_____. "Scenarios: Shooting the Rapids." *Harvard Business Review* 63, no. 6 (November-December 1985): 131–142.

Wathne, Kenneth, Johan Roos, and Georg von Krogh. "Towards a Theory of Knowledge Transfer in a Cooperative Context." In *Managing Knowledge: Perspectives on Cooperation and Competition*, edited by Georg von Krogh and Johan Roos, 55–81. London: Sage Publications, 1996.

Webber, Alan M. "What's So New About the New Economy?" *Harvard Business Review* (January-February 1993).

Winn, W. D. "Design and Use of Instructional Graphics." In *Knowledge Acquisition from Text and Pictures*, edited by H. Mandl and J. R. Levin. Netherlands: Elsevier Science Publishers B.V., 1989.

Wriston, Walter B. "Dumb Networks and Smart Capital." *The Cato Journal* 17, no. 3 (Winter 1998).

Wurman, Richard Saul. *Information Architects*. New York: Graphis, 1997.

Index

Butterworth-Heinemann Business Books . . . for Transforming Business

Developing Knowledge-Based Client Relationships: The Future of Professional Services
Ross Dawson, 0-7506-7185-8

Diversity Success Strategies
Norma Carr-Ruffino, 0-7506-7102-5

5th Generation Management, Co-creating Through Virtual Enterprising, Dynamic Teaming, and Knowledge Networking, Revised Edition
Charles M. Savage, 0-7506-9701-6

Flight of the Phoenix: Soaring to Success in the 21st Century
John Whiteside and Sandra Egli, 0-7506-9798-9

From Chaos to Coherence: Advancing Individual and Organizational Intelligence Through Inner Quality Management®
Bruce Cryer and Doc Childre, 0-75067007-X

Getting a Grip on Tomorrow: Your Guide to Survival and Success in the Changed World of Work
Mike Johnson, 0-7506-9758-X

Infinite Wealth: A New World of Collaboration and Abundance in the Knowledge Era
Barry C. Carter, 0-7506-7184-X

Innovation Strategy for the Knowledge Economy: The Ken Awakening
Debra M. Amidon, 0-7506-9841-1

The Hidden Intelligence: Innovation Through Intuition
Sandra Weintraub, 0-7506-9937-X

The Intelligence Advantage: Organizing for Complexity
Michael D. McMaster, 0-7506-9792-X

The Knowledge Evolution: Expanding Organizational Intelligence
Verna Allee, 0-7506-9842-X

Leadership in a Challenging World: A Sacred Journey
Barbara Shipka, 0-7506-9750-4

Leading Consciously: A Pilgrimage Toward Self-Mastery
Debashis Chatterjee, 0-7506-9864-0

Leading from the Heart: Choosing Courage over Fear in the Workplace
Kay Gilley, 0-7506-9835-7

Learning to Read the Signs: Reclaiming Pragmatism in Business
F. Byron Nahser, 0-7506-9901-9

Leveraging People and Profit: The Hard Work of Soft Management
Bernard A. Nagle and Perry Pascarella, 0-7506-9961-2

Liberating the Corporate Soul: Building A Visionary Organization
Richard Barrett, 0-7506-7071-1

Life Work Transitions.Com: Putting Your Spirit Online
Deborah L. Knox and Sandra S. Butzel, 0-7506-7160-2

A Little Knowledge Is A Dangerous Thing: Understanding Our Global Knowledge Economy
Dale Neef, 0-7506-7061-4

Marketing Plans that Work: Targeting Growth and Profitability
Malcolm H.B. McDonald and Warren J. Keegan, 0-7506-9828-4

Navigating Cross-Cultural Ethics: What Global Managers Do Right to Keep From Going Wrong
Eileen Morgan, 0-7506-9915-9

A Place to Shine: Emerging from the Shadows at Work
Daniel S. Hanson, 0-7506-9738-5

Power Partnering: A Strategy for Business Excellence in the 21st Century
Sean Gadman, 0-7506-9809-8

Putting Emotional Intelligence to Work; Successful Leadership Is More Than IQ
David Ryback, 0-7506-9956-6

Quantum Leaps: 7 Skills for Workplace ReCreation
Charlotte A. Shelton, 0-7506-7077-0

Resources for the Knowledge-Based Economy Series

   Knowledge Management and Organizational Design
   Paul S. Myers, 0-7506-9749-0

   Knowledge Management Tools
   Rudy L. Ruggles, III, 0-7506-9849-7

   Knowledge in Organizations
   Laurence Prusak, 0-7506-9718-0

   The Strategic Management of Intellectual Capital
   David A. Klein, 0-7506-9850-0

   Rise of the Knowledge Worker
   James W. Cortada, 0-7506-7058-4

   The Knowledge Economy
   Dale Neef, 0-7506-9936-1

   The Economic Impact of Knowledge
   Dale Neef, G. Anthony Seisfeld, Jacquelyn Cefola, 0-7506-7009-6

To purchase a copy of any Butterworth-Heinemann Business title, please visit your local bookstore or call 1-800-366-2665.

Ross Dawson is recognized as one of the most innovative thinkers worldwide on the evolving role of knowledge in business. He is the founder and Chief Executive Officer of Advanced Human Technologies, an international consulting firm based in Sydney, Australia, that specializes in developing the information and knowledge capabilities of investment banks, portfolio managers, professional service firms, and other knowledge-based organizations. Ross is a regular speaker at international conferences, and he has published over 50 articles on international business and knowledge management in major publications.

Prior to establishing Advanced Human Technologies, Ross's positions included working in London as Global Director—Capital Markets at Thomson Financial Services, in Tokyo as Asian Director—Capital Markets, and in international stockbroking with Merrill Lynch. He holds a B.Sc. (Hons) from Bristol University, UK, and is certified as a Master Practitioner of NLP. He has extensive international business experience and speaks five languages.

Ross Dawson is available for speaking engagements. Advanced Human Technologies helps its clients to enhance their knowledge capabilities and decision making, and to implement the principles of developing knowledge-based client relationships.

Ross Dawson can be contacted at:

Advanced Human Technologies
Level 22, AAP Centre
259 George Street
Sydney NSW 2000 AUSTRALIA
Tel: +61-2-9255-7877
Fax: +61-2-9255-7883

or

580 California Street, 16th Floor
San Francisco, CA 94104 USA
Tel: 415-439-4890
Fax: 415-283-3301

E-mail: rossd@ahtgroup.com
Website: www.ahtgroup.com